I have often heard the remark, "Life would be so much easier if only humans came with an owner's manual." Coburn Tuller, in this volume, has provided that much longed for manual. Mr. Tuller does not ask us to engage in any higher consciousness gymnastics here. The simplicity and power of this work can be accessed by acknowledging the obvious.
Ken Boschert
Imagine Magazine

Nearly every page of this book is a mirror. If you look into it you'll see yourself, not in a mean way, but in the most loving light.

In What in the World is Going On Here?, Coburn Tuller covers more than 100 subjects ranging from doubt to creativity, ambition to joy. No rock is left unturned- allowing the reader to discover the riches and insights beneath.

What in the World is Going On Here? is practical, perceptive, and written in a warm, conversational tone. Like the musings of a friend on along, quiet afternoon, this book is as comforting an easy chair. But don't let that fool you.

This is a forever book. One that you'll turn to from this moment on.
Leading Edge Review

What in the World is Going On Here?

COBURN TULLER

Butterfly 1995

Copyright c 1995 by Coburn Tuller

For permission, serialization, condensation or adaptations, write to:
Butterfly Po Box 2001, Springfield, MO 65801

Library of Congress Card Number - 94 - 096508

ISBN - 1-886322-17-1

ORIGINAL COVER ART BY KIM MORELOCK

PUBLISHED BY

utterfly

Po Box 2001
Springfield, MO 65801
1-800-727-1636

Printed in the United States of America

Dedication

To Us

Table of Contents

Chapter 1   1

What's Going On? 1

The Situation 1
Power 3
Where do we go from here?   11
Doubt 15
Life Without Hope   19
The Cult of the Personality 22
Anger 24

Chapter 2   27

How We Think 27

The Mind   27
The Pyramid 29
Change   30
Love, Joy and Celebration   33
Entertainment   34
Creativity   38

Chapter 3   41

Going Within 41

The Inner Journey   41
Deserving   44
A New Understanding   47
Love and Light   48

Who We Are   49
Regret   51
Rebellion   54

Chapter 4   57

Letting It Flow 57
Acceptance   57
Trust   60
The Religious/Spiritual Life   65
The Process of Transformation   68

Chapter 5   71

The Power Of Old Ideas 71
Fame   71
Education   73
Achievement   75
Ambition   77
Pride and Allegiance   81
The Search for the Center   84
Doubt and Control   86

Chapter 6   91

New Ideas For Growth 91
Growth and Light   91
Releasing the Old Method   95
Encouragement   95
Structure   96
Simplicity   98

Chapter 7   103

Moving Past The Future 103
The Past   103
The Future is Now   104
The Control Issue   110
Recognition   110
Getting Hurt   114

Challenge   116

Chapter 8   119

Goals and Growth 119

Punishment   119
The Four Steps of Growth   123
Goals   127
Identity   128
The Real World   131
Intimacy   134
Self Centeredness   136

Chapter 9   139

Aspects of the Self 139

The Ego   139
Separateness   140
Success   143
Creativity # 2   144
Happiness   147
The Challenge of Change   148
The Observer   151

Chapter 10   155

Exploring a New Method 155

Evolution Revisited   155
Infatuation   158
Exploration   161
Goals #2   163
Opportunities   165

Chapter 11   167

The Path of Service 167

The Missionary Tradition   167
Becoming a Center   168
Purification   170
Self Expression   172

Dreams   173

A Positive Attitude   176

Chapter 12   179

The Problem with Problems 179

The Inner City Puzzle   179

Inner Joy   181

A Brief Moment of Doubt   182

Desire, Accomplishment and Failure   185

Competition   189

Fear   190

Adventure   192

The Devil Created   194

Risk   195

Striving   196

Chapter 13   199

Time and Eternity 199

The Clock Ticks On   199

Focus   200

Being and Becoming 202

Changing Beliefs   203

Work and Freedom   204

Money   209

Chapter 14   213

Transformation 213

Intention   213

Motivation and Growth   215

The Energy Matrix   217

Happiness   219

Acceptance   220

Chapter 15   225

The Freedom of Knowing 225

The Truth Shall Set Us Free   225

The Signs of Growth 227
Fear   227
Anger and Love   232
Superstition and Evil   233
A Choice Is Presented   235
Need   236
Emptiness   238
Abundance   239

Chapter 16   241

The World We Live In 241

The Secret of Life   241
World Wide Change   243
Fear and Transformation   244
Knowledge and Intuition   245
The Eternal Questions   247

Chapter 17   249

Beyond Belief 249

Shame   249
Experience and Learning   254
Energy and Flow   256
Sexuality   258
Tension and Release 260
Love   263
Murphy's Fear   264
The Search for Love and Joy   266

Chapter 18   269

The Journey Home 269

The Source   269
The Spiritual Path   271
The Concept of Opposites   272
The Payoff of Negativity   274
Humiliation 275
A New Image of Self   277

True Success   279
The Light at the End of the Tunnel   280
Rebellion Revisited   281
Experience as Teacher   284
Authority Figures   285
Perfection   288

Epilogue 293
Index--295
Suggested Readings 311
About the Author 313

Introduction

set out to write this book because I wanted to help change the world. I didn't have any illusions about myself as being 'already there.' I knew I needed to change as well and I imagined what this change would entail. I thought I would probably learn something of value, get in touch with more of myself and hopefully release some pains and bad habits. I might even experience some kind of deep realization. But I really had no idea the depth to which this process can take us. I had never had any experience like this before, so there was nothing in memory to prepare me for the journey. But I began it anyway with only myself to guide me, or so I thought.

I guess I figured I was alone and wandering towards some nebulous destination whose location was lost in the mists of confusion. I knew how to get to any place on the earth, but I didn't know which way to go to find the Source of Light within. I was a little afraid of what I might find, but more than that, I simply didn't know where to turn. Knowing the Source was within should have been a clue, but the pull of the external world was still too strong in me. Only gradually did I become ready to let go of this world so that I could expand into the next. I suppose I was a little wary of the journey but that was only because I didn't understand it. I wanted to understand and experience it, and so it began.

We can look at Spiritual Transformation as the beginning of a new understanding along with an emergence from old beliefs. Like a cocoon, our present system of beliefs and knowledge has provided an environment in which we were able to live comfortably while building and experiencing a life. All of our deepest questions about who we are and why we are here were answered by these ideas, providing us with the mental security necessary for exploration and expansion of the physical, emotional and mental spheres of living. We have learned much from our adventures in the four corners of the Earth. We have journeyed far and discovered much about the World and its riches. Our relationships have nurtured and taught us about Love and continue to challenge our emotional understanding. Our minds have ventured from the depths of the oceans and the intricacies of the atom to the highest mountains and the vastness of outer space. But we have not yet explored the depths of ourselves. It is time to come out of our protective sheath of thoughts and feelings so that we can grow further. By expanding, we can discover our direct connection to Divinity where understanding is immediate and intuitive instead of laboriously mental. It is time to learn just what our minds are designed to do for us, and where they are hopelessly inadequate.

Our mental sheath has helped us immensely in our everyday existence. It has given us a sense of security and been able to explain the basic questions we have about life, at least somewhat. Its method of carefully sifting through data and considering every possible angle is a slow, halting process, but one excellently suited to scientific experimentation. By trial and error we have developed ways of growing food and remarkable systems for the manufacture and distribution of goods. We can marvel at the mind's computer-like ability to organize and store information, and see how the mind's structures enable our schools, cities and businesses to operate in an orderly fashion. Yet when we try to use the mind to fathom the deeper aspects of our lives we find that it falls short. In these realms, the interlocking systems of knowledge and beliefs bring endless debate and confusion and do not easily adapt to new information and insight. As such, these structures keep us firmly anchored in the level of understanding we have grown accustomed to rather than allowing us to expand into the realms of intuitive perception. It is time to discard this old cocoon, and rather than weep because we are losing something that was once so useful and precious, rejoice that the butterfly within is finally emerging into the Light.

Preface

When we look at modern life, we must admit that Joy is not one of its most apparent characteristics. Although we have made great strides in guaranteeing the pursuit of Happiness, at least for some of us, the directions we have taken that pursuit have been pnly marginally successful at best. Some would say that we merely need to find another direction, and there are many suggestions for the best road to follow or how best to repair the present one. But since we are what we think, the answer more probably lies in our thought patterns rather than our zeal for conquest. We do not lack in either imagination or exuberance, but wisdom appears to be in short supply. Perhaps the answer is to not really travel at all, but to stay put for a while and seek the answer within. We are precisely what we think, and it is there that we can make the most improvements with the least amount of effort as well as the most success.

In this book we will be talking about how our present thinking affects our Life Experiences. If we want happier Lives and more Loving relationships, then we need to change the ideas on which we base them. The present systems of beliefs does not produce the Life we want to experience. So we will be exploring the relationships between the present or old way of thinking, and the new way, the Spiritual Way that is now dawning on this Planet. We will look at how simple changes within these basic ideas about living can make dramatic and wonderful changes in each of our lives, and how collectively this will heal all current troubles on Earth. It's a kind of 'how to' approach that demonstrates the value of totally Positive

Thinking and the Life enhancing benefits of meditation. We need to clear the mind of all negative thought material, and plug into our Spiritual Source within. This is the only way we will evolve into the wonderful Divine Beings we are designed to be. It is a magnificent journey ripe with challenge and surprise, brimming with Love and Goodwill, and completely full of Joy and ultimate Success. Let us begin.

I will be using certain terms interchangeably throughout the text both to provide variety and subtle nuances of meaning. Though I use the more traditional term, Soul, I also call this part of us the Center, our Source and Essence, or the Higher Self. I call the way most of the world now approaches life the present way or method, the present thinking, the current thinking or the old way. In contrast, the new way of thinking from the Center of Love and Light is called the new way of thinking or Being, or the new method. In all cases I have tried to be consistently clear. I hope you benefit from reading this as much as I have from writing it.   Coburn Tuller

Acknowledgments

A book of this nature has a long history and involves most of what I have learned so far. If I were to thank everyone who has helped me, it would take more pages than we have. All of my teachers and friends who have shown me so much about who I am and what they believed to be true and good about the world we live in would have to be graciously included. And I would have to mention my enemies as well, for in them I saw the most self defeating aspects of myself., aspects I trust I have learned to grow beyond. I thank them for these reflections. And then there are my mentors, those wonderful fools who took the time to show me something of beauty and significance.

To Howard, Linda, Polly and the rest of the gang at SMSU for more than I have room to mention. And two very wonderful ones. To John Woody, that crazy soul who let me loose with a room full of cameras and editing equipment to explore any avenue I found interesting, and who told me the Secret of Life. And to Kay Brown who introduced me to dance and mime, for so began my exploration of the intuitive realms of energy and expression of something greater than my individual ego.

To my family and friends for their tireless support and especially my sweet Ellyn who teaches me more about Love everyday, and whose wonderful knowledge of books and sense of editing helped immensely to fashion a readable volume. To Ron Brown for encouraging me at the beginning and introducing me to the more esoteric aspects of Macintosh and to Ken Boschert for much love and help with many things. I am also indebted to Kim Morelock for the wonderful cover art and Lea Vetter for help with layout and design. And to Elaine Hines of Renaissance Books for her kind guidance and wonderful suggestions. To these and to all, my most grateful thanks.

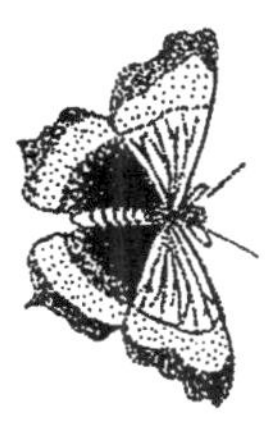

We are Love,
We are Light,
We are One with all Life.

Chapter 1

What's Going On?

The Situation

The process of Transformation ultimately begins in our own minds and continues until we learn to be in conscious control of what we are thinking. We do this by getting in touch with our Higher Self. This is the journey at the dawning of the New Age, the age of humans guided by intuitive perceptions. Some of us experience initial fear at this change and at the newness of spiritual living. So instead of expanding further, we resist learning to control the mind and allow it to continue its amusing insanity. But in order for intuitive perceptions to be received and understood, the mind must be quiet and under conscious control. Thus we find ourselves caught in a mental tug of war between the fearful traditions of the past and the obvious truths of the present expansion. We must become aware of the thoughts in our minds and learn to reprogram ourselves to think positively. Unless we learn this well, we will continue to be at the mercy of our own conditioned thinking, doing the same song and dance we were taught when we were small and easily influenced. We must also learn to know ourselves thoroughly in all ways.

There are many who cry out and will try any method offered in hopes of quieting the mind. What a seemingly sad situation that some of us are being driven crazy by our own minds, by a part of ourselves that we do not know how to stop.

1

And as a result, we are being afraid and hating and killing each other because of these thoughts in our minds, thoughts which we do not like and over which we believe we have little control. What is needed is a method for quieting the mind, a way to turn off the ceaseless chatter and in the ensuing silence, begin to hear the solace of the Soul's Song. One can never hear the soft murmur of Divinity while the ego-mind is clamoring for attention. Within the Soul's silent spaces are the words and images we are looking for, the words of comfort and images of Joy that will change our lives into the wonderful experiences we all know they can be. In scenes like movies and dreams, we can begin to see the true inner self. In many ways it is a dream, our wildest dream coming true where everyday is full of growth and challenge, every hour a joyful celebration of life.

When we look at the world as it is today, we ask ourselves why it is not full of Joy and celebration, why there appears to be so much sadness and anguish, so much fear and anger, and so much disappointment at what is missing. What is missing is Love and Joy, the very Love and Joy that we have the power to create in our lives. We are beginning to understand that we are what we think, so that we will become joyful in exact proportion to how much we believe we are joyful. If our experience of joyfulness is so easily changed, then everything else can be also. It becomes clear that all the pain and suffering in the world is quite easily cured by a change of attitude.

The world everywhere seems to be full of tension. The media and entertainment industries paint a picture of danger lurking everywhere with outbreaks of violence on every corner. There is much hatred and fighting going on and most of it over territory. Many indigenous peoples in the world are rising up and demanding a homeland. They are fighting for something they can call their own whether it be the newest Russian splinter group or a battle over turf on the streets of New York. Either way, the principle is the same. We are fighting and driving and scheming for our own personal success. Leaders would have us believe that this is all in the best interests of everyone; it keeps the economy going and gives us something to live and strive towards. But the most important aspect is that it is for us. It really doesn't matter whether it's a new car or a new country, the reason for pursuing the dream is entirely self-centered. Even traditional religion's major thrust is for personal salvation, the saving of one's individual soul. And all of this self-centeredness produces a world composed of people totally absorbed with their own destiny and only interested in anyone else's if it has a direct effect on theirs. We have created a culture and a world that is nothing more than a web of interconnected self-interests with some kind of imposed order that attempts to keep it happening smoothly. The problem is that many of us refuse to play within the established order and when that happens, the entire order begins to break down. This produces chaos and confusion and a frenzied rush to reestablish order or in many places, several groups hoping each to establish their own particular brand of order. These groups want control because they believe, with control, they would be able to establish an environment that would produce happiness. Happiness takes many forms.

All of us want to feel secure, to know that we and our children will have the necessary resources to produce and sustain a good life. Yet it has been shown that if we took 2% of what we spend on warfare and used it to feed, cloth, house and heal, then every person everywhere would have everything that they need. So there must be some other force operating here that bypasses logic and appeals to the prideful ego, and this is the idea of control or power. If only we had control, our lives would be better. Yet this control is only of the physical circumstances. When we fully understand that as we think so we are, then we begin to understand and control the mind, recognizing it as the mechanism that produces the life that we experience. All of these aggressive groups who are conniving and fighting for their happiness are looking in the wrong place. In seeking to establish order on the outside, they are allowing disorder to continually reign supreme on the inside, a disorder that can only continue to manifest in their lives. Their quest is doomed before they even start because their understanding is as unevolved as their method.

Power

In my experience, I have run into this time and again in the form of, "If only I had the power, I would make things better in this world." This is, of course, an improvement over the desire to use power for one's own selfish gains, but it is a desire for power nonetheless, and in the desire for power lies its corruption. 'Power corrupts and absolute power corrupts absolutely' the old saying goes, but it never says why. The desire for power is the key because it implies that having power is necessary in order to bring about change. This is old thinking. In the light of our new Understanding, we know that change happens from the center outward and not by the exertion of some external force. So the whole system of desire for and acquisition of power is part of an outmoded form of living, a form that is no longer necessary and obviously counterproductive. It is destructive because it focuses on the ego's desire to change things rather than allowing the change to emerge from the deeper level of the Soul. The ego's focus is too shallow and so desires things that are either impossible to attain or unimportant to the growth and happiness of a human being. We must relinquish the desire for power by understanding its limitations before we can allow our true essence to come forth into manifestation. This brings up another important point.

The only reason we think we need power to get what we want is because we believe either, a) that other people are obstacles in our path of acquisition or, b) that there is a limited amount of something that we need to be stronger to attain. Both of these beliefs break down in the light of our new Understanding. There are no limitations because all is abundant and the more we share the more we get, so other people are not obstacles but the very means by which we acquire the most. It's amazing how backward the old thinking really is. While we give lip service to the importance of relationships and genuinely feel the need for Love, the mind's attachment to physical things prevails in an alarming number of cases. We even treat life experiences as if they are things to be acquired like so many dream vacations. Yet physical objects and events, like us, are also made of Love and Light and with these energies they are created. We do not need to have control of this creative process but rather only need to understand how it works and allow it to happen. Releasing the need and desire for power is the first step to our ultimate attainment of everything, including real power.

We might think of these major ideas like power, selfishness and focus on the future as large boulders that block the stream of life from flowing. Some of these obstacles have been large enough to dam up the flow completely, and those with power have attempted to build their own dams and thus keep most of the stream's contents for themselves. Our life streams have been full of such obstacles and while the water swirling around them has been dynamic and at times beautiful, it does not compare to the stream in full flow.

When we fully understand the power of our thinking, then there will no longer be any reason to think negatively because that only produces negative results. The old adage of the end justifies the means is finally shown in the light of its true absurdity because whatever thoughts we use to create anything will be part of the creation. We are seeing this in every aspect of our daily lives. Aggressive business practices build companies that spread sorrow and disaster wherever they grow. We continually fail to build lasting, loving relationships because of our fear of intimacy, and our dreams of Joy and peace are founded on violence and so never materialize. We see how our old ways of thinking have caused our present predicament and yearn to develop new ways of thinking that will produce better results.

With this new Understanding, it is crazy to worry about the future because that worry can only manifest. The very thing we worry about will become part of our lives. We can eliminate worry and so begin to change the way that we think. It is as simple as that, and as complex. Since we are thinking at the rate of 60,000 thoughts per day and since so many of our thoughts can be seen to be negative, the task of changing our thinking can at first seem overwhelming. Perhaps we should focus our attention on classes of thoughts and by changing the class, change all the thoughts that are part of that class. For example, fear thoughts.

All the fear thoughts have one thing in common, fear. For instance, the fear that we will not have what is necessary to be happy. By changing fear to trust we instantly alter the entire meaning of this thought. Instead of fearing that we will not have what we need, we now trust that we will. This simple replacement turns our lives around and just as we have experienced the fruits of our fear, we now get to experience the fruits of our Trust. We can now manifest our Trust. There are three dimensions to this type of manifestation.

The first dimension occurs when we think. The thoughts in our heads manifest as the dreams and fantasies of our waking life. If we begin to feel the presence of these thoughts then we have manifested emotionally as well. With fear as our example, we at first have fearful thoughts and then begin to experience the disquieting emotion of fear. Our manifestation now has two dimensions. If our fear becomes strong enough, then we can manifest an actual three-dimensional, physical experience that involves fear. When I was younger and poorer, I drove my car without benefit of insurance. It was always a test of my trust to do this and I was continually plagued by the fear of having an accident, ruining my car and plunging myself into massive debt. This fear was not particularly strong, but more like a continual nuisance that was getting progressively stronger. One day while I was heading home, a car ran a stop sign and passed inches in front of me. I understood in a flash that this was a precise representation of the balance of my fear and trust at that moment. I trusted that nothing was going to happen but was afraid that it might, and this fear was almost to the point of manifesting. I was probably thinking that I was pressing my luck and it was this bit of unsureness that caused the other car to come so close. It was a warning from within my mind that I had been dwelling too much on this possibility so that it almost came into being. It was time to do some inner work and release this idea.

The wonderful thing about this process is that it is from the inside outward, so that by substituting Trust for the fear on the inside, the Trust is automatically manifested on the outside. We become our own television repairman realigning our selector so that it stays tuned to the channel of Trust and Love. One way to approach this realignment is with a new Understanding of our process of thought. When we begin to see our thoughts as the script by which we produce this three-dimensional experience, then all thoughts become equally powerful. In the present world system, fear is a very strong thought that manifests everywhere and seems out of control. One does not intentionally go to the inner city and take a leisurely stroll at night. There is too much fear and that fear makes people do fearful things to others. Yet Love is equally strong and will produce just as easily and much more positively. The truth of this idea can be quickly proven by beginning to think and feel Love in all waking moments. By doing this, we soon perceive the change. Yet many of us claim to have little or no control over our thinking.

When you think about it, we have ultimate and complete freedom over what we think. At any moment we can conjure images in our minds of anything from the silliest jokes to the most dazzling flights of spiritual perception. We can create any kind of scene that we want at any moment. So these other out of control thoughts must just be bad habits, collections of thoughts so habitual that they appear to be beyond our control. We have complete control over what we want to think at any given moment as any simple visualization technique will easily demonstrate. The lack of control is only a perceived reality and can be changed if we really want it to.

So fear becomes only a thought like any other thought and we realize that we only think about fear because we think it is an important consideration. Indeed, the prevalence of fearful situations in the world seems to preclude its importance. But with our new Understanding, we realize that fear is the cause of the present world situation, not a result of it. We are learning that our fear is only as important as we believe it is and that it gets its apparent power from our focus. "As a man thinketh, so is he," the proverb tells us. We have successfully turned ourselves into fearful humans dwelling on a planet full of fear by focusing on fear. We can just as easily become humans experiencing Love and Joy by changing our focus to these other, more positive aspects of living. By changing the thoughts that we think, we can change our world. And when two or more of us gather together in the name of Love and Joy, then we will produce it together. By changing fear into Love, the world becomes a different place and we begin to create a beautiful environment where all humans manifest lives full of Love and Joy.

Our present world experience is caused by a fundamental misunderstanding of the nature of energy, a fundamental misconception of what life is all about. If for one moment we could see ourselves as other galaxies see us, we would be amazed. Where we see ourselves as powerful, superior beings carving their destinies out of the rock of reality, they see small children digging in the dirt and fighting over it. Where we perceive ourselves as intelligent beings demanding control of our destinies, they see creatures who have not the faintest idea how to manifest energy in their own best interests, and so create fear and misery in the misguided attempt to create Joy and Love. If we want Love and Joy, then we should begin to create it the easiest way possible, with our minds. We need to replace the old methods of competition, striving and warfare which have never produced anything but the opposite of what is really desired. There is one fundamental concept that must be changed before any of this can happen, and that is the idea that the world is real.

As long as we believe the world to be a real, three-dimensional place, then the only way to facilitate change is to change the actual three-dimensional circumstances. All of our aggressions, our schemes and hard work are attempts to accomplish these physical changes. We see ourselves as builders, as sculptors who must fashion the clay of existence into the desired products which we call acquisitions. But the new paradigm shows us that we are really transmitters and that our thoughts transmit their content into three-dimensional form. We are more like the television picture than the television set, more like computer software than the physical circuitry. Indeed, the television picture and the computer's virtual reality are providing us with the most accurate model of what we truly are. We believed in the past that the pen is mightier than the sword, that words have more power than armed coercion. We are learning now that the pen and the sword are one, that they both create their own reality.

And so our Understanding of Life comes full circle. The truths in all the old scriptures are being substantiated by quantum physics, and the split between science and spirit ceases to exist as anything more than a historical event. We have known that we are what we think and yet we are just now beginning to apply this understanding to our lives. Indeed, how do we apply such a simple yet far reaching concept to our everyday lives. The paradigm of the transmitter can help us.

Since our experiences are the projections of our thoughts, they become a feedback loop that tells us what we are thinking and feeling. Our life is like a series of scenes in a movie whose script is our thoughts. If we do not like the content, then like the director we can yell, 'Cut,' and work with the actors (the various aspects of ourselves) to produce a new scene. And since there is no timetable or budget for this particular movie, we can rehearse and rearrange as much as we want until we get it right. Understanding that the three-dimensional world is a play place for learning takes all the worry and strain off of our efforts. When we begin to see ourselves as children learning to use the tools of mind and emotion to produce three-dimensional forms, then we are truly on our way to becoming conscious creators. And it is all inside of us, manifesting outwardly. As the ancient saying goes, "as it is within, so it is without," and the full circle happens when we finally begin to truly understand this ancient truth and apply it to modern existence.

We begin to change our minds into ones full of Love because we know a mind full of Love will produce a life full of Love. The key to happiness is to begin to think happiness, the key to our salvation is to see ourselves as saved, and the key to a life full of Joy is to imagine we already have a life full of Joy. And so we can create a world full of Love and Joy and happiness, a heaven on earth. As the Master Jesus said, the "kingdom of heaven is within us," and we are now bringing this kingdom out to experience its majesty. This heaven within is itself based on another concept, the soul.

The old concept of the soul carried with it the idea of the eternal conflict between good and evil. Our souls were seen as the battleground for these two immense forces and our decision to follow one path or the other determined our eternal fate. This is understandably a simplistic concept of life, life as a test of our loyalty to a divine king, a being of great benevolence and mercy but who will turn the unfaithful over to his sidekick, a fiend known for his treachery. Historically, this concept predates Christianity by about 600 years and while it represents a fair guess as to the nature of reality, at least from the perspective of 600 BC, it is a concept that can hardly be considered accurate 2600 years later. In fact, since all is a manifestation of our thinking, then the conflict between these two forces in the present world system has been caused by this kind of thinking. The belief in good and evil is the energy which has created it. By telling our children that they have within them the source of great evil, we have encouraged many of the more adventurous to explore that possibility, and with amazingly grisly results. If we can create such a monstrous situation by focusing on the possibilities of evil, imagine what can be produced when we focus on the beauties of Love and Light. We will produce a world beyond our wildest imaginings, a world which is already being created in many of our lives. We can be thankful that we are seeing the truth about our creation before it is too late. We can also be grateful for the present world of violence and suffering because it has forced us to look within for a better way.

We humans are odd in that we learn the most when we are backed into a corner. The present world condition has caused many of us to search inwardly for a solution because all outward solutions such as scientific advances, warfare, or politics have failed to make any real change. And when you think about it, if life since the beginning of time had been absolutely wonderful, we would have had no reason to look any further. A world without problems would require no solutions and we would still be living in the mythical Garden of Eden, a place full of Love and Joy but without conscious understanding of the underlying principles that govern creative existence.

As we see ourselves as Light and allow that Light to shine forth, we become the perfect reflection of who we really are. The present history of the world can then be understood as Light that has been colored by emotionally tarnished thinking, diffused through layers of self-centeredness until very little light actually escaped. The present state of the cinema with its penchant for the darker side of life is a testament to this filtering process and is forcing us to evaluate the effect these movies and television have on us and our children. Even the greed of unscrupulous producers is teaching us the harmfulness of filling minds with images of glorified violence and is causing many to call for a halt to such encouragement. Many of us have had enough and are yearning for a new Understanding of who we are and how thought energy manifests in the lives of our children. It is said that when the time for change arrives, everything will point in the necessary direction. And we see it thus becoming clear in every aspect of our culture and in every country in the world. What we need to do now is to remove all the filters and allow the Light to beam forth in its full brightness. And we can do this by reprogramming our transmitters.

Where do we go from here?

When we begin to reprogram our thinking we run into a number of things. The first is the idea of change itself. In order to change we must be willing to change. The present world order despises change because there is always the fear that loss will ensue. We even cling to misery because we fear change might make it worse. This is the most pathetic instance of negative thinking we have because within its grip no improvement is possible. Just the opposite, the focusing on fear of things getting worse makes them get worse and so there is set up the endless recurring misery of a downward spiral. Even positive change, if allowed into the consciousness, is viewed with such doubt that it is a wonder that anything changes at all, let alone for the better. So first up, we have to deal with the fear of change and its companion, pride.

Many of our present thought structures rely on pride to keep them going. They are handed down like treasures from generation to generation with the stipulation that they be kept close to our hearts and never forgotten. Fear of change makes us hold onto the ideas of the past as if they held all the secrets to successful living. Yet we constantly look to the future and pray that it will somehow improve. This is confused thinking. If the ways of the past are so good, what are we praying for, and if they are not producing the kind of life we would like, why don't we let them go? It is time to loose our death grip on the misconceptions of the past, no matter how dear, and replace them with concepts that make sense. It is time to lay aside the prideful heritage of our ancestors and cease to identify ourselves by the piece of dirt we or our parents once inhabited. Realizing that we are made of Love and Light brings us together in Love and Light. Thinking that we are citizens of widely differing lands keeps us apart and encourages strife. This change is a real stretch for our consciousness.

We are all part of one vast human consciousness. We express ourselves in a multitude of cultural and personality forms, yet recognize our overwhelming similarities, our Oneness as the children of Love and Light. Now that we know who we are, we can explore why we are here.

When we see ourselves as the expression of Love and Light, then our purpose on this earth is to allow these qualities to manifest. We can do that by saying 'yes' to all the most beautiful parts of us that we wish to share. We can dedicate ourselves to learning how to be more loving and full of Light every moment. The more Light we share, the more our path will be enlightened. The more Love we share the more we will have to give and receive. By manifesting and sharing our Love and our Light we will become brighter and stronger and will create the Kingdom of Heaven on Earth where all else will be given unto us. We are here to learn this and to manifest lives founded upon this growth in Understanding. Every time we learn, we grow, and every time we grow, we share, and every time we share we learn even more. And this upward spiral continues until we see Divinity face to face and know ourselves to be part of this Divine Perfection. We are becoming conscious creators of our Destiny because we have learned the Secret of the Universe, that all is Divine and naturally manifests itself when we allow it to do so. This implies a certain control over our thinking.

Control is the big word these days. Every imaginable ethnic or cultural group is clamoring or fighting for self-rule, for control of its Destiny. Yet they are fighting in the outer world rather than learning to control their Destiny from within their minds and emotions. They will never produce the happiness they strive for because their anger and violence insures that they will find only more anger and more violence along with its legitimate offspring, suffering and misery.

Many groups fight for autonomy, a homeland, a place that they can identify with as theirs. Yassir Arafat has made a career out of trying to establish one for the Palestinians and has taken this kind of struggle to new depths of treachery. Yet this identification with a particular place on the earth's surface and the rampant need for such a place in order to feel that one is a whole person is an example of very unevolved thinking. As humans we should be identifying with the soul, with the source of Love and Light within us and not some quarrelsome chunk of dirt. Yet this is showing all of us just how important the feeling of being connected really is. In the pursuit of this goal, these groups have been willing to commit all manner of atrocities to other humans which has only further degraded their cause. "The end justifies the means" could be their cry and they have taken this old belief to its logical and ultimately destructive absurdity. Yet now we applaud Arafat's new diplomacy and have bestowed upon him the Nobel Peace Prize in a valiant attempt to encourage him to stop. The true shame of this situation is that by establishing a homeland built on violence, he will only reap more violence and indeed, he is already having trouble controlling the anger and explosiveness of groups he helped train. Unless he can somehow infuse this situation with tremendous Love and positive peacefulness, he will reap what he has sown and his people will never enjoy the peace and contentment of their place in the sun. By using violence and chaos to establish a new order for himself, he can only hope to see even more of both.

Yet if we asked these groups what they really wanted, they would answer, happiness. To think that happiness and abundance can be found through the vehicle of violence is very foolish thinking. It is thinking and acting that is grounded in the ego/mind and so subject to its inherent limitations. Meanwhile, others have been focusing on the soul and its growth. They are releasing interest in the things of the ego and embracing the things of the spirit. The net result is that by the time Arafat finishes building his ideal Palestinian state, no one will care. In time, even the Palestinians will ask, why did we make so much fuss over a matter of so little consequence. Perhaps his legacy can at least teach us that. And when he falls, as he inevitably will, he might wonder what he did wrong, never understanding that in choosing treachery as his means, he insured his own treacherous end.

In learning to be conscious creators we are fulfilling our Destiny as Humans. We have been given the opportunity to exist on his planet in order to learn how to utilize energy, energy which takes several forms. We have a physical body which allows us much mobility and is capable of interacting in many wonderful situations. We have emotions that can fill those experiences with Love and Joy, while with our minds we observe, explore and try to understand this phenomena. In addition, we have the new frontier of Spirit that we are just beginning to investigate. We have been given all of this so that we might learn of what energies we are made and how best to utilize them. It's as if we were thrown onto this planet with bodies, minds and emotions but without a manual on how to use them. We have been writing the manual since time began and are only now beginning to perfect it. This is our purpose, to perfect our knowledge of these energies and then use them to manifest a joyful world of Love and Divine Celebration.

We are emerging from confusion and darkness into the light of Understanding. We are learning exactly what the mind is and what the emotions are and how they are part of these beings we are becoming. A fascinating aspect is that there are no road maps to this journey. It is a new direction, the beginning of a new type of awareness. It is the type of quantum change equal to the birth of the conscious reasoning mind.

We can imagine what life was like before conscious thinking because we can observe it in our children as they grow. Thus we can imagine what the world might have been like when everyone responded according to only pain, pleasure or gross emotion. Then the thinking mind began to develop and written history began, a history which has flourished during the last four hundred years. Not that our world is a perfectly reasonable place, but I'm sure there have been some improvements since men behaved more like animals than conscious thinkers. The problem is not that our thinking isn't capable of producing a satisfactory environment, but that our thinking is still tied to concepts left over from the dark ages of fear and instinctual behavior. The dawning of intuition as an additional factor in our consciousness, coupled with the new Understanding of the use of Spiritual Energy, should produce a quantum leap in intelligent living.

The first step in our development occurred when we became self-conscious. We were able to see ourselves as unique entities separate from everything else even if still tightly identified as a particular group. Many aboriginal tribes still function in this manner while others have begun the journey from group identification to personal self-consciousness. The important point is that with the dawning of intuition, we are recognizing that our individuality only applies to the perceived reality of the transmitted three-dimensional, personality mechanism. Each of our movies appear different but we realize that at deeper levels we are completely connected to each other and to everything else. So we are beginning the journey towards Oneness, bringing our individual consciousnesses with us. As such it is a whole new world dawning that is both built upon the conscious understandings of the ego/mind and yet extending into the wonders of the soul/mind.

Doubt

In working with a friend plagued by alcoholism, we were trying to discuss what he needed to do now that he had been through treatment. He seemed to understand that it was important for him to change, but he expressed doubt that change was possible. His main reservation was that even if he really tried to help himself or work with a recovery group, what possible good would it do? The idea of doubt was so strong that just the attempt to consider improving was met with immediate and complete failure. This mind doubted everything except, of course, its own doubt of which it was completely certain. It is amazing that a man who cannot trust anyone or even his own mind, yet trusts his own doubt explicitly. When he told me that he had no intention of stopping drinking, I knew that I would have to let go of him as an employee. The main difficulty I faced in this situation was letting go of the aspects of him that were reflections of me. His doubt was my doubt. His desire to slowly fade into oblivion was my hidden desire to do the same. The suffering we both felt was reason enough to give up on life, and so the all-consuming doubt. I was fortunate in that I was able to learn this from him and move on to a life based on trust and confidence while he remained in a clouded world, doubting the value of life itself.

So this person has faded from our association and we

thank him very much for having shown us these aspects of ourselves. Someday he will also learn this lesson and move on from his world of doubt. It is important for him to have the choice of whether he will heal or continue to degenerate. This made me aware of how I was beginning to heal and how this experience was part of that process. In releasing him I also released those degenerating aspects of my consciousness and thus learned more than I had known before.

I meet with people quite often to discuss their growth in awareness. I notice after some of these sessions that the client really has not understood what was said. The words were all in English and in the correct order and the feeling that is transmitted is quite profound, yet the client often times does not comprehend what is being suggested. For instance, the Master's statement, "The kingdom of Heaven in Within you." I have always assumed that Jesus meant what he said, yet most organized religions based upon these teachings believe just the opposite, that Heaven is a physical place located somewhere in the galaxy, but definitely outside of the self. So prayers are directed to this being who exists in this far away place. In other words, when they read the word "within" they actually understand the word "without." So I began to wonder how we can hear one thing and yet understand exactly the opposite. There must be a underlying structure within the mind which allows us to do this. And so there is. Our minds hear what they have been conditioned to believe regardless of what is actually being said. One of the things we get to understand is how we have been conditioned and how to reprogram this thinking machine we call the mind. One of our major programs is the idea of opposites.

Prior to Christian cosmology, Heaven was full of many gods, one for every major element of the world. The gods of sunlight, of the ocean and war and the goddesses of agriculture, healing and the moon. The early Christians borrowed the idea of good and evil from Zoroaster and the concept of the One God from Judaism, and reworked them into the concepts of the two great beings, God and Devil. This introduced the concept of opposites into the very fiber of existence. This belief in opposites in constant conflict has given rise to all the competition and fighting the history of the world has recorded. All of this fighting has, in turn, established a desire for order. If we want to stop the fighting, then we need to look at the basic attitudes about Life that are causing it.

We can begin with the idea of the fear of God. If we fear Satan because he's the bad guy, why do we fear the Good Guy? There should be one of them that we can trust. It is a result of the way fear spreads. At first only the immediate source of fear is seen, but pretty soon fear takes on a reality of its own and we begin to see it everywhere. Being totally afraid of everything has allowed us to see the insanity of this fear and thus discover the truth of manifested energy. Because as our fear has manifested itself throughout our world, so can our Love manifest when we believe in it as much as we now believe in fear. We are taking the truths of the ancient scriptures and applying them to the present while bypassing the current thought system.

The most interesting aspect of this change of focus is how resistant to change many of us remain. We are being shown the door by which we can escape the absurdity of modern existence and still we cling to the miseries we have come to expect as the best possible life style. The key concept necessary to help bring about this transformation is that the older thought system is based almost entirely on fear. So naturally, the first obstacle we will encounter is fear, fear of change, fear of losing what little we have, fear that this new way will prove to be false, fear that we will not be able to be spiritual enough to allow this new life to manifest in our lives, and on and on. Fear everywhere. And this is good, because it only reinforces the truth that the present system is built upon fear. Understanding this, we are freed to transcend this belief in fear and immerse ourselves in the energies of Love and Light. We go within and begin to manifest this new world order. By doing so, we can circumvent some of the mental anguish involved in the change.

We have already discussed the fear of change with its built in loyalty to the old ways, but there is also an emotional aspect to this change. When we change, we often experience a sense of loss. Even when we manage to free ourselves from blind adherence to old ways of thinking and begin to allow ourselves to expand, we still experience the slow, slipping away of the present life system. All of our hopes and dreams, all of ɔur efforts to achieve and create a life based on that type of thinking have to be released. Our cherished goals and dreams of future prosperity are tied to very strong emotions like faith and hope. It really doesn't matter that we are already experiencing more Joy in every moment. It really doesn't matter that the truth of "we are what we think" is incredibly clear and already producing joyful results, we will still experience the loss of the old ways as an emotional purging. And this is good.

When observing this phenomenon, it is interesting to observe just how much emotional energy we have tied up in hopeful future projections. We realize that a good portion of our emotional life was spent yearning for better times to come. We have the joy of releasing those yearnings and allowing ourselves to manifest Joy now. Not tomorrow, not someday, but this very moment. This sometimes takes some adjustment. We have been so used to living in the future that living in the present seems odd. But after a short time of experiencing more Love and Joy, it is quite easy to get used to. We experience the loss of a dream but gain a marvelous reality. In time, we willingly release the entire concept of future dreams and embrace the concept of the moment. It is part of a remarkable change of focus.

As long as we remain inside the mind, then we will be subject to all these ideas with which the mind is structured. By getting our focus out of the mind in meditation, we can allow the energies of the Soul to permeate our being and produce a new sense of self, a new sense of purpose, and a new sense of Being. Changing our focus is a process that involves two major aspects. One is the practice of focusing on the Soul energies in meditation and allowing those energies to manifest in our daily lives while the other is the releasing of all the old ways of thinking, feeling and behaving. There is a tremendous clearing of all that is outworn and no longer useful. One of these outworn forms is desire.

Every time we have a desire, it is covering something. It is a projection into the future of what is seen as missing in the present. More accurately, it is taking what is remembered as missing in the past and engaging our desire system to try to create it in the future. Either way, it is an attempt to make up for some perceived lack. We can replace this kind of thinking with the knowledge that we are already perfect as we are now and thus produce the perfect platform for growth. As long as we focus on what is missing then something will always be missing. We can never be satisfied in the present moment if we continually strive for a better tomorrow.

This change of outlook brings about a different kind of living, one that is based on finding the Joy and learning in each experience. The old way is to attempt to restructure reality in line with desire. The new way is to see the Joy in every moment and allow that Joy to expand and let the now take care of itself.

I suppose my present meditations can best be summarized as Being in the present moment. My mental energies are focused more on understanding and releasing old ideas than in trying to utilize those ideas to produce the ideal future life. I find myself being more receptive to what is going on around me. It seems that before I was so busy looking for a certain kind of flower that I couldn't be bothered to stop and smell the ones that were already there. And indeed, it is doubtful that I saw them as flowers at all. There was so much forward momentum that I was unable to be still, even for a moment. A man traveling at eighty miles an hour does not know what he is passing and in that headlong search for Destiny, we do not experience the joys of each potentially Love-filled moment. We really do not live at all, but only drive ourselves ragged chasing after a future which never arrives. Being in the moment, we can experience Love and Joy now instead of hoping to find it in some future fulfillment. Of course, this kind of living is based on a new kind of Trust.

Life Without Hope

7   Trust has in the past been confused with hope even though they are two very different ideas. Actually, they are opposites. Hope is based in fear, in the belief that nothing will make the present situation any better, but things might get better later if certain all powerful beings intervene on our behalf. So hope really keeps things from improving by transmitting the idea that they will not improve, at least not right away. The Universe merely cooperates with this kind of thinking as it would any other, and the envisioned future never arrives. And all this time

we thought Hope was our only salvation, our only hope, when in fact it is one of the main ideas that keeps us stuck where we are. We do not need to keep Hope alive, but rather allow it to fade away like any other outworn item in our lives. Hope only believes in a remarkable but distant future whereas Trust acknowledges present perfection.

It is hard to allow our Love and Light to manifest if we do not trust that it will. So we must go within and see for ourselves the fountain of Love and Light that is there, not hope that it will be there by and by, but find it now. We must get quiet and allow these energies to flow from our Center, for only then will we be completely sure of what we are doing. Only then will we be absolutely enthusiastic about the change we are experiencing. Yet many of us need proof before we will allow ourselves to change.

Personally, I find it odd that we can hope and work for future bliss without any kind of proof yet find it difficult to begin this process of change until some kind of proof is offered. Proof is so important to the present world system and yet the most important things we do, our relationships, our projected desires, in fact most of our waking endeavors, are earnestly gone after without a shred of evidence that they will be successful. We insist on proof and at the same time do without it, or completely ignore it if it shows its logical head. This is just another example of the insanity of the present system of thinking, a system that constantly limits our growth.

The young people we meet with for discussion are continually running into these kinds of limiting ideas and express their confusion about this mental dilemma. They experience a form of split mind as part of them is proceeding with this transformation while the other, older part seems locked into the ideas they grew up learning. The only real problem is that we are so used to thinking the other way that it is entirely habitual. And, as one man pointed out, all sentences begin with the pronoun, 'I.' Everything that is thought by the older mind is centered on the ego, an ego that is full of fear. So this ego is constantly badgering the person to go after this, to ignore something else and making endless judgments about everything. All of these judgments as well are also 'I' centered. The result is that even the willingness to proceed with spiritual transformation is met with this ego asking the same tired question, "What's in it for me?" And the problem here is that there is very little in Spiritual Transformation for the ego except a diminished influence within the self, a situation which it abhors and fights off with all the powers we have allowed it to accumulate.

So all thoughts are self-centered and the language we use is also structured to use 'I' as the beginning of each sentence. The language must also change. In place of 'I' we can substitute 'We.' In place of self-centeredness we can substitute Soul or Human-centeredness, recognizing that what is good for all of us is also good for each of us. The main reason we have been so self-centered is that we have believed that there exists only so much stuff, so much food, so many acres of land, so much love and respect, and we had better get what we need while we still can. The new Understanding is that there is infinite Abundance.

"Seek ye first the Kingdom of Heaven," the Master said, "and all else will be given unto you." He didn't say seek the kingdom of heaven last, but first, yet our true inner Essence of Love and Light is generally the last thing we seek. When we do seek Love or Joy, we usually look outside of ourselves. He also didn't say we would only get a few things, or that we had to work really hard in order to get anything at all. He said all things will be given. We will be given all that we need if we pay attention to the essence of our true selves. How could we have misunderstood such clear instructions and why do we continue to hesitate? It is our conditioning in this older way of thinking and living that we must now decide to leave behind us like old shoes that no longer fit. If we indeed all want to experience Love and Joy, and as we understand that the best way to accomplish this is to begin imagining that we already have these things, then it is time to begin thinking in this new way.

Oddly enough, the very selfishness that makes us desire to love and be loved is the biggest impediment to Love the world has ever known. We are so afraid of losing that we become afraid to share. When both partners are consumed with worrying if they are loved or loved enough or whether or not the love will last, then very little real Love is possible. Only when we put self interest aside can we truly allow Love to flow. It is an amazing paradox how the self-centered desire for Love can be so filled with fear that it stops the very Love it wants so badly. The end result is a culture full of lonely people who fear true intimacy. When we fear anything, anything at all, then fear is all that we allow ourselves to experience.

We can substitute a new spirit of exploration for this two sided paradox of desiring/fearing. Each day can become an adventure as we learn and grow and become these new beings full of Light and Love. When I first began to think about things, I felt guilty for wanting these things for myself. I thought that it would somehow be more noble for me to help others achieve Joy and Love while being unconcerned with my own happiness. It finally dawned on me that I was really afraid to try out these new ideas in my own life. It was much easier to tell others what to do than do it myself. This mind trick bit the dust when I realized how ridiculous my ego mind was being, and I began to bypass it for the deeper insights of the soul. These deeper insights have the ability to change our lives and our world. We are a highly educated yet quite barbaric world. It is time we became wise.

The Cult of the Personality

This era of our culture is marked by the worship of the personality. The music and movie stars are seen as people who have something special and many of them have hosts of imitators and look a likes. Yet their abilities as entertainers do not necessarily guarantee deeper insight into Life or any other special qualities. Often, just the opposite is true. Actors are the most remarkable case because they are worshipped and highly paid for pretending to be someone other than themselves. As such they reflect our deep desire to be someone else and break out of our dull routine, even if only for a hour or two. This stage in our learning is marked by dissatisfaction with our personality self, our small self. Our lives seem small and boring when compared to the 'stars.' Yet, when we begin to cultivate the expectation of adventure in our everyday lives, our lives become filled with more adventure and Joy than all the movie screens in the world. We begin to grow past our fascination with personality and observe an exciting new self emerge. And this excitement is so much more fulfilling because it is our lives and we and our friends who are the main characters. This self is much different from the personality.

The cult of personality can be defined as those who are concerned with the appearance of the smaller self, having the latest look, the appropriate career or becoming someone of stature within a particular sub-culture. This is a process of developing a self that satisfies an inner need successfully. This success runs the gamut from providing a support for the self image or a feeling of belonging all the way to a packaged commodity intended for public consumption. The Spiritual Path on the other hand is a process of allowing the Higher Self to manifest without interference. Where the personality is designed to produce a certain effect perceived as valuable by the ego/mind, the Higher Self naturally manifests the life experiences necessary for optimum growth and understanding. In this sense, the personality with its entirely active approach to life-making can actually interfere with the agenda of the Higher Self, producing much less growth and much less happiness than if the Soul was allowed to do its thing. If nothing else, the modern world of famous personalities with their notorious troubles are helping us to see the absurdity of their situation.

They want so badly to be loved that they drive themselves to become talented and famous in hopes of being loved by all. The tragedy is that fame immediately forces them into isolation to escape the constant badgering by groupies and the media. Those who truly want Love would do better to go to the source of Love within rather than trying to find it in mass adulation. The best laid plans of the personality always go awry because they are based upon false assumptions about the nature of reality. It is better to have one good friend than millions who wish to gaze upon the star.

The personality appears to be an expression of the self, but like the moon it is actually a very weak and filtered reflection of the true source of Light. As such it motivates us to pursue goals of little real benefit to the larger Self. And the control factor comes in when achieved goals fail to produce the happiness that was expected. The personality, in its narrow understanding, assumes that not enough was achieved and so spurs the hapless host to go after more and ever more. This can become a frenzied drive which sweeps anyone in its path to the side. The saddest part of the story is that the Love starved ego, because it craves enjoyment, begins to enjoy the race and even the ruthless crushing of others in its pitiful quest for happiness. It begins to use others in this quest without regard for sharing or Love, the two activities that would produce the joy that it seeks. And in this angry and misguided control for the ego's pleasure, we have the history of the world's troubles. Yet all the time, shining like a star deep in inner space, lies the source of all Light, the source of all Life, the Higher Self. The truth in the ancient paradox is obvious. "He who finds his life shall lose it and he who loses his life shall find it." Only by losing the false sense of self the ego has developed will we ever know true happiness. All these centuries, we humans have been looking for sustenance and Joy in the wrong place. It is time to change ourselves from anxious seekers after pleasure, to calm and contented experiencers of Love and Joy.

Anger

I was involved in a business situation where the client was intent upon controlling the outcome. This person was very forceful and used various manipulation techniques in an attempt to get me to satisfy all of the company's needs for a fraction of its actual value. I was used to this kind of intimidation because it was the technique my mother had used so effectively and was the reason I had been so angry at her. Perhaps the most unsettling aspect was to realize that I was still dealing with this anger/control mechanism 25 years later. A quick review of previous business fiascoes clearly showed that I had been experiencing this very problem all along. But now, rather than get even angrier at Mom for having saddled me with a defective brain, I instead determined to figure out and release this mentality so that I would never, ever have to experience it again. I saw here displayed all of the major mental problems I had going for me. There was anger, resentment, guilt and doubt all combining to make my financial success a struggle of mammoth proportions. This was my conditioning and the perfect place from which to explore the possibilities of change.

What I really saw when I looked deeper were layers of emotion and distorted thinking. There was the ever present resentment for my parents as well as guilt for feeling such things towards those who had raised and cared for me. There was also anger at myself for having fallen for this conditioning in the first place. Then, there was fury at all of the life experiences that these emotions and thoughts had ruined in the past as well as doubt that I would be able to do anything about any of it now. I was effectively held in a conditioned form of suspended animation and like Prometheus, doomed to live out the same torturous events eternally. But when I looked at this tangle of thoughts and emotions as an impartial observer, I noticed an underlying structure.

On one level was firmly intact all of the ideas of doubt and negative self-worth that I had accepted as well as a history of being manipulated. Over that was a second level of rebellion against this conditioning along with all the negative, stressful emotions associated with it. I could see that what I needed was not some form of reconciliation between these two, but a dispersal of both layers and a focus in an entirely new direction.

For starters, I began to initiate the idea that I was in control of my experiences and that by changing my thinking, I could change my life. This was an amazingly empowering idea. I found that I could release my poor self-image and insist upon fair treatment. And with the success of this attitude I was able to begin to eliminate the anguish over my past poor performance and forgive everyone involved, including myself. This act of forgiving opened up the true meaning of the lesson I needed to learn. It was not so much that no one had the right to take advantage of me or that, by God, I had better look out for myself, but rather that I had the power and intelligence to decide what was fair for me. I saw that their attempts to manipulate me were a reflection of both of our desires to be in control and our fears that we were not. By simply releasing the idea of control completely, I came to a more centered state where I simply presented my case and allowed the others involved to make their own decisions. They were completely free to decide to do business with me or not, but they were no longer free to manipulate. In essence, I became disassociated from the outcome because I understood that I would always be taken care of regardless.

What is amazing about this process of transformation is the simplicity of the ideas involved. They are very easily understood and there are so few of them that the entire structure of energy and its manifestation can be expressed in a few key concepts. Compared to the mountains of information required to understand the present system, this is indeed a significant breakthrough.

The more we understand that we are the way we think we are, the more we can begin to change our thinking. Those who are resistant to change will have to put up with their present lifestyles. Those who doubt will have to release the doubt and replace it with Trust because Trust is the foundation of this new way of thinking and being. Without Trust there can be little progress because doubt automatically casts doubt upon whatever it is we are thinking about and interferes with its manifestation. But if we Trust, then all the positive creative forces of the universe combine to bring our mental images into Being. One person's heaven is another's hell. Two people side by side can be having completely opposite experiences, but when we pay attention to our inner Light and allow it to flow out into three dimensional form, all will be well.

Chapter 2
How We Think

The Mind

It is impossible to see the mind clearly from within the mind. This is like trying to see the ocean while swimming on its surface. We can see and feel the water but have no idea what is happening a few feet away, let alone on the ocean floor. Only plunging to the depths will reveal its true secrets. The mind is a wonderful organizational tool, but is not really set up to make intelligent decisions. It knows only the past, so how can we expect it to predict the future? The best it can do is to repeat the patterns it has learned. This would be fine if everything we have experienced before brought us peace and Joy. If that were the case, then we would not be striving so hard to understand what is going on, nor would we be interested in changing anything. But we are interested in changing, even changing the way we perceive life. So we are involved in two major lessons about ourselves. The first one is understanding the limitations of our conscious minds. While minds are very adept at remembering details and are the center from which we consciously observe and record our experiences, they do not perceive the whole picture. The second lesson is to focus our attention on the Center, the seat of the Higher Self, and allow its energies to manifest, knowing that it perceives the much larger picture of who we really are. By doing so we are not losing anything but are rather adding a whole new dimension to our range of experiences while rearranging the structure of our thinking.

We must first understand the past as a process of learning rather than a battle for survival or affluence. All past experiences have been lessons designed to help us attain a more perfect Understanding of Life. This realization helps us to release all the hurts and resentments connected with memories. Our past is no longer viewed as having been a failure because we realize that is was not a competition where success was the goal. The past (and the present moment) are for learning through experience, and true success comes only when we learn to be joyous. This Understanding helps ease the stresses of day to day living and smoothes out relationships. It brings about the end of conflict and striving for the acquisition of goods and the perfect mate. Relationships, too, become wonderful opportunities for growth and sharing instead of coalitions for the mutual satisfaction of needs and desires. As such, we open ourselves to all aspects of relationships rather than the limited ideas we may have had before.

When we realize the present error in our focus, we can begin to release the old patterns and habits and so reclaim all the energies locked up in memories, in disappointments, in hopes for the future and misunderstandings about the present. This energy becomes once more available to the Self where it can be used to further create the new life of Love and Joy. All the energies tied up with sadness can be used to create happiness. The negative self image can be dismantled and its components restructured to produce a self full of confidence and zest. And the process continues in all areas. This is the true meaning of the Christian phrase, 'the dead in Christ shall rise,' because it refers to all the parts of us that have lost sight of the Light. This resurrection is but another instance which points to the dawning of the new age of Joy, the time of rejoicing and heaven on earth that all scriptures foretell.

This process of the negative becoming positive is the first step in our expansion. The next step involves leaving the concept of opposites behind. As long as there is good and bad then we will seek the good and try to avoid the bad. If everything is instead viewed as an experience given for our learning, then we no longer have the need to judge. It is experiencing rather than judging, it is 'walking a mile in another man's moccasins' before deciding anything about him. Non-judgment implies a world of experience where good and bad, right and wrong, beautiful and ugly do not exist. It is a world where everything simply is and we no longer interpret things in terms of our own egos. This is a path through the center of these two opposites where all is Light. When we know this to be true beyond a shadow of a doubt, then will we begin to transform ourselves and the world.

The Pyramid

If we use a pyramid model to look at our thinking, we can see that there are certain key ideas at the top from which all ideas underneath derive their meaning. These key ideas are the gate through which the Light of manifestation enters and which determines how it spreads throughout the structure. Imagine that the pyramid's tip is plugged into the source of Light and its makeup determines how much and what colors get transferred to the layers underneath. This process of filtering and channeling of Light continues until it touches the ground and establishes a four sided foundation, physical manifestation. The four has always represented the earth. The four corners, the four winds, and the four directions are reflections of this, as is the fact that most of our buildings and properties are square. The point is, if we concentrate our efforts on these key ideas, these elemental filters at the top, we can more easily change the entire pyramid than if we started at the bottom and laboriously worked our way up through layer after layer. Psychoanalysis represents the process of working from the bottom upwards (or from the outside inwards) and is ample testament to the slow pace of this approach. It is much faster to start at the top where it all begins.

If we examine the usual collection of these central ideas in any of our minds we will find two major ones, hope and fear, engaged in endless conflict and earnestly trying to outwit the other. It is no wonder that our lives seem so fragile and happiness such a rare commodity. I suggest that we replace these ideas with two others, two others that we know to be the true Essence of our Life Energy. These are the very two ideas that we are so hopeful and fearful about. They represent all that we so deeply desire and everything we are so afraid we might never see. They are Love and Happiness.

As we can immediately see, both of these desired ideas are positive which automatically eliminates conflict. Both of these can also exist at any time, in any place and under any conditions. These ideas are independent of all the limitations of the world with its present tumultuous rantings and represent the sum total of our passionate desires as well as the height of our most sublime intuitions. And these two concepts are really the two aspects of the one eternal truth, Light, as so wonderfully represented by the Sun in our solar system. The Sun, the source of light and warmth, the source of all energy from which life flows. And this Sun has its counterpart within us which further explains the ancient parable, 'as it is without, so it is within.' If we take our pyramid analogy one step further, we see that the point at the top is actually more like a center, and the Light radiates in all directions like a transmitter and produces our three-dimensional reality. Like a hologram, our lives are projections from this Central Source. So when we place the single idea of Light at the center, everything emanating from that center will be filled with Light. This Light filled existence will produce its twin offspring Love and Happiness, and our lives will be all that we have ever dreamed possible.

Change

This is a fundamental change in the way we think. It replaces the two basic, key ideas in our minds with new ones. It is the letting go of many old, cherished beliefs. The belief in evil, for instance. That belief produces evil and since most of us do not enjoy evil, one wonders why we are so resistant to releasing its influence in our lives. I think the key is that all of our perceptions still function within the present mental system where holding on tightly is considered a virtue and openness a dangerous departure from the norm. But we need to open up intuitive perception so that we can begin to explore these new realms of Spirit, realms of which sense perceptions are totally unaware. One idea that might help explain reticence to become Spiritual is the general notion of what the spiritual life entails. Most religions that we in the West are familiar with paint a picture that is full of renunciation. The initiate gives up the normal lifestyle of his culture and dedicates his energies to good works or to some cloistered form of prayer and fasting. This is understandably unappealing to many and is another example of the idea of opposites playing havoc with Truth.

Only if Life itself is perceived as a choice between God and the World can the life of renunciation be considered more spiritual. With this idea in place, we are forced to choose one or the other with our eternal reward at stake. We, as human guinea pigs, become pawns in a witless game between two super powers bent on testing the depths of our faith. This is not a formula for a life of Love and Joy but rather one torn between two very strong desires, the desire for happiness in this life and the desire for eternal bliss in the next. The picture painted by early religion was that these two paths were mutually exclusive so we ended up having a world conveniently divided into puritans and philanderers, monks and sinners. This produced a world of extremes which was only recently toned down by the separation of church and state in America. Now, at last, one could live a life of the senses all week and fulfill one's holy obligations in a couple of hours on Sunday morning. This was much handier, but still involved a split with the holy being viewed as the loftier and more important part of Life. It is now possible to see past the fallacy of opposites where both paths become the same.

The two paths were perceived as opposites because the method of attainment in each was different. The earthly path was characterized by the process of acquisition. One went out into the world and carved one's fortune out of the hard rock of adversity. In contrast, the holy path used faith in the beneficence of Deity as its sole tool for manifestation. One merely prayed, knowing that the Divine Presence would make its plan known and all things would be given to he who believed. These are perfect descriptions of the active and receptive paths, the male and female, the Yang and Yin. But rather than see them as opposites, we can now begin to understand that they are really complementary.

Like men and women joined in love, the active and receptive are actually two faces of the same unity. Only the idea of opposites in Western thought made them seem so black and white. And indeed, the focusing on male and female as opposites has given rise to all the conflict between the sexes that Western culture is famous for. The strength of this idea is amazing, and has affected the very foundation of western society. Any other idea is equally strong and would have an equally fundamental effect. Let's give unity a try and see what happens.

If we take this idea of unity and apply it to the conflict between the sexes, the conflict melts away leaving only Love in its wake. When we insert the idea of unity into the conflict between the two paths, we become aware that all Life is One and the earthly life and holy life are merely expressing the one Life Energy in different forms. If we take the idea of unity and place it on the very top of the pyramid, at the very Center of our holographic projector, then all conflict is washed away by the rushing forth of Love and Joy, the two aspects of Light.

We can bring all of our energies together in unity, flowing from a central point within. How different this is than the current psychological models which admit the existence of many voices within us. To them we are besieged by the ego and will, by desires and memories, by ego, id and collective subconscious urges, all clamoring for attention. It is no wonder so many of us are either confused or crazy, we have a whole family of bickering voices inside our own skulls. "Let thine eye be single," one Master said, pointing the way to calm, peaceful living, pointing the way to a mind and emotional structure centered on one intention, the intention to become One with all creation. And we start this process of becoming One within our own mental and emotional selves. When we become centered, when our eye becomes single, then we know true peace and contentment. We are no longer at the mercy of errant fears within. We are no longer subject to the vagaries of external fortune. We realize who we are and it is unshakable, giving us a peace that surpasses understanding.

Love, Joy and Celebration

Love, Joy and Celebration, what a superb mantra to place within our minds and watch as these amazing thought forms flow into manifestation. This is the process we are undergoing, a process of replacing the words and ideas in our heads with new ones. Fear is replaced with trust, anger and sadness with Joy and the frenzy of acquisition with allowing our true Inner Selves to manifest in a Celebration of Life Eternal. When we begin to change thusly, we find ourselves surrounded by others interested in changing as well. When the student is ready the teacher appears. This truth works both ways and we soon find ourselves teaching and learning exactly what we need most in order to grow. Instead of the alienation and loneliness many of us now experience, we have the opportunity to share with many others. Instead of a life that seems to be going nowhere, we have a challenging future of continuous exploration and growth. Instead of every man for himself, we have the nurturing relationships of a community of souls journeying on the Spiritual Path. All of this gives us a strong sense of identity and purpose.

The present culture's acknowledged purpose is to have a good time, to experience a wide variety of situations and to have all of our dreams come true. As a system built on acquisition, it has shifted from merely acquiring what it takes to survive to the drive to accumulate happy times. It is interesting that we do not focus on the state of Happiness within, or Contentment, but rather identify this state with active experiences. We tell each other about all the fun things we have done and hope to do in the future. We discuss in the most intimate detail our life plan and long term goals and yet seldom mention how we feel at the moment. A happy life, then, is perceived as one that has had a large and varied collection of experiences. And with the proliferation of night spots, videos and packaged vacations, it is possible to stay busy experiencing almost continually. Yet does this constant stimulus bring happiness or merely stave off the ever present threat of inertia and boredom?

Entertainment

The modern concept of being satisfied focuses on outward stimuli. Our music and entertainment are examples of the constant need for input. We seem to believe that we cannot be happy unless something exciting is going on, well, at least something going on. At times it seems impossible to find a quiet place to meditate because everyone else has all of their entertainment machines going full blast. What does this say about our culture, that we have lost the ability to entertain or enjoy ourselves? I think the question goes deeper and rests on the very idea of entertainment itself.

The very fact of separating life into work and entertainment puts an automatic premium on entertainment and makes work out to be the villain. We have become a people who despise their work and immerse themselves in packaged enjoyments during leisure. Even splitting our lives into two parts robs us of the very unity we actually desire. I have heard many say they wish their work was more enjoyable and that their leisure was more meaningful. Neither one, it seems, really has any connection to their real existence but are merely what they do with their time. When we begin to see our work as an exciting challenge it will become so and our leisure time becomes more and more involved with our own growth as Spiritual Beings. This growth spreads rapidly into groups of us sharing our experiences and helping each other to expand. We begin to be excited about our own lives instead of focusing on the make believe lives of media personalities. All of a sudden, everything that we do is intimately involved with us and the days of boredom and apathy are gone. Instead of trying to get away from it all we become completely involved in getting into the very center of it all. It is the exploration of the final frontier, inner space. And it is a place where everyone can go and everyone can be successful.

The new purpose we gain from growing and sharing has in its makeup all of the characteristics we say we prefer. Rather than being consumers of passive entertainment we become active players in our own exciting story. Rather than experiencing Life as make-believe interactions in relative isolation we get to experience Love and share in the learning and growth of ourselves and others. It is a dynamic, interactive lifestyle rather than the lonely, sedentary one. It is everything we really wish we could have and so much more. Why do we delay? Because we are still so used to operating our lives in the old ways. We are still being consumers rather than active participants.

We are so used to being totally programmed, to making things happen, that it is at first difficult to allow things to happen. Even if all that we actively plan is our inactive entertainments, the active principle is still operating. The new way exemplifies the Zen paradox of doing by not doing. By allowing things to manifest from the Center outward, we can not only accomplish so much more in much less time and with much less energy, we will also be much more satisfied with the end results. Yet the idea of having to work hard to get anything done is so strong that it gets in the way of this new method. It must be released before the process of allowing will be successful. We must release all doubt and open to Trust. We must say 'Yes.'

Saying 'Yes' is the key to the new Understanding and is based on the knowledge that by saying 'Yes' to Love and Joy we are opening ourselves to those experiences. The old way taught us to say 'No' most of the time. If we did say 'Yes' it was often more of an okay than an enthusiastic embracing, and usually came only after much analysis and deliberation. Sometimes, this deliberation process took so long that the opportunity was long past before any decision was made. 'Better safe than sorry,' the old adage goes. But given the level of fear in the old way, it is perfectly logical that we could have difficulty making up our minds. After all, saying 'Yes' is tantamount to a commitment and a commitment is a serious decision affecting the most important thing in the universe, our own little future. So fear and self-centeredness combine to make forward momentum difficult and for many, impossible. The very term 'making up our minds' implies the kind of quarreling factions most of us identify with conscious thinking. It describes a mind paralyzed with indecision. Rather than say 'Yes' to life, we go around and around through an endless cycle of possibilities, each of which rests on the perceived results of past experiences. We are attempting to make decisions about the future based on shreds of memories. It is a process of deciding without vision and based almost entirely on the fear of what will happen if we make the wrong choice. On the other hand, trusting and saying 'yes' opens us up to the wonderful possibilities before us, possibilities emerging from a true Understanding of how Life Energy works in cooperation with thought. I have seen many students get stuck in this very place because though they really wish to trust and grow, they are held back by their fear of making a decision or mistake. Fortunately, there is a way around this dilemma.

Whereas the traditional decision making process is a careful weighing of probabilities, saying 'yes' to the universe is based on fact. The old way believes that the future cannot be known and is filled with danger. The new way knows that the future is a simple process of our present thoughts manifesting. We no longer need to stare with dread into the misty recesses of time, praying for vision and safety. We only need to make sure our present thoughts are wholly positive so that they will manifest a positive future. So, we turn our attention within and begin to purify our minds of all negative thinking. And this is easily done by saying 'yes' to the process of purification. We merely have to trust that we will be shown what we need to understand and release, and we will see these thoughts and their corresponding emotions perfectly reflected in our lives. This process is automatic because it rests on Truth. Our thoughts and emotions are already manifesting in our lives every moment of every day and always have. It's just that we are only now becoming aware of them. This is a process of inner discovery where we learn to perceive the true underlying structure of three dimensional experience. As we grow in the understanding of this process, we become more and more conscious of our creative power because we see that we have been creating everything that happens to us all along.

What a wonderfully freeing realization! We are no longer at the mercy of fate or under the control of any person, organization or supposed state of the world. We are free to create the absolute life of our wildest dreams for which we already have everything that we need. We do not have to wait until we have amassed a fortune or until we have managed to build a vast support network. We do not need to bide our time until the economy improves or until the stars are in the right positions. We are completely self-reliant. We have complete control right now and the results will be incredible and immediate, which is what we really want anyway.

There has been a lot of criticism lately of the younger generations lack of responsibility. The old guard complains that they are not willing to work for what they want and expect to have everything handed to them on the proverbial platter. Yet these ideas of hard work and slowly building up a fortune are in direct contradiction to the new truth. We create our life experiences by our thinking, not by the sweat of our brow. The only reason hard work has ever paid off is because our thinking told us it would. This is what the Master Jesus was trying to show us with his demonstrations of healing and creation. In our ignorance we have called these demonstrations miracles, attributing them to some kind of divine intervention to which only He had access. We completely ignored his statement, "All that I have done ye can do also, and even greater things can you do." He was showing us that the true creative nature of life is, "ask and ye shall receive," that our words and our thoughts create their content and that the asking is a process over which we can have conscious control.

Just think of all the benefits this new Understanding gives us. For one, we become in charge of our own lives. We no longer need to seek for sustenance from others but rather will be able to share from a Center of absolute Abundance. Most of the problems associated with modern life can be traced to lack, lack of love, money or the necessaries of survival. We are learning now that there are no limits of anything, only the perceived limits of the old way of believing. All is abundance. "In my father's house there are many mansions," refers not to the rooms of a mythical castle, but to the absolute abundance of all things. And these are not small rooms or hovels, but mansions, each of them a work of creative manifestation like the world has never seen. It is time we began to claim our rightful inheritance of Abundance, Love and Joy. It is ours for the asking.

So what is involved in this process of growth and purification? It is like giving our minds a shower, a shower of Light from within. By going to the source of Light in the Center, we can allow this Light to permeate our entire being and wash away all dark patches from our thoughts and emotions. Light will remove the filters that our conditioning has placed within the mind and so allow the Light energy to flow through us undisturbed by erroneous beliefs. This is the ultimate in creativity because the Light does not have to twist and turn through the many layers of the personality, but rather manifests directly and effortlessly from the Center outward.

Creativity

True creativity is far different from the current view of it. The present idea seems to be that pressure is good because it forces us to create, a creation that we would supposedly not attempt without this external deadline. It is entirely obvious to me that all the external pressure does is force us to say 'Yes' to the project. When we are backed into a corner and have no other way out, then we say 'Yes,' however begrudgingly. Unfortunately, many of us wait until the last possible minute to say 'Yes' and so increase the stress ten fold. Some of my artist and theatre friends have taken this kind of behavior to new heights and so display its shortcomings most clearly. By observing, I began to see the double edged hook of the creative process.

Artists attest to the thrill of creativity but remain relatively unaware of the frightful lack of self-confidence that often inspires the creative drive in the first place. Taking on a new project involves an exciting leap of faith but the ensuing doubt about one's ability to produce often leads to stalling. Waiting until the last minute, then, is a combination of waiting for inspiration and building up enough deadline stress to overcome fear of failure. It is an interesting process whereby the ego forces the self to take on more than is comfortable in an effort to prove its own genius. Yet the common experience is that the project always gets done and this phenomenon provides fodder for the belief in the 'magic' of the creative process. It is this 'magic' that is so addicting because in its flow one feels the energy of Life pouring through. Yet all that has really happened is that the artist finally said 'Yes,' and the creative energy within was released to do its job. How much simpler to say 'Yes' right away and avoid all the stressful unpleasantness of fear-filled procrastination. Of course, this implies a new understanding of the creative process, one devoid of affiliation with the ego.

If there was not a weak self-image then there would be no need to push the self. If there was not a doubt as to the value of the self then there would be nothing to prove. We all want to think of ourselves as special, but trying to build a specialness based on achievements is missing the point. The best we can hope to accomplish through achievement is the respect of others when what we actually want is a feeling of worth inside of us. Trying to get this feeling from others is like trying to quench our thirst by having someone else tell us about drinking water. It is second hand and not very satisfying. Only by going to the Center and discovering our own Source will we ever feel totally full-filled.

Even Christians who believe that God is outside of themselves still realize that they must let the Christ Energy into their hearts in order to fully understand the Love of God. They do not understand that Love is and always has been within us, but they at least realize the transforming properties of Love if it is allowed to occupy the Center or Heart of Hearts. It must be inside before it can manifest in the life experience. Artists and others who create wonderful things are not showing us the superior nature of their own personal creative abilities, but are rather demonstrating what we are all capable of producing if we would only say, 'Yes.'

The other problem with artistic creation is that it is often a solo flight. Even in film or theatre where many artists collaborate, it is often times more of a battle of egos than a unified, cooperative effort. Everyone clings to their own individual vision of the finished project and begrudgingly submits to the top dog. If we cross this analogy over to everyday life, we have a world full of individual egos all clamoring for their own particular vision of the future. There is some cooperation, but only if the goals are similar. So we have political parties and special interest groups and all out war in many countries, all the result of ego visions in conflict, and all based on the idea that we need to work (or fight) together to get what we want. We all seem to believe in the need to make things happen. I often wonder if we are afraid of what might happen if we don't make things happen. In this new paradigm, we begin to understand that we all want the same things and that we can all have them so much more easily if we allow them to manifest rather than fighting each other for them. Gone then will be the eternal conflict of egos. Gone will be the scrambling for limited resources. There is plenty of everything for everyone. There is total abundance in all areas, but so far the only real abundance we have been able to manifest is one of suffering.

Think about it. Our ways of thinking, our greed and anger and fear have produced a world consumed with greed and anger and fear. And these insane thoughts have in turn produced a world filled to the brim with incessant suffering and disheartening situations seemingly beyond all hope of cure. If we can create such great suffering with thoughts that produce suffering, imagine what we can create when we begin to think of Love and Joy and Cooperation. And the most insane part of this whole scenario is that what we are really trying to create with all of this hate and anger is Love and Joy.

We only use fear, greed and violence because we have been taught that this is the way one get things in this world. False, totally false ideas that have led to all the disasters in the history of man. We must begin immediately to change this way of thinking. Now that the true cause of our misery is clear, there is no longer any reason to delay the immediate intention to completely transform our lives from the Center outward. Let us begin!

Chapter 3

Going Within

The Inner Journey

As a race of beings known for its incessant urge for exploration, I find it interesting that going within is met with such resistance. You would think that the existence of an entirely new level of reality, a level of existence filled with Light and Love and almost totally unexplored would bring the adventurous out in droves. This is a pioneer's dream, virgin territory in a world described by a few ancient traveler's but never before encountered by the masses. Yet many seem reluctant to even approach the entrance to this new land of Abundance and Love. There have always been a few Prophets and Masters who have walked this path and returned to tell us. There have always been holy books that tried to describe the territories known as Heaven and Nirvana, but never before have we as an entire race of beings been poised on the threshold of such a monumental discovery.

We stand now upon the crest of the Hill of Understanding and can for the first time view the valley below. Our weary eyes behold the vision of a world full of Love and Joy. It is the land flowing with milk and honey that the Hebrews wrote about. It is the Happy Hunting Grounds of the Native Americans, the Heaven of the Christians and the Nirvana of the East. Only now we know that we do not have to physically die in order to enjoy and experience it. We only have to let our egos fade away, we

41

only have to release the false idea of separateness and step across the bridge of trust into the valley of unity. When we allow our egos to die, we are reborn in the spirit and we rise again. The dead in Christ shall rise, the Christian texts tell us, and it is this rebirth into the spiritual world of Love and Light that this verse refers to. This small change of consciousness, from ego centered to humanity centered, from I centered to Us centered, will bring about more positive change than we have yet to witness on the earth plane. Understanding the ego might help in this change.

We are all of us aware that the present world system does not work. Organized religion is beginning to acknowledge that they have failed in their attempt to make the world better through preaching and missionary work. The present political systems are hopelessly inept at accomplishing anything of value. Politics itself is no longer the career of the community minded, but has become the haven of the most egocentric persons on the face of the globe. And how wonderful this situation is for us. We can no longer depend on the Church, or on our elected officials, or on science to fix the world for us. We are thrown back on ourselves. We must initiate a grass roots effort. And now we have the perfect Understanding of where the true power lies. Our older systems failed to transform our world because the people involved were not transformed. It is too much to ask an egocentric person to become a senator and immediately drop his egocentricity. There are a few who manage to keep their own self interest under control, but for most, the temptation is too great. But we now know that real change does not come from the outside but from the inside. We have the power to change the world and are doing so this very moment. And we are doing so without regard for what anyone else thinks or might be doing.

In the old way it was important for everyone to be pulling together because it was believed that only in concentrated group effort would any real progress be made. But that supposes that the purpose of Life is to produce things. We understand that the true purpose of Life is to learn and to grow. If others wish to expend their energy in the pursuit of acquisitions, then that must be the best way for them to learn. We can totally support them in their choice while choosing for ourselves a different way on a new and more sensible path.

In the early days of the spiritual movement in America, in the late 60's, even to suggest that the American Way was not the absolute best was heresy. Many thoughtful young people were branded as Communists for even asserting that the American Dream could use some improvements. And those who questioned the American system were dismayed that their questions were viewed as criticism. That a system so enthusiastic about the scientific, inquiring mind should fail in this test of self analysis is enlightening. This is a basic contradiction within a system that professes interest in making things better for future generations yet is so afraid of change that such growth becomes impossible. There was a vast difference between what was being said and what was being done. It is no wonder that new generations seem so disillusioned, they realize that a lot of what they have been taught to believe has little substantiation in everyday experience, even for the teachers. But we can now leave all of that behind us.

When we focus on what we need to do to manifest our own best experience, then we are no longer concerned with the perceived problems of the current system. We understand that as our thinking changes, our world will change. And when enough of us have made this transformational change, the entire world will change according to the law of critical mass. We need do nothing else but make sure our own house is in order. In focusing on everyone else's problems, we have kidded ourselves into the arrogant position of thinking that we are perfect. It is a very safe procedure for us. As long as we focus on the problems of the world, we do not have to look at ourselves. We also fool ourselves by thinking how magnanimous we are being, how noble and self-sacrificing by concerning ourselves wholly with the welfare of others. This is one of the oldest lines in the book, the old 'I'm only doing this for you' routine. It is time we get the guts to look at our own foolishness and stop blaming everyone and everything else for our unhappiness. The new victim mentality has got to be the lowest form of egotism I have ever observed. It is the ultimate manifestation of seeking our happiness outside of ourselves. To think that someone else is responsible for our misery is the ultimate cop out. We alone have true control of our thoughts and we alone can change them. All the legislation in the world will not make up for one minute's worth of self-destructive thinking. And if we have been conditioned to think in destructive ways, then it is our responsibility to change it. No one else can do it for us. And as mentioned earlier, if it were not for the problems our thinking is causing us, we would never be in a position to attempt this kind of transformation. So instead of belly aching about all of the opportunities we have missed and about all of the advantages we have been denied, we can rejoice in the knowledge that all of them have brought us to this point of ultimate Understanding.

Besides, the victim mentality is based on the assumption that there is a certain level of affluence guaranteed by being born in the West, that there is a certain prescribed way we should all be treated and clothed and nurtured and that anything else is an injustice against humanity. This is but another example of Life being viewed as acquisition, only these "victims" are angry because they have not received their due. Yet the truth is, we all receive exactly what we ask for. The negative and destructive ideas in their minds, as in all of ours, have manifested perfectly. If they now desire something else, then they need to learn to think in more positive terms. All the shouting and petitioning in the world will not get them what they want. Anger and violence can never create Happiness. If we want true Happiness, then we will have to learn to ask for it by name, and with Joy and enthusiastic expectation in our hearts. But first, we must believe that we deserve it.

Deserving

Deserving is another idea that is central to our present thinking, the idea that we have to do something to be deserving of love, to be worth our salt. This sets up the practice of driving ourselves to produce something the world considers valuable. It starts in grammar school with the competition for grades and approval and continues into the working world. This idea of proving our worth is just an idea and is not based on observable fact. There is not a shred of factual evidence that we do not deserve unless we contribute something of tangible value. If it were really true, then we would drown our babies as soon as they were born. Babies produce nothing of tangible value and yet we adore and care for them, often to distraction. Somewhere along the weaving line of maturing, the idea of 'you are beautiful just the way you are' becomes 'you have to strive to make yourself better and develop skills to make yourself valuable.' All of this sets up the heartbreaking stories of failure and disillusionment that plague our cultures.

In a culture that focuses so much on success, failures are the more common occurrence because competition sets remarkably high standards. There always seems to someone somewhere who can do something better. This produces the inevitable distress, frustration and rebellion we see everywhere we look. When we learn that we are all the wonderful children of Love and Light, then we have nothing that needs to be proven. We have no reasons to enter into stressful competitions or push ourselves to the limit in order to prove that we are worthwhile. We are worthwhile! We are little bits of Divine Energy dwelling in three dimensional form. Everything we do can be imbued with this Divine Energy and we can glow and shine like brilliant beacons of Joy and Light, just like our beautiful babies. So we have something we get to unlearn. We need to release from our minds all of the ridiculous, limiting thinking about deserving we have inherited and replace it with the truth of our Divine inner natures. And we do this by recognizing this nature and allowing it to manifest in our personal lives.

How different this is than the present world of acquisition and power. In this world, though all desire it, only a very few make it to the top. Everyone else has to settle for whatever they can get and somehow come to terms with the obvious fact that they are not the best. This makes many of us strive to be the best at something even if it is being a con artist or mass murderer. The desire to be the best, to be famous has created whole generations who thirst for recognition in the form of exposure or money. If recognition is the game, then it really doesn't matter how one achieves it, an idea which has led to all the modern abuses reported by the media and tabloid sensationalism. It is time we turned our attention within and stopped the pitiful and desperate clamoring for ego recognition, replacing it with the far more secure knowledge of who we truly are within.

The Olympic Figure Skating scandal of 1994 demonstrated what happens when success is more important than any other aspect of Life. We welcome these traits in our movies and books, yet deplore them in three dimensional reality. We need to decide if we want these traits or not. To say 'yes' to them on one level of reality, like movies and dreams, is to say 'yes' to them on all other levels as well. We must project creative images that are cleansed of these ideas of striving and success and replace them with the gentle allowing of our true inner selves to come out. We can wholeheartedly thank these tabloid heroes for showing us the absurdity of this kind of thinking. They have aptly demonstrated in their lives the foolishness of the thoughts we have all held sacred for hundreds of years. In seeing them manifested so precisely, we are finally able to recognize their true content and begin the process of changing them into more positve ones.

The first thing that happens when we begin to manifest our true inner nature is that we all see that we are totally beautiful, totally surrounded with Abundance and completely capable of becoming anything we can imagine. We find ourselves open and loving and able to share what we know with others. We immediately become sparks of Divine Energy instead of lumps of flesh trying to prove our worth. It is a situation where everyone wins, where everyone is the best and all are totally successful. We can start by focusing on the joys of our everyday life. If we can not see the Joy in our day to day existence, then it is a sign that we are not seeing what is there. The only difference between a good day and a bad one is attitude, and going to the Light within can help change our attitudes about absolutely everything.

We have been looking at Life as if it were some kind of game. The rules of this game stated that we only had this one chance and it was important to make the most of it. And so we have tried so hard, so very, very hard to make every minute count that we have lost sight of the larger picture. In focusing on accomplishments or the quality of our experiences and possessions, we have forgotten the fundamental truths of existence. So much so, that we even treat Love as a commodity. We have become stuck somewhere between the opposite poles of 'the sky's the limit' and 'I'll never amount to anything.' Yet the answer to this dilemma is so very simple.

When we focus on the Center and find our true Essence, then we no longer need to strive so hard to become. We realize that we have been standing at the doorway of Life clamoring to be let in when we already are in. We discover that all of the things we truly want for ourselves, Love, respect, Abundance and Joy, already exist within us. We understand that the human race does not have to be a race at all, but an incredible flowering of our Being from within. We are not human doers, we are Human Beings! It is time for us to acknowledge this truth. It is a very subtle change we are going through but with incredibly vast effects.

By a simple change of focus from 'I' centered to 'We' centered, by shifting from ego controlled to soul expanded, we change everything without effort, without competition and without fear of failure. And this change begins to manifest immediately. What more could we possibly want? Well, how about a system of thinking that explains everything.

A New Understanding

Religions as we understand them are systems of thought whose purpose is to help us have the most successful total existence. As such they address beliefs and behaviors in this Life designed to produce Happiness here and insure eternal bliss in the next life. It is interesting that in many traditional Western religions one must work very hard on earth for little apparent gain while in the afterlife everything we need is provided automatically. That is beginning to change as some religions preach prosperity for both now and the hereafter. Modern Western political systems are also designed to help produce the best possible Life for the greatest number of us. We are really talking about the same type of system and it is only recently in history that the church and state have been separate enough for these systems to operate independently.

The world's history is full of wars being fought over

whose set of ideas are the best, over whether the church or state should rule, and most nations and religions have never been shy about imposing their beliefs on others if they got the chance. Some of these wars were fought over what appears in hindsight to be trivial matters, slight differences in procedure or issues that were actually cultural and had no real bearing on the true nature or truth of the belief system. Everyone, it seems, has been sticking up for their own cherished beliefs and thus there are zillions of denominations, all with zealots willing to die for the sake of dogma. Perhaps what we need is a system of beliefs that is not so controversial, one that addresses the essence of all of them without getting into the petty details that have led to so much separateness, misunderstanding and utterly senseless suffering.

This new Understanding would have to explain the laws of physics and the confusing notions of psychological theory. It would have to provide a model for new political, religious and social systems as well as point the way towards Happiness, Joy and personal fulfillment for every Life form on the planet. In short, it would have to be a solid basis for solving all of the world's present problems and still contain an understanding that would allow continued growth and exploration. It would also need to be very simple so that everyone could understand it, yet have enough truth and exciting possibilities to satisfy the most adventurous intellectual. It would have to echo all the hallowed traditions of ancient wisdom as well as integrate seamlessly with modern theoretical science. In other words, it would have to both completely explain and offer an understandable way to access all levels of human existence, physical, emotional, mental and spiritual, and be capable of producing total satisfaction and happiness for everyone. That is a very tall order but fortunately, one that is easily accomplished with one simple truth, that we are a projection of Love and Light. This one simple statement is the basis for a complete and universal Understanding.

Love and Light

Life can be explained as a series of projections in an ever expanding universe. The Light of our souls projects outwards into the level of mind, which forms those energies into thoughts. Those thoughts then project their content into emotion and finally into physical manifestation. The world as we know it is a result of the combined projections of all of us together while the universe is the result of the combined projections of every Life form that exists, and is the outward expression of what we call God or Divinity. As we go within ourselves further we find Divinity again as the Source of the Light which is our Being. Within and without is the same energy in different forms of manifestation. The only real problem that we have right now is our inability to perceive the existence of anything beyond the five senses.

In effect, our current knowledge of the world limits us to dwelling on the physical, emotional and mental planes. We have blinders to all the myriad other levels of reality and yet we intuitively know of their existence. That is why we can trust that things will be better. That is why we strive so hard to learn and why we explore everything that comes within our aura. We know Life can be more than it is and we are looking for it always and doing everything we can think of to make it happen. Watching a small child taking everything in and everything apart shows us our creative exploration operating in top condition. We explore everything, so it was only a matter of time before we began to explore the levels of Spirit. That time is now. And with this simple Understanding of how Life energy works within us along with the intimate knowledge of our true makeup, we are well on our way.

Who We Are

What a remarkable planet with incredible forms of Life! We ourselves are only just beginning to become all that we are capable of being. So far we have been limited by our thinking. We have been dancing to the beat of drums played by those with little true knowledge of rhythm. Our religions have told us that we are inferior to God. Our social systems have told us that we must sacrifice ourselves for the good of the greater number. And so we try to make the best of it and hope for Joy and Bliss in the future. Yet as we continue to evolve and become brighter with each day, we realize that Joy is no longer the private reserve that only a few humans get to experience. We are no longer interested in a system which produces a few jewels to be admired, a few special people to be adored and emulated. We are in the process of developing a new world based on mutual Love and respect, a respect grounded in the knowledge that we are all the Children of Light. We leave behind the limitations of the older way of thinking. This is not to say that the older way is bad, but only that it has built in limitations that can easily be bypassed with a quantum leap in positive Life experience. We are not giving up anything, only leaving behind systems that are no longer in line with our new Understanding.

There are very few of us who would attempt a cross country trip on horseback when cars and planes are so convenient and accessible. Yet within our thinking many of us cling to systems of thought equally as antiquated. We can always go back and experience them in fond memory, but to attempt to utilize them as everyday methods is ridiculous. We cannot go back to old ways even though many still believe it would be better.

If we look at the old ways, what is it about them that we imagine we miss so very much? Is it the Joy of those days and the neighborliness of those ways? Of course, anyone who really studies earlier times does not come away with a feeling for everyday joy, but rather of much hardship and stern resignation. Nostalgia is very big, but do we really think people were happier then? We don't respect or admire our old people yet go on and on about the old times and pay huge amounts of money for old things. But even supposing that some aspects of life were better then, is it not equally possible that we can be even more joyous now than we imagine they were then?

This idea of standing by the old ways has to be one of the most limiting beliefs that we currently possess. It is a belief with the power to keep the evolution of consciousness at a complete standstill. It's as if we would rather bask in the romantic nostalgia of the past or in vague dreams of the future than attempt to become satisfied today. We would rather live within our emotional imaginations than truly experience the present moment. If we wish to experience a Life of Love and Joy then we must divest ourselves of this attachment to the past. This particular nonsense is really a whole generation of people doing what they consistently chide other not do, crying over spilt milk. To think that yesterday was better than today is an example of insane thinking. And to think that tomorrow cannot be better than our wildest dreams is to put such severe limits on the human spirit that we might as well all give up right now. And that's a very good idea!

Why don't we just give up? Give up all the worry and the fear, all the strain and stress of working so very hard. Let's give up all the wishing for the past days of glory and the yearning for a better future, and instead focus our attention on the joys of the present moment. Why don't we eliminate all of this inner bickering and give to ourselves a single vision, a vision that shows the earth and all of its inhabitants living in Love, Joy and Celebration. We are what we think and it is time we stopped thinking in these old, self-defeating ways. When we let go of these old thoughts, we can allow these new ones to take their place. Let us release the nostalgic desires of yesteryear, desires that by their very nature can never be fulfilled, and let us replace them with desires that can be fulfilled. Why expend so much energy on dreams we know can never come true? Let us beckon to the Source of Love within us to fulfill our most cherished wishes for Love. Let us bring the brilliant Light we find within out into the present moment so we can see what is happening within and around us. Let us throw off the blinders of limiting thought and propel ourselves into the 21st century instead of lamenting that we cannot live in the middle ages. It is time to grow! And we can do that by allowing our true inner natures to emerge from their cocoon of misunderstanding and ignorance.

Regret

One of the major limitations we place upon ourselves is regret. It is another of the types of thinking that keeps us glued to the past. But we can rewrite our own history. What has happened is done and we cannot change that, but we can change our understanding of it completely. For instance, I use to spend a lot of time chastising myself for lost opportunities. There were many romances and many business and social opportunities I passed up because of shyness, lack of self-confidence or down-right lack of awareness that an opportunity was being graciously offered. But I can see now that these experiences enabled me to search for a way to heal the inner hurt and turmoil I felt. Every-thing that happened, including my regret, was a perfect reflec-tion of my thoughts and emotions at the time. Without this inner turmoil I might have never discovered that my thinking was the cause of these situations, and that it was also the cure. Oh, what freeing power to know that we can heal ourselves and completely revamp our entire Life experience. What a bless-ing to become conscious creators, fully in charge of our desti-nies. It is a triumphant emerging of the Spirit within us.

We can only find this inner peace if we look within. Often our restlessness only allows us to feel good when we are active. When we have to sit quietly we are at the mercy of our own negative thinking. So we remain moving at all times, at least mentally. Some of us can go whole lifetimes without re-ally seeing this process of avoidance. 'Keep them busy, keep them happy,' seems to be a motto. Yet it is so very important to be able to be happy when sitting alone in a quiet room. If we are unable to accomplish this, then we will never be truly happy no matter how many thrills we experience. But because we have been taught to fear aloneness, we limit our access to the gate that leads to the peace we wish to experience. The fear of being alone is so very prevalent and is actually founded on the false idea of separation.

In our modern cultures we have perfected the art of be-ing cold towards others. We do not know our neighbors and can feel totally isolated in the midst of the most crowded city in the world. When we add the fear of intimacy, we have a formula for the sadness and misery our world is becoming fa-mous for. And this loneliness is the admitted cause for all sorts of insane behavior. The profound lack of Love causes so much stress within the individual that it is bound to explode in all sorts of neurotic imaginings and aberrant behaviors. This is only possible because we have developed the ability to completely ignore other people. We have become so totally wrapped up in our own pursuit of Happiness that we have forgotten how to be friendly and kind, even to those who are supposedly our most cherished friends.

We see the people on the streets but our main concern is how best to avoid them. We know that we should spend more time with our children but we have our time all rented out in the rush to satisfy our desires. We would like to be able to relax and enjoy ourselves once in a while but our isolation from everyone else makes it necessary for each of us to have everything so we can do everything ourselves. Lawn tools and vehicles and leisure toys, there is so much stuff that each of us simply must have to make life easy and enjoyable that there is no time left to take it easy or enjoy anything. We have been fooled into the predicament of working for things instead of living. And everyone suffers and works and looks forward to retirement when, at last, there will be time to enjoy life, at least in theory. There is nothing wrong with tools and furniture and lifestyle items, but if we cannot ever enjoy them, then we must have them for some other reason than their usefulness. That reason is self-image.

Self-image, the battle cry of the late 20th century. Since most of us do not have to worry about basic physical survival, we have shifted our concerns and worries to the content of our self-image. As a result, we work harder than we ever have and under much more stress. All the labor saving devices and the mechanization of industry that was supposed to free us from the drudgery of ceaseless work has not fulfilled its promise. And it is not industry's fault or the government's fault, it is our thinking's fault. We have been conditioned to believe that there are always shortages and problems in life and that hard work and drudgery are inevitable. These thoughts are in the mind and must manifest somehow. If there is not a real danger of starvation or physical hardship, then the mind will find something else to bitch about. The result is that we have whole generations complaining that they have not received the love, money, support, etc., that they needed to be totally fulfilled people. Their car isn't new enough, their house big enough or their bank account fat enough to support their intended lifestyle, a lifestyle that would be considered total luxury by any other standard than their own. It is not anyone's fault that they find themselves in this predicament, it is the fault of their thinking which is so full of problems that it creates them even where none exist. We pity the psychotic whose vivid imaginings produce fear and despair without apparent stimulus, yet we do not understand that we are doing the same things in our lives. We are being unhappy and totally depressed over situations which do not exist. And this depression only makes things worse for everyone involved.

We have whole segments of our society that are basket cases, unwilling and unable to do anything for themselves except scream for someone else to make it right for them. As long as we look for what is wrong with our lives we will find it. Perhaps we should begin to look for what is right about our lives. Perhaps if we concentrated on the good parts, on the wonderful potentials we have and begin to build upon those potentials, everything would become better. This process cannot fail to work because we are what we think, and thinking of how good everything is will make it so. We are beginning the exploration of inner space where one small change within produces immense and welcome changes for us all.

Rebellion

I was thinking about rebellion this morning while meditating. As I allowed the Light to flow from the Center, I began to feel pockets of tension release which were accompanied by an image of myself when younger. I saw myself being forced to do things I didn't want to do and remembered becoming determined to punish those responsible by not liking them. After all, that is what they did to me. If I did things my parents didn't like they would tell me, "You know better," and I would feel emotionally rejected. Now it was my turn and I became dissatisfied with them. So I stopped giving them love, I got angry and rebelled for all the things they had done to me. It was a situation in which everyone lost. They lost a son and I lost both my parents and more. By willfully shutting down my flow of Love I sentenced myself to a life without it. Of course, Love always manifests eventually, and there were times when I could set aside this situation and allow myself to experience some for brief periods. But soon the sadness, confusion and anger would return.

Now that I have understood these events from an adult perspective, I can see that all of this treatment was an attempt to lead me down the right path. However foolish or unevolved their ideas and methods may have been, my parents' intentions were sincere and I have 'turned out all right.' It is intentions that are the most important aspects. So I can release my rebellions which have only hardened my heart and kept Love from flowing. This has effectively kept everyone unhappy and accomplished absolutely nothing positive for me, except an odd sense of power. If we are powerless, which we are as young children, the only thing we can do is withhold love or rebel behind backs. In a world of power struggles, children have few weapons. Regrettably, the ones we develop at that age do not serve us well as adults. If we continue to use them, then we are trying to build mature respect with children's tools. If it was the best we could do then, it is not the best we can do now. Love is much stronger and gets much more accomplished than rebellion ever thought of doing. Rebellion and anger can only produce a reality that is full of rebellion and anger. After a while we get tired of that. It is a poor substitute for strength and Understanding and never produces positive results. I guess I finally got tired of being angry and doing nothing to heal my hurts, and so I began to experience Love. In my quest to feel more Love and Joy, I was able to release these old ideas that were once so sacred, because I understood that they did not give me what I really wanted anyway. Someday we will all grow up and allow ourselves to Love again.

If I'd known then what I know now, there's no knowing who I'd be.

ANONYMOUS

Chapter 4
Letting It Flow

Acceptance

Ellyn pointed out to me that I was at times forcing this writing project into being rather than allowing it to manifest. I was pushy, stressing and actively straining to get this job done as if the universe would not allow it to happen without this external push. This is a very common idea, that nothing will happen unless we make it happen. Where did this idea come from?

If we look at nature it is obvious that a lot of things happen everyday without anyone making it happen. The sun rises, the seasons come and go and the animals and plants go about their activities. Do we really think that every animal and plant willfully plans its day, or is it more like they are all being controlled by some supreme being with a penchant for detail? As a theory from older times this has some merit. In earlier stages of mental understanding the only way we could explain the complexities of nature was to have some sort of grand engineer orchestrating every movement from a master switchboard. But we have come to understand that the orchestrating mechanism is part of the essential structure of all things, as in DNA. In other words, the mechanism for controlling life energy resides within the energy itself. So, understanding this underlying structure is the best way we can learn to be in harmony with it, a situation which creates our own best advantage. By understanding Spiritual Energy, we also learn how to utilize it for the benefit of all.

This is the beginning of a new phase in the evolution of consciousness. Learning to Trust and opening the flow of Light from within, we will soar to new heights of experience and sharing. We will find that merely releasing all preconceived notions of who we are, what we need and where we would like to go will open up tremendous new possibilities that would never have been recognized if we remained thinking in the old way. There is no way of knowing in advance what this change of consciousness will bring because all we can really know now is limited by our present thinking. With our present thinking we can only continue to project the reality we have been experiencing. If we were satisfied with that reality we would not be contemplating this change, and only by changing will we ever know what the change will bring. It's like going on a vacation to a place we have never been and for which there is little in the way of literature. We do know, however, that it will be beautiful beyond anything that we have so far experienced. We know that it will be filled with Joy and Contentment, with Love and Light, and with sharing and growth and exploration of the true inner nature of us. What we do not know are the details. But considering the disarray that many of us experience when we project for a particular future experience, and considering the mammoth disarray that all of our collective projections have created in the present world system, it might be better to concentrate on the major qualities we would like to experience and leave the details to some wiser source of consciousness, our Higher Self.

There are really two processes going on here. There is perception of what the Soul has in mind and there is active cooperation with it. In my own experience, I am noticing the difference between the things I make happen and those which seem to manifest effortlessly. In my set designs, I still sometimes get nervous about whether the projects will get finished on time and I worry about details. As the deadline approaches,

I get even more frantic and end up working long hours until all is complete. It isn't so much the long hours I mind, it is the nervous, uptight attitude I sometimes get caught up in. That attitude causes much fretting and frustration and removes all possible joy from the experience. But there is another factor that I find even more interesting.

The sets that I build for large corporations seem to go easier than the sets built for the country music stars in Branson. Part of it seems to be that the corporations do not have an identifiable ego/personality at the top whereas Branson sets are built to please a single individual. I don't know why I perceive these Branson sets as more stressful. It's true that the deadlines are shorter and the projects are usually something I have never done before, but those ideas have never stopped me before and the history of our company is one of continued success and steady growth in the design and execution of projects. I think it has more to do with my attitude towards Branson which I consider to be a remarkable but not very evolved phenomenon. But it is interesting all the same as a lesson to help my growth in Understanding.

So I began to suspect that the quality of my Branson experience was a direct reflection of my attitude about it. With this in mind, I began to apply the lessons of Joy I had learned from my personal life to the work environment. After all, if I could so dramatically increase my happiness at home by focusing on the opportunities for growth and sharing, the same outlook ought to work just as well on the job. And, of course, it has. I am finding new enthusiasm in this change of direction in my professional life, a direction that is an accurate reflection of the Light I am allowing to flow from within. This change is the epitome of 'ask and ye shall receive' and teaches us this truth. And what a difference this concept is to the present one which only explains a few parts of being human, and does a fairly poor job of even that.

So in our quest for a new Understanding we look to the new arena of Spirituality which has a few very simple yet profound concepts at its core. We are attempting to reorganize the mind so that its thinks positively, so that it understands all experiences as manifestations of Divine Energy and sincerely attempts to contact the Source within. Seeking first the kingdom of heaven and knowing that all else will be provided, knowing that the future of our world is in our hands is tremendously empowering.

When I apply this new Understanding to my everyday, I notice that all of the stress disappears. Where before I would be concerned with making enough money from a project as well as getting it done on time, I now understand that my needs will be provided by this work I perform and it will naturally go smoothly and be perfect in its manifestation of my intentions. My life is always the perfect manifestation of my inner state and I am always learning and growing. The more I learn, the more I have to share and in sharing I find my true Joy. It is one thing to feel the thrill of a new realization and another to see the light of Joy dawn in another's eyes as well. That is why I am excited about this writing. The more we allow these kinds of thoughts to echo within our minds, the more we will manifest these ideas. It's like a song that runs around and around in our head, a song which helps our joyous outlook to grow with the experience of Joy following close behind. By sharing what I have learned, I surround myself and others with this song of Joy to the benefit of all. So I welcome the opportunity to help encourage growth and Understanding in every situation I encounter. Like the sun itself, the Light within continually shines forth. The more we are aware of this the more we will allow it to flow unrestricted by negative thought habits. The process of allowing things to happen is a new idea for us and involves a new Understanding of Trust.

Trust

The central idea at the core of our present thinking, at the tip of our pyramid of thoughts is fear. Fear is lack of trust and is the reason we feel we have to make everything happen in the first place. We believe that we are not provided for, that it is every ego for itself and so we go about the business of forming desires in our mind and then trying to get them to come true. It is this very forcing process that is the cause of all the problems because it narrows our focus to the accomplishment of only the particular job at hand. We become so busy satisfying our present desires that we have little time for anything else, including enjoyment of the things we have already manifested. We are involved in an endless race from which death appears to be the only escape. So these ideas at the very center of our thinking are the ones which need to change. The idea of lack and living in an unfriendly universe exists there and so influence every thought that we have, every time that we think, every day of our lives. In meditation we can go to the Core of our Being and see these ideas circling like miniature planets around our Inner Sun. By going past then into the Light itself, we can sense their limiting effects and allow them to change into brighter reflections of our True Essence. The idea that we are not deserving transforms into knowledge that we exist in the sea of Abundance. The idea of an unfriendly universe becomes the Understanding that the Universe is Us, a wonderful place full of Light. In fact the only place there is darkness is within our own minds. And this darkness is so easily removed by allowing the Light to flow from within us.

We as humans have a peculiar habit and that is feeling dissatisfaction. Sometimes we are dissatisfied with what is, but often we focus our attention more on what is not happening. If only I were rich, if only I were more beautiful or stronger or smarter. In other words, we are concerned, upset and worried about things that do not exist. This is its most perplexing aspect. It would be considered understandable to be upset because something had happened which was causing us some discomfort, but most of our unhappiness is because of things that have never occurred. Of course, most fears are about things that have never occurred, but that doesn't make it any more logical. How have we evolved into a species who constantly worries and frets about what might happen but rarely does, and why have we allowed this to be? Both of these stem from the same basic misunderstanding.

We have allowed ourselves to become full of fears because we believed the world was unfriendly and an ever present threat to our well-being. This is a misjudgment that is now fairly easy to correct. Once we realize that the world is a reflection of the Divinity within, we can allow that inner essence to manifest rather than the fear. The other part of this basic misunderstanding is the idea of the future. It is difficult to worry and fret about the present moment so when we shift our focus away from the nebulous future to the gloriousness of the present, all vestiges of fear and worry fade away like so much snow on a bright sunny morning. In focusing on what is missing, on nothing, we rob ourselves of everything.

We can only think one thought at a time. If we are thinking about how dissatisfied we are, then there is no opportunity for anything else to happen. In effect, we have locked ourselves into a frozen state by focusing on a negative thought. If we were to focus on the possibility of change, change would occur. If we would try to see the beauty of each moment we would see it in every detail of every day. But focusing on the negative keeps our attention riveted in a place where only negativity can exist. It is our own self-created hell. It is like a child who has received a different gift than he wanted and is so upset over not getting, that he cannot enjoy what he did get. He may not be able to change the gift, but he can certainly change his mind about it. Our life experience is the same. Just as we create it with our thinking, so our thinking can change it. The process is so incredibly simple that any child can do it and so can each of us. To change our world we only have to change our minds, but to change the way that we think we first have to change our attitude about what our minds are telling us.

Most of us believe everything our minds say. While we might laugh at the silly things some of our friends or acquaintances believe, we are very serious about everything that we believe. We need to understand that our minds are not the source of truth about any situation but only a storage house of old perceptions we call memories. When we encounter a new experience we immediately search our memory banks for a former experience that most exactly matches it. By this haphazard process of comparison, we arrive at what we believe is an accurate understanding of the present event. We don't go into a movie house telling ourselves that we know what is going to happen, yet we do that with our lives. We go to see a movie hoping to be surprised with something new and wonderfully entertaining, yet in our lives we try very hard to know everything that is going to happen before it does. And we do that by hanging onto memories and continually projecting their content onto current experiences. No wonder we keep having the same situations occur over and over again! We're afraid to try anything new, even within the relative safety of our own minds. So we go to a movie, an even safer place, for our adventurous experiences while all the time wishing that our lives were more exciting. Well, we don't have to be Indiana Jones searching for the secret jewel of power to have an exciting and rewarding life. We can search within and find the true jewel of our own untapped power to manifest a Life of Joy and Happiness beyond the wildest dreams of modern cinema, and even far beyond our own.

It is interesting to notice what kinds of challenges we run into when we attempt to change the mind. First of all, we recognize that there are really several minds at work here. There is the mind that has the thoughts and the mind that has attitudes about the mind that has thoughts. So we can both think that we are the most incredible person the world has ever seen and know that we are completely full of it. We are our own best booster and our most severe critic at the same time. And many of us have even more voices: the one who wants, the one who despairs, the one who loves and the one who shies away, the one who tempts fate and the one who fears. There is this whole group of people living inside our skulls which only compounds the question of who to listen to. The usual result is that we listen to each voice part of the time. No wonder we are so moody. Depending on who we are listening to at the moment, we can be entirely different people. Like the Medusa we are ordered about by aspects of personality over which we have little control. And all this occurs because we believe everything we hear in our heads. Perhaps it's time we developed a new voice, one which can put all of these others in perspective. It is useless to try to make up our mind. We can never truly understand the confusions and complexities of the mind until we step out of it to a new and higher perspective, and this can only be accomplished from a different viewpoint, the viewpoint of the Soul.

From the Soul's perspective we are all the emanations of Light. The Soul does not spend eons of time trying to decide who is better. Whether it is better to be black or white, male or female, smart or simple are not questions that the Soul considers. The Soul is interested in our similarities rather than our differences. The only reason we have been so consumed by our differences is that we have been vainly trying to bolster weak self-images. And admittedly, a self-image grounded in the personality with its myriad of demanding voices has to be quite confused, frustrated and in need of propping up. No wonder we are all so nuts! We have been trying to achieve a sense of security about ourselves while standing in the midst of total inner turmoil. If we lack any of the marks of success or beauty or intelligence which our culture values, we try to find what we need within realms where we can function. We take pride in our physical strength or clever conniving or in the fact that we are an American or Caucasian, Black or Hispanic. The only reason we need to find all of these excuses for pride is because we have been taught that they are necessary. So we look outside of ourselves for whatever shred of self-respect we can find while the fountain of sustaining Love lies quietly within waiting to be discovered.

I was thinking about the search for happiness as way of life. All cultures differ on what constitutes this happiness, but most agree that it is desirable. As a result, most of us expend all of our energies in its pursuit. Americans believe in the accumulation of wealth, the traditional Hindu in a large number of children and the Eskimo in doing what is best for the larger community. The Orthodox Jew has hundreds of yearly observances that guarantee a holy and therefore happy life while many Christians make the best of the trials of the present world while working towards an eternal reward. Yet it is puzzling that with all the attention this search for happiness gets, how little seems to be actually found. Happiness is the Holy Grail, the elusive Secret of Life for which the adventurous have always gone in search. The search should be much simpler now that we know the Grail's true location. For now we can turn our adventurous lust for exploration to the uncharted inner realms where all can be found. So we substitute the idea of exploration for the pursuit of happiness. My Grandson Ezekiel knows this and is constantly exploring everything he sees. His enthusiasm is unbounded and infectious. And we can learn much from these children. As they explore the new environment of the three dimensional world they have so recently entered, so we can explore the wonders of the spiritual world we are just beginning to enter. Ezekiel agrees; exploration is the best.

If we do not explore, then we limit ourselves to the same experience we had yesterday, and we desire this change more than anything else. It is not really happiness that we want after all, it is the chance to explore new vistas, new worlds, to go where no one has gone before. It is this exploration of new experiences that brings interest and, two key ingredients of happiness. Perhaps the most attractive aspect of inner exploration is that we can all do it. It is not just for the rich and affluent or for the powerful and respected, it is available to everyone. The ultimate adventure in the present world is reserved for only a few, the lucky ones we call them. But on the Spiritual Path, we all experience the most incredible chance for adventure and personal growth and in the process become certain of who we truly are. We not only get to experience the wonders of inner adventure, we also get to improve our self image and experience much Joy and Love, all by looking within.

The Religious/Spiritual Life

Focusing within is the Essence of the Spiritual Life and is often quite different from being religious. Most Western religions believe in a Supreme Being that is outside of the self rather than inside. They generally consist of a system of beliefs and associated behaviors designed to produce a successful, that is, religious life and afterlife. They accomplish this by conditioning the parishioner through religious teachings in the form of scripture, sermon and song. These conditioned thoughts and feelings then naturally manifest in a life experience consistent with these teachings. Religions intuitively know that we are what we think and thus expend vast amounts of resources to insure that their particular way of thinking is passed along to new generations and converts. All of this is external conditioning, building a character within the mind of the practitioner. The only reason they believe they have to do this is because of what they think will happen if they don't.

Most Western religions see the world as full of catastrophes, and blame them all on an inner nature which they call Evil. Now this is very different from the spiritual approach which understands that the inner nature of man is Light, the Divine Spark or Soul. Religions also believe in Souls but seem to be more interested in saving than in understanding them, implying that they are somehow corrupted at birth and need to be reconditioned. Spiritual teachings insist, on the other hand, that the perceived evil in the world is all the result of not knowing that we are Light. In other words, by thinking that we are basically selfish and evil, we have manifested that kind of experience on this planet. All the character conditioning in the world will never save us from this perceived evil destiny because these particular thoughts have to manifest just like any others.

The more we think about evil, the more it manifests. We are living in a time where many are embracing evil as a working concept for their lives. After all, we have been told since infancy that we are basically like that, and we see it all around us and read about it in every country in the world, so why not? Everyone else is doing it. This predicament will only change when we change our minds about the nature of who we are. Only then will we begin to experience true Peace and Joy, and show others by example what kind of Love and Happiness can be experienced by focusing on the Light within. There are many who are now deciding to allow this inner change to begin. The Spiritual Path is the path of change and we are now in a world situation where inner change is the only way out. We have tried every form of outer change from diplomacy to nuclear attack and still the onslaught of conflict and violence cannot be stemmed. Only by finding true peace within will peace manifest in the greater world experience.

The Spiritual Path thus leads to Peace and Contentment within and to Peace and Happiness throughout the world. The best that religion has to offer is personal salvation. Many religions are hopelessly ego-centric teachings and thus subject to all the pitfalls of egotism we have witnessed for centuries. The Spiritual Path replaces ego-centered teachings with soul-centered ones. It replaces greed and acquisition with sharing and growth. It replaces the goal of personal salvation with an expansion of consciousness that embraces the Oneness of all Life. And the approach itself is entirely different.

Instead of making things happen we allow them to manifest. This is what all spiritual teachers have tried to show us. Jesus, Buddha, Mohammed and others have all encouraged us to look to the Soul or the God within as our true Source, and to allow that energy to manifest just as they did. It is interesting that most of the religions based on the lives of these great teachers should still continue to be such self-centered, outwardly focused entities. But the religious leaders who followed these great ones were not nearly as evolved as they. So the deep wisdom of the Buddha became the prayer wheels of the people and the parables of Jesus became hardened into inexorable dogma. We were not able then to understand what was truly being said and demonstrated, but we are now. We are beginning to realize the full truth of their teachings and the full impact these truths can have on our lives. That is the true blessing of the present world experience. Like the Phoenix, we are emerging out of the ashes of our own destructive intentions. In a position where a change of consciousness is our only hope of peace and happiness, we are prepared to initiate that change. And what a glorious emergence this transformation is becoming.

This spiritual transformation takes place in the mind and produces heaven on earth. The new ideas of Light and Love manifesting from the Center will produce a world experience consistent with these ideas. In contrast, the religious transformation is believed to occur in the soul itself. But rather than having a large effect on this life, it is geared more towards ensuring a heaven, or haven, in the next. As such, the focus is on beliefs and behaviors that will produce this eternal reward. Some of these ideas and behaviors are quite noble yet the focus is hopelessly misplaced. It is far too easy to do all the right things while thinking about something else, and this has produced the hypocrite. But if we think about Love and Light, then only Love and Light will manifest. It is an automatic manifesting system whereas the religious tradition involves bending one's individual will to the will of the higher power.

Wills are very difficult to bend and though sometimes bent by force or persuasion, they easily and quickly go back to their former shape. We have learned that it is fruitless to force anyone to do anything yet we continue to try because we have not learned any new method. The new method is to go within and allow the truth of who we really are to make itself known and then flow out in magnificent manifestation.

The Process of Transformation

I was thinking today about how the ideas of the present age carry over into this new direction. For instance, the old idea that hard work is necessary in order to survive. Most of us have never known a day without food or shelter, yet we continue to work just as hard for other things that are, to us, just as necessary. More, always more, and always a struggle. Even those in the proverbial lap of luxury still experience the need to be working towards something. What is interesting is that this idea of having to work very hard is the antithesis of allowing our inner energy to manifest. And many of us, when first becoming interested in the Spiritual Path, begin by working very hard. We read extensively, do yoga and constantly search out the errant thoughts in our minds. If the secret to a new life is to eliminate older thinking, then, by God, we are going to get busy and work hard until the job is done. And the sooner it is done, the better. Rather than allowing these new energies to manifest, we are totally engaged in forcing them with all the determination and drive we can muster. But after a while, we begin to see that our constant searching for errant ideas only helps produce them. We are what we think, and if we think our minds are filled with the wrong ideas, then it will be so. There can never be any happiness or Joy while we are doing battle within our own minds.

It is only when we release the inner struggle that we have the opportunity to become satisfied and happy. Any errant thoughts that are interfering with this process will surface to our attention and can then be easily released. The first idea we have to release is the idea of struggle. If the struggle for survival merely changes into the struggle for spiritual enlightenment, then the change has been quite superficial, a change of subject rather than a change of direction. The idea of struggle is now known to be nonsense. We are what we think and so we only experience struggle because we think it is necessary, not because it is the nature of things. When we remove the reason for its necessity, then it disappears. As long as we believe that it is necessary for progress and that competition is the best way to insure survival, then it will be so and the world will continue to display its current patterns of insane behavior.

Also on its way out is the faith in some superior being to fix everything for us. The age old concept of trying to please an all-powerful deity in hopes of gain can now be released. We can replace this archaic concept with the knowledge that we have within us the Source of our own beneficence and that we access this Abundance with our thinking. This higher power within, this Soul voice has more Understanding than all the databases in our world. It is the source of wisdom, knowing what is best in every life situation, and it is just beginning to open its treasures to us.

The Western concept of life as the accumulation of goods and focus on the future is a poorly written story told by a fool. The fool is our ego which only knows its own desires while being blind to everything else around it. And the story is the same tired tale handed down from generation to generation since the dark ages of man's history. When we look at the living conditions and the immense level of ignorance of former times, we are appalled. Yet we think nothing of living our modern lives by the same beliefs as those earlier times, beliefs which work just as poorly today as they did 5000 years ago. The names may have changed, but we have the same villains, the same suffering and the same uncertainty that has plagued us since the beginning. We are ready to move on and we have the new Understanding that will allow us to do so. We no longer have to wait for some Supreme Deity to descend out of the clouds and save us because we realize that we are part of that Divine Energy. We are creative beings like the Father who created us in his own image. Those who are waiting for the return of a fiery savior had best look within and welcome the dawning of that Divine Fire within them, for it is only when we all become filled with Divinity, when we all are flowing over with the Christ energy, that the world will be saved.

So within our selves, we are asking our inner Source to show us what is truly going on so that we may learn and grow, and so that the world as we know it will be completely healed and begin to shine like the diamond in the sky that it truly is. This changes the way we look at everything.

Chapter 5

The Power Of Old Ideas

Fame

I was thinking about a friend's question involving sexual expression. Basically, she asked what the world's objection was to making a living from some aspect of sexuality. Prostitutes have done so for thousands of years and the modern world has turned sex into one of the largest and most profitable industries going. Yet it seems that those who are so focused on the surface, physical aspects of the world are missing the most important aspects of it, regardless of their apparent fame or fortune. They are mistaking the appearance of things for the true reality. Paying attention to how one looks or dresses, to the housing or career that one occupies, or what kinds of experiences one has had is missing the point. "What profit it a man to gain the whole world and lose his own soul," the old saying goes, yet many of us still bend all of our energies to worldly acquisitions and pay little attention to the level of our Understanding or the amount of joy we actually feel. It is interesting how the physical aspects of life have recently taken such a large jump in popularity.

It is to the point that those who are idolized the most are those who have the appearance, the look of success, without any regard for what their true inner qualities might be. This leads to tremendous copying of the latest fad and personality cults made up of little mockups of the original. It is only the

71

surface characteristics that can be imitated and yet many hope to somehow accrue part of the magic they perceive the star to possess by dressing the part. This is the oldest form of sorcery on the planet, sympathetic magic, and is no more reliable these days than it was thousands of years before books began to record its spells and incantations. It is perhaps saddest of all when some of these stars actually believe they do possess some secret dazzle that makes them superior to the rest of us. By looking deeper, we realize that we all have within us all sorts of marvelous qualities, deep and wonderful aspects of which these surface glimmers are but weak shadows.

Star worship is actually based on the idea of certain personalities being greater than others. The truth is that we are all capable of anything anyone else can demonstrate, so these 'stars' are only showing what is possible. If we began to look at ourselves like we look at them, if we saw ourselves as these beautiful and talented characters in our own movie, if we saw all of our friends as our Oscar winning supporting actors, imagine what our lives would become. Instead of wistfully admiring total strangers we would love ourselves and instead of wondering what it would be like to be an incredible person we would be one. By having this focus in our lives, our lives would become like our favorite movies but with one important difference, we would realize we are the stars!

I see ads for contests where one can win a night on the town with some celebrity, but why bother when we can share every moment of our lives with people of this caliber. We are all people of this caliber. There is nothing special about any of these idols that is not also special about us. The only trick to their immense success is that they have taught us to believe in their specialness. So we flock to catch a glimpse of what's-her-name when our own mirrors would reveal as much beauty, and we stand in line for hours to view romance we could more wonderfully experience ourselves. We can begin the process of moving past the movies, because we can realize that they are based on false beliefs about Life, namely, that some people are gifted above others and that some life experiences are more interesting or exciting than others. All Life is brimming with

Love and Light which will manifest the moment we decide to allow it to do so.

Another example would be the sports stars with their physical prowess representing the ultimate in human development. This idea had its flowering in the 50's when baseball was king and Joe DiMaggio married Marilyn Monroe. This royal pair began a life together as America watched breathlessly. That dream soon ended but the sports phenomenon continues to focus young minds on physical success and competition as the measure of manhood. Yet the supposed success of the stars, of the few winners, does not offset the tragedy of the multitude of losers. If we look a few generations before this one, wit and knowledge were the measure of greatness and we had our Mark Twains and others. If we follow this line we see how the lecture circuit gave way to radio and it in turn to movies and television. The focus has been subtly shifting from content to appearance. It is interesting that in this time of Transformation, the major focus is on the bare surface appearance and yet is poised to plunge to the very Center of reality. In the generations to come we will universally realize that all Life is magnificent, that all of us are superb expressions of the one Light that is our Source. It is time to leave this ridiculous structure of measurement behind us and substitute a new system based on higher Understanding. As long as we focus on the outer appearance, our inner growth will be excruciatingly slow, and the amount of real happiness we experience will be minimal.

Education

This leads to inevitable changes in the current education system. The minds that are coming into incarnation are in some cases so advanced that the current system is boring at best and totally useless at worst. The memorization of facts and their associated concepts only guarantees that the present world chaos will continue by conditioning the leaders of tomorrow to think in the same shallow way as those of today. In effect, the game of life we are teaching is no longer an accurate model of how Life energy actually functions. We are doing a great disservice both to our children and ourselves by continuing to invest in this travesty of truth. It is no wonder that the rules the old system makes are being broken so often by so many. When a system fails to produce the correct results then it is usually replaced. This system is producing the exact opposite of what it was designed to make possible. Instead of order it has created uncontrolled violence and high level fraud. Instead of safety and hope it has created an atmosphere of fear and dread. And instead of happiness it had produced only confusion, disillusionment and anger. As a result, the focus has shifted away from working hard for the future to indulging in the pleasures of the moment. And who can blame the younger generations who have witnessed the crumbling of values and the deterioration of the society these values were supposed to insure. Yet the momentary highs of rebellion and drugs do not produce any more of a lasting happiness than the older values.

Our youth is stuck in a world which cannot make them happy and an educational system without a clue as to how to change that fact. We need to teach about relationships and loving, about sharing and growing and forget about how many battles took place where. The time is ripe for a new Understanding. There is so much more going on than the surface appearance and all are now ready to begin the exploration of those depths. We might laugh about the hillbillies who say that white lightning is the biggest thrill of all, but we cringe when we realize that we have so far failed to find anything any better in the physical realms. To do so, we must go beyond mere physical thrill seeking, and this involves letting go of the past and its conceptions of life.

One must let go of the past in order to escape its conditioning. All of the ways of bolstering our self-image, all of the ideas about how the game of life is played must be released in order for the new Understanding to take form in our minds. There is only room for one thought at a time and the present mental understanding is hogging all of the space with grossly inadequate information. We are so much more than just bodies that feel emotion and have thoughts. We are marvelous creative beings whose possibilities have not even begun to be demonstrated. When we are driving the wrong way on a journey we usually turn around and go the best way we can find. It is now time for all of us to change directions, a direction that will take us where we truly would like to go. And so we release all of the past and focus our attention on the present moment.

Achievement

I was in on an interesting conversation yesterday. Two of my friends were discussing what it takes to be successful in the world. They talked about what they wanted to do with their lives and how they intended to get to that point. One wanted to be rich and famous and felt the only way was to get recognized as someone who is good at performing music and thereby get hired for ever more lucrative gigs. The other just wanted to be rich, to live his life out on a little dream farm and produce award winning artistic designs. What was interesting is that when it was my turn to answer, I said that I wanted to be as centered as possible. This started me thinking about how we access our present situations.

For those who have the means of survival and comfort, the desire for acquisitions turns towards experiences. The latest hot spots in the country, the most exotic vacations, the worlds of art or high finance lure many with their lurid tales of adventure and excitement. But it occurred to me that going within was also a very strong desire for experience. Gone are the days when the Spiritual Path led to the cloistered monastery or the mountain top temple. We are talking about experiencing what it is like to be joyous, loving, spiritual beings in the everyday world. And the hunger to feel this Joy and live this Life of Love and happiness is stronger than anything else.

Like a present from some gracious benefactor, I was being given the opportunity to find the Fountain of Youth and taste all the luxuries of Spiritual Bliss. I immediately sensed that this desire is deep within all of us and is only focused on the physical things because we have not been informed that there is anything else available that will fill the bill. Modern religion has failed us because it does not offer Joy and celebration. In fact, many of them frown on almost all forms of enjoyment as if to suffer were somehow a virtue making one worthy of future reward. It's odd how a religion that so believes in making a joyful noise unto the Lord can yet encourage such quiet misery. So perhaps the yuppies are right, and the key to happiness is to have as many and varied experiences as possible. It just seems easier and faster and better to find those experiences within rather than searching the globe to discover their elusive havens. The secret seems to be desiring to learn and grow and wanting to share with others, to share Love, Joy and everything that we are. By allowing this Joy to flow from within us we can easily accomplish a thousand times more Joy and Happiness than all the ego-centered drive the world has ever known.

I observe with interest that as my drive releases I feel very odd at times. I am so used to diving headlong into projects that the idea of allowing still seems foreign. Of course, I could dive headlong into allowing myself to grow, but that is a basic contradiction in terms. It's like we take our drive that we are used to using in the pursuit of acquisitions and try to use it to pursue spiritual Understanding. This is a problem with some metaphysical teachings which focus on power, on making things happen. In the process of making things happen, the true gift of Spiritual Understanding is missed and the lesser goal of power rears its grisly head. Those after power will use metaphysical truth to go after the same ego-centric desires that have marred the present world experience, and so miss the whole point. Until the ego is no longer a factor in the decision making process, the results will be the same as they are now. Only when the Soul provides its intuitive counsel will our experience change for the better and our lives become calm and centered. I think what has been bothering me is that even though I want to do some writing, I have no drive and so can get nothing rolling. But I am sure that this is also part of this change. If I am to write these things, then the opportunity and motivation will present itself at precisely the right moment.

I am, of course, writing these things that you are reading, but the opportunity and motivation came many months after these initial words were recorded on tapes. By that time I had all but forgotten about the writing project because I was concentrating almost all of my energies on daily meditations and sharing with others who come to talk of these things. One day, the change occurred and I began this new adventure. It will happen to all of us who truly seek the Source of Light within and allow those energies to manifest in our lives.

There are some fundamental changes in our perspective that we can expect. For instance, we replace the idea of destination with the concept of journey. It's remarkable that when we talk about beginning a journey on the Path of Spiritually, so many of us immediately look to the end. We try to locate a goal and bend all of our energies towards achieving it. It's a linear way of looking at things. But the Spiritual Path is not so much a path as an expansion, and more like a journey which departs but never arrives. It just keeps on going and growing. We have to shift out of our regular mind and perceive the Spiritual Life differently, as a process rather than a goal. We do not have to set the goal of attaining fulfillment, we only have to realize that it is ours for the asking. We do not have to wait for certain desires to be satisfied before we can be happy, we can start enjoying everything immediately. And we do not need to find the key to unlock these mysteries of Life, we only have to release old fears and limiting ideas and allow the energy to flow.

Ambition

An old friend was over last night. He wanted to discuss a key idea, ambition. He was seeing that he did not, for instance, want to have a relationship with a woman, he was ambitious to have one. He was anxious for a relationship because it meant that someone would take care of his needs. He needed someone to believe that he was a special person. When he decided to approach the Spiritual Path, he immediately had the ambition to be a great teacher and already felt that he knew everything he needed to know. It was necessary that whatever he did, he be able to do it quickly and perfectly in order to satisfy his ambition. What was bothering him was not so much wanting to be wise or to share love with a woman, but the fact that he was driven towards accomplishing these goals. How can one be driven to succeed on the Spiritual Path? Of course, behind this is the negative self image, being afraid he might not be able to achieve any of this. Our attention shifted to the idea of worthiness and the work we feel we must do in order to deserve what we want. As if the very fact that we are here does not guarantee us anything and we are continually having to strive for everything we get. We are like pawns caught in some cosmic joke of which we are unaware, vainly searching for the punch line so that we can understand what is going on in and around us.

But we are here, and our very presence indicates that we are part of the scheme of things. This is another example of the precept, if something can be thought, we will at some point think it. So because we can think up the idea of unworthiness, we have created a whole slew of ways to feel that way. It has caused us so much suffering and heartache that it needs to be completely released from our thinking and cleansed from our emotions. Since we believed that we had to achieve something in order to be worthy, we have had to work very hard at achievement. The only problem is, as soon as one thing is achieved, we feel the need to do even more. The expectations grow with every new day, with every new generation until our children inherit a world in which life is clocked at 75 miles an hour and everyone has to run to keep up. The idea of achievement has done all of this for us.

And what are we unworthy of, survival? There are many parts of the world where this idea of not surviving is manifesting quite clearly. While ambition can in some cases make up for this unworthiness, it is only an overriding effort and not a cure for the disease. Our dis-ease is with ourselves. Because we feel unworthy, we do not like ourselves, and we do not like ourselves because we feel unworthy. This is an impossible situation, the proverbial Catch 22 that can only perpetuate the situation. The only solution is to realize the insanity of this thinking and allow the idea of unworthiness to release from the mind. Then we can replace it with the truth that we, by our very nature, are totally worthy because we are an expression of Love and Light. And if this thought of unworthiness, with all of its twisted logic and emotional grunge, can have such a profound effect on the world, imagine what a truly positive and logical thought can produce. Just imagine what effect the positive ideas of Love and Joy will have and we are well on our way to creating that kind of life experience for ourselves and everyone we meet.

If we think the world is Light and Love then it will become so. And the incredible simplicity of this transformational process becomes immediately clear. Somehow we got the idea that only Buddha, Jesus or Mohammed could make this kind of world come true. After all, they had special powers because they were the Sons of God. But we know now that we are all the Children of God, the Children of Light, the spark of Love and Light Divine. And when we begin to allow ourselves to express this Love and Light, we are amazed at how quickly it begins to manifest in our lives. Our uncovering of this truth has been a gradual process of an evolving awareness. We see that by filling our minds and hearts with Light and Love, the world of Love and Light becomes our everyday reality.

In my own life, the idea of unworthiness has manifested in many types of ambition. To be a writer, dancer, actor, teacher and clown were for many years the goals for which I strove. I felt I needed some external proof of greatness in order to justify my existence. What is most interesting about this is that now that I have managed to let go of ambition, all of these possibilities are beginning to happen in my life. The feeling about doing some of these things is, 'Why not?' It is clear to me that many times the soul, in its attempts to guide us along the path of our greatest learning, will encourage us to desire certain lifestyles, will allow ambition to take us in directions we probably would not have explored without its drive. Ambition can be the vehicle through which we learn skills as well as grow in awareness, and when we become aware of our true place in this world as helpers and healers, those skills and talents can be used for the greater glory of us all. It is one of those rare moments in our lives when we see how everything we have ever done and all that we have learned and experienced has prepared us for the task at hand. We all know how to do so many wonderful things and with those abilities, we can all be of such help in healing ourselves and the planet. This will help us to see that our energies have been well spent. We have not wasted our time, as the old saying goes. We are all learning and growing at our optimum and most perfect rate.

As we allow the Soul to manifest through our Being, we realize that all of our desires of the past, all of our dreams, our connivings and schemes were but attempts to find our fulfillment in external circumstances. We were trying to find the key to Happiness and the door that leads to joyfulness. Now we have discovered both the key and the door, because the key is our ability to focus on the Source within us, and the door is our Understanding of our true Essence. By knowing that we are beings of Love and Light we pass through that door into the land of Eternal Joy. Thus we continually become more of who we are truly meant to be.

Think how interesting it is that those of us who have been so unwilling in this lifetime to accept any kind of authority, who have been accused of being so arrogant, confused and disrespectful were merely responding to the truth that we intuitively knew. Each of us should be answerable only to the urgings of our own inner guidance, so to label dissatisfaction with the norm as simply youthful rebellion was to only partially explain the objections. Of course, many did not really understand the true nature of their frustration, but rather only that something was not being addressed. The desire for Happiness is so very strong in everyone, it is too bad that so many insist on a single cultural path of its pursuit as the only alternative. This is even more so considering the fact that so many pursue and so few attain this goal. You would think that someone would realize the game was not working and speak out. Well, someone did, and they were called every name in the book. It is amazing to what great lengths some will go to protect their investment even when it has not produced the happiness they hoped it would. In the name of pride we follow the path we have initiated even when ultimate failure is assured. This idea has huge implications.

Pride and Allegiance

As humans, we have prided ourselves on the strength of our allegiance to the traditions and ideas of our birthplace. It's as if nations have believed themselves to be in competition to produce the best person. The Arab, the American, the Englishman and Frenchman all think they are the absolute perfection of humanity on the planet. Every culture is full of deep pride and honor for their cultures, even to the point of disowning or killing those who break away from the norm. Every tribe believes that they have the one true way and that everyone else is questionable. Therefore, whatever the tribe wants is the most important thing. The problem arises when one tribe wants something that another tribe has. The attacked tribe had better be able to stop them. Where they are kind and nurturing to their own, towards others they are 100% treacherous. This allegiance is something one is willing to die for and is the basis for one's self image. This is not advanced thinking and yet many tribes throughout the world are trying to go back to this archaic and mutually destructive kind of living. Many others have not even begun to evolve past this early thinking. If we look at this idea more intently, we see that it has split and gone two directions.

One is the direction of multi-cultural allegiances and the other is in the direction of the ego. In the larger world, the United Nations represents the supreme attempt to provide a forum for world wide cooperation. It attempts to combine all of the smaller allegiance groups like NATO under one roof. It is a helpful step towards unity yet there is difficulty finding a common ground when everyone still thinks selfishly. The best it can do is offer the idea that by cooperating we will all come out better in the end. Yet cooperation for selfish reasons is still selfishness and subject to all the pitfalls of such limited thinking. There will always be those who pretend to cooperate until they have established enough of a power base to go their own way, as Saddam Hussein has recently shown us. Nevertheless, the UN is an attempt and will be invaluable once world centered thinking replaces the ego centered thinking of most member nations.

The other extension of this idea makes the tribe we owe allegiance to our own individual ego. This is a philosophy known as existentialism. If nothing matters except what each individual can obtain for himself, then the fabric of cultural cooperation breaks down, as indeed it has almost everywhere. Yet even this breakdown of law and order has its valuable lesson. The most important thing we learn from this is the obvious limitations of our present thinking. If our system was a good one, this kind of deterioration would not be taking place. Good theories are ones which always work. It is worth noting that because our entire thinking is based on self interest, it is the flagrant self interest of existentialism which is breaking it down. Within the heart of every tyrant lies the seed of his own destruction. The very fact that we continue to be self absorbed automatically leads to the present conditions in every part of the world. Only by replacing this thinking will this cycle ever stop and go in a new and more positive direction.

New directions require new methods. The main hindrance to peace is the use of force for selfish reasons. Yet the use of force for humanitarian reasons isn't any better. Force for any reason only reinforces the belief that force produces results. If present trends continue, we could easily reach a point where the United Nations is policing every country in the world. If a police state is undesirable, what would a police world be? Force needs to be understood as an unreliable method for attaining goals and released from our thinking so that it will no longer manifest. This is the key to personal safety as well. No one can be hurt by anyone else unless they are attracting such an experience with their thinking. This fearful thinking can be totally subconscious, but the fear is present on some level and so produces the fearful results. You may be able to stop a man from killing by tying him up, but you will not stop his killing thoughts. It is the thoughts which ultimately kill, the body only does what the mind tells it to do. As always, the key lies within the mind, but since the ego mind is so tied up with this kind of destructive thinking, we need to go beyond it to where the air is clear. Only the Center is clear because it is the Source which is always pure. This is the new rallying point for all of us.

Instead of being so wrapped up in our own trite little dramas, we can expand to see the world differently. Since we know that all is abundant and we get everything we need by sharing, it is ridiculous to continue to function from the selfish ego's point of view. The ego can only cooperate because of what it believes it will get in return. The Soul cooperates because that is its nature. Like stars combining to illuminate the night sky, we shine as beings of Light together. Where there is Light, there is Life Abundant. Where there is selfishness, there is only unrewarded struggle. The choice is ours and the task is to let this truth be known to everyone we meet by our example. As the Master Jesus said, "No man cometh unto the Father except as I have done," meaning that no one becomes enlightened except by allowing the Light to flow and shine in every way. Thus we unite ourselves in the Light which is far different than uniting us in allegiances of cooperative self interest.

We are building a new kind of allegiance based on a common Understanding instead of a common fear. Being afraid of each other is not an efficient way to keep us peaceful. You can't make anyone peaceful, especially when his entire cultural programming is screaming for vengeance or notoriety. These major traits must manifest as all traits manifest, so their very existence threatens the evolution of consciousness. As long as we hold onto old allegiances, we will never be able to embrace any true ideas of Unity. Allegiances keep us separated from each other. Once an Englishman, always an Englishman, the old saying goes, and once a terrorist always a terrorist. Let's transfer our allegiance to something which will give us the most Joy and allow it to create a new and wonderful world. Rather than connecting as physical bodies in mutual defense and shared fears, let's join together as Beings of Light in Harmony, an allegiance to the Essence of who we truly are instead of who we pretend to be.

We will go past this idea of allegiance just as we go past all of these other limiting ideas. The concept of banding together against a common foe breaks down when we realize that it is our own thinking that has been the foe. This is the cosmic joke. We have been running around trying to destroy enemies that actually live inside of us, enemies that are only erroneous thoughts in our minds. Thinking that we had enemies and struggles created them for us to deal with, and we have been dealing with them for thousands of years on the outside without apparent success. Now we can go within and deal with them where there is a decent chance of succeeding. Any fisherman knows that the best fish are found in the deepest recesses of the lake. Our Essence and salvation do not skim the surface, but dwell in the very depths of us. It is there that we will find the true Source of our Being and enthusiastically embrace it.

One could say that this is the wave of the future, but it is really the now moment, a completely new territory, the one thing that we have not truly explored yet. We have explored and researched, and many of us still live in the past. We have libraries and museums full of the past. If we have learned anything from all of this is hard to tell, but it certainly hasn't helped make us more joyous. Then there's the future. It is what we dream about and work towards. The future is what we live in most of the time, waiting for the clock to say 5 PM, waiting until we retire, waiting until we have enough money to relax. We wait and work and dream, but the true promise of tomorrow never comes. We are forced to settle for what we get. I would much rather feel Joy today than hope I can feel it tomorrow. And when we ask ourselves why the joy doesn't arrive, why the same old cycles keep repeating and who is responsible for this state of affairs, the answer is simple, we are. It is all the result of our thinking, thinking that we can change.

The Search for the Center

We all want to feel the flow of Life and we all strive to do so. Some of us try to make it happen, others use money to attempt to buy it, but it eludes everyone except those who know the secret. To paraphrase Robert Frost, we dance around the circle and suppose, while the secret lies in the Center and knows. This dance is what we call Life, but without knowledge of the Center it cannot be life, but only what we imagine life to be.

We do not know who we are or what we are doing, we only pretend that we do because we have been taught that this is it, and we all cooperate in that pretense. If we can cooperate in this kind of imaginary game, why can't we cooperate in a new game with a basis in real Understanding? Only because we are afraid of losing what little rewards this older game provides. Fortunately for many of us, the rewards are too little and are too much trouble to be seriously believed. This allows us to move beyond them and encounter the true nature of spiritual reality. When one theory reaches the end of its usefulness, another surfaces in our consciousness. Another way this is often said is that when the students are ready the teacher appears. We are the students and we are ready to replace this older and less effective operating system for a better one, one that is in line with our new Understanding and that produces more acceptable results. We no longer care what happened in the past nor worry about possible events in the future. We focus our attention on what is happening now and thus insure our immediate and continued Joy and Success.

In focusing on the present, we simplify life remarkably. We no longer have to worry about who we are, we just are. We don't have to struggle to survive because everything is provided when it is needed. We only have to allow our inner Essence to emerge from behind the walls we have built to hold it in. All of the rules of behavior and carefully crafted personalities we have erected can be seen as obstacles to the passage of Light and our ultimate experience of Contentment and Joy.

Perhaps now that we know there's another way, we will follow it. And interestingly enough, now that we have found the key to our own destinies, now that we know the source of everything is within us, we have no further use for rebellion. Let the old guard continue to pursue their hopeless goals and peddle their flawed philosophies. In time, the inefficiency of the path of power will become obvious even to those inextricably involved in its furtherance. Then the Joy and Love created by the true path of Light will appear as the fountain of hope that it truly is. The Joy and Love of those embracing this path will demonstrate its virtues for everyone to see. All will then welcome the Spiritual Path as the way we can return to the land of Joy and Bliss that is so keenly felt within all of our heart of hearts. And the differences will be clear.

We are not trying to attain power to satisfy our own personal desires but rather allowing the true power within to manifest its perfection in three dimensional form. As this Light grows, it lightens everyone's experience. The rest of the world can go about its self-centered business but all will eventually return to the Light. There really is no other way though there may be many who doubt it.

Doubt and Control

A friend came over today with his usual load of doubt. He doubts everything including his ability to love and be happy. He even doubts his existence at times and his right to be here. He understands that he is what he thinks and so he sees how his doubt manifests in misery, yet he still doubts and is frustrated at his inability to understand and release this hindering thought. We finally arrived at the process of releasing the doubt by focusing on something else, namely, the Center. He realized that he was so consumed with trying to get rid of the doubt that he was thereby making it stronger, and by doubting his ability to release doubt was giving doubt ultimate control over his life. It seemed amazing to him that he could even doubt his ability to release doubt. After all, he didn't doubt his ability to doubt. He knew he was very good at that, but he feared he would never be able to grow beyond it. Thus he felt at the mercy of his own mind, a mind that had become the enemy with him as the one and eternal prisoner.

I mentioned that I had once been in that position and how disheartened I had felt. Yet the simple exercise of focusing on the Center and allowing the Light to flow erased all doubt in his mind, at least for the moment. Afterwards he sat quietly and then began to fear that this feeling of calm and sureness would fade, doubt again. And so the cycle continues. Yet each time he responds to doubt by releasing it and realizing his true nature, the doubt gets weaker. Only when he gives it power by being afraid of it does it have any power at all. It has taken a while for him to understand this, but I notice that he is coming over less often and says he is meditating, that is, allowing the Light to flow, much more often than he used to. I do believe him because I can see the results. For the many months when he only thought about his doubts and wondered why he could not conquer them, no progress was made. But as soon as he began to see past the doubt and reconnect to the Source of Light within, he began to grow in strength and confidence. Like flowers, we thrive on Light, not on darkness. As long as we dwell in the recesses of our minds where our greatest fears and doubts live, we will never grow. Fear and doubt hold us in that space. We must make the step out into the Light. We must move our focus out of the dungeon to where the Light can be found. My young friend understands this now and is on his way.

Fear and doubt are two of the old gods that we are moving past. We have worshipped them long enough and sacrificed much in our attempts to appease them. Because of fear we have erected elaborate institutions for mutual defense and created vast arsenals with incredible destructive powers. Fear is a destructive thought and so has spurred us to produce the means of our own destruction. Doubt has led us to build vast defenses as well, but these walls are internal and keep out new information and experiences. If we doubt everything except what we can see, then we limit ourselves to living in the same world as prehistoric man. Our tools may be more advanced, but we still use the same five senses. Our doubt, which we have glorified by calling it the scientific method, keeps us functioning as we have always functioned. It effectively blocks any new understandings that are outside what can be observed with the senses and their mechanical extensions. This keeps us experiencing life on the same level as cavemen, and with the same primitive results.

What is interesting about science is that it is an attempt to reduce life to its smallest parts and thereby gain knowledge useful for its manipulation to satisfy our needs. Life as the universe was too vast to be able to predict, let alone control. But the small parts, those parts smaller than us seemed to be where we might exert some power and influence. And indeed, we have managed in chemistry and physics to create rather intricate and apparently useful items that have made physical existence more comfortable. All of this has been the result of the dissection of nature and its rearrangement. Yet whether we understand life any better from this experience is debatable. Since so much of our scientific knowledge has been used to create ever more effective means of destruction, we would have to admit that the overall benefit to humanity has been a mixed blessing. Perhaps the problem has been not so much our desire to have a better life, but the way we have chosen to approach it.

Two things about the approach jump out at us; the separation of life into minute parts, and the focus on control. Study of the small parts can never yield knowledge about the whole, and it has been our narrow view of life that has caused all of the problems so far. If each person can only see as far as their own desires, then we will never advance into any kind of world consciousness. Only when we understand the whole can we function with knowledge of the true picture of reality. Until that time we remain separate individuals with differences more pronounced than similarities. This idea of separateness will never allow unity, and only unity can bring us together in peace.

The other part is control, and is perhaps the weakest idea we have ever had. To think that we, as tiny dots of matter, should be able to control the destinies of everything else on Earth is the most supreme arrogance and is based in fear, not on strength. Our true strength lies in mutual cooperation and in allowing rather than controlling. It is a simple fact that science has not fulfilled it's imagined dream of making life better, but of course, it couldn't. Science is built on the twin ideas of separateness and control, both of which are now acknowledged to be inaccurate approaches to effective living. We must come together in Unity and we must allow the Love and Light within us to manifest if we are to grow and prosper. To do anything else is to remain where we are. We must expand and feel the flow. This flow is close to what we call serendipity.

It is interesting that even in the midst of the perfectly ordered and arranged life, the life that is totally on track and happening according to plan, the desire for serendipity still exists. We spend untold years getting our lives just so and then sit in our perfect living rooms and wish for something unforeseen and magical to happen. Who does not enjoy waking up to a blanket of new fallen snow or dream of vacations that refresh and inspire? If everything is planned, then nothing can be spontaneous, and we complain about the lack of spontaneity even while busily planning every detail for years in advance. The yearning for serendipity is the religious idea of being blessed, good things happening as if from nowhere. Yet it is really just allowing the moment to manifest and when it does we are always joyfully surprised and delighted. Only our fear makes us think that the moment can manifest to our detriment. When we learn to allow the Light to flow at all moments, then all moments will be full of delight and surprise. Then life is flowing and we feel like we are in the main current. Serendipity, spontaneity or divine blessing, they are all names for the way we would really like our lives to be.

Of course, we really need to go past all of these ideas to fully understand this process. Divine blessing is a concept that depends on some superhuman being to discharge these blessings. This has led to all the forms of trying to influence such deities with sacrifice and good works in order to receive. This is an odd concept of Abundance because it has someone who is in charge of the flow. No wonder we elected to try to control this flow ourselves. We wanted to go past the idea of having to please or bribe some divine figure in order to get what we thought we needed. Yet serendipity is an equally difficult concept. Since there is no personality in charge of it, we could only believe that it just happens by a process we call blind fate or luck, a concept closer to chaos than we liked. So the question becomes, what do we do now? It seems that we need to find a method that includes both complete control and surprise and delight. So the impetus for science was right, we do need control, but of thoughts rather than minute and separate particles of matter. And the continued desire for serendipity is fulfilled by allowing the Soul to manifest its delightful Essence. Thus we find the place where both ideas are united as One. This is the whole idea of unity.

For unity to work, it must replace all ideas and be able to satisfy all needs. In the present system, the best we can hope for is that good will triumph over evil. Yet the result will always be defeat for some part of humanity, and that is not unity. Only when everyone wins will we be satisfied, only then will we be united as One. Even the present concept of God is divided with His eternal conflict with the Devil. The triumph of God that traditional religion prays for is misunderstood. They wish to see a triumph by success in battle, but true success comes with Understanding and that takes us to the Unity of all Life. We cannot fight and hope to be unified when we win because the very act of fighting insures continued conflict. We must reach a point in our knowledge where all is Divine, not divided. When we are One, then we shall finally be at peace.

This Oneness releases us from the pursuit of our individual destinies. We can allow ourselves to be joyful and loving in all situations instead of worrying about whether there will still be time to attend to our own agendas. We can release our frenzied quests to be unique and special and yet be totally connected by realizing that we are all uniquely special expressions of the One Light. Focusing on our unique differences limits us to those manifestations while focusing on our unique similarities opens up the new world of Joy and Love for us to share.

Chapter 6

New Ideas for Growth

Growth and Light

Tonight I was meditating and sending Light to the various parts of the body where I feel pain, behind the heart, across the shoulders, the upper thighs, a whole system of interconnected areas. I have been aware of these connections for some time and have tried chiropractors, relaxation and meditation techniques. This evening, just allowing the Light to penetrate and infuse the areas, I saw the image of a tired, old man. A tired, aging man, a little stooped and weighed down from the amount of work required to keep things going. At my present age I am hardly old or stooped and this image is in even starker contrast to my new Understanding of myself as a Child of Light. Yet I recognized this image, it is the same as my father had of himself when I was growing up and probably the same as my grandfather whose only picture I have shows him as old, stooped and with a cane. And I was amazed at how these concepts transfer so easily from generation to generation. My grandfather may have been that way because of the hardships of his life, but his son would have been young at the time. Yet the image is passed on like a heritage from father to son through as many generations as we allow.

It is time for this image to change. Indeed, it is time for all old images to release their influence because they are all based upon some ancient person's understanding, or rather, misunderstanding. I was amazed how easy it was to see this image when concentrating on the Light within, and how easy it was to release this old idea. I observed how the Light healed these areas and enlightened all aspects of the self. All I had to do was simply remain relaxed and observe the changes taking place. With the observation comes the beginning of change because we are finally aware of the situation. Such a simple change of focus brings about such monumental possibilities.

When I focus on the Center deep within, I sense a new beginning. I see the Light begin to shine and the sphere of cloudy darkness that has enveloped these areas begin to disappear. This parallels the clearing process that the world itself is going through. The Light in the Center is glowing strongly and is beginning to allow the shirking off of the darkness that has enveloped this planet. The planet that has been dull and gray will now become blue and green, yellow and golden with the light of the sun, bright and sparkling like a diamond in the Center of the sea of Life. We are those diamonds, those gems of Divinity that have manifested on the earth. Our being here can bring about a joyful celebration on the earth, an expansion of Light into this other plane of existence.

In each of our lives we strive to uncover this inner self. We allow this self to emerge from behind the barriers we have erected to keep it inside. We allow that frightened part of us to come out, that has been both afraid to emerge and afraid that to be a Child of Light would not be acceptable. In a world that has prided itself on remaining faithful to ancient beliefs, we have been waiting in the wings for a chance to try our new ideas. In a world that prides itself on its power of destruction, we have been waiting to encourage true creativity. Like brilliant beacons, we have been harbored in the dimness until it became our chance to shine. In the interim, we have been going within to find the Source of Light because we have tired of trying to find it in outer manifestation. Our outer manifestation is only a reflection of the Light we bring to it. The time has arrived for us to show what we have learned from our inner journeys.

As we begin to focus on the Light and see ourselves as

manifestations of Light, the world begins to lose its glamour. We understand that the purpose of our desires and adventures has been to show us the Light and not just for our enjoyment. As we see the Light and focus on it, it becomes brighter. We realize that it doesn't take hard work or luck, it doesn't take talent, perseverance or gumption, it only takes focus.

We begin to realize that the purpose of our Life experiences is to teach us how to expand our Light and our Love. That we are here to encourage this expansion in ourselves and others is our destiny. And as this Light and Love expands, our Joy and Happiness expand as well. It is interesting that we get to experience more Joy and Happiness by focusing on the Light than we could ever have experienced by focusing on desires we hoped would bring us Happiness. By going directly to the Source within, we experience so much more. And we realize that this is because we have been mistaken in our basic Understanding of the world.

Where we saw pleasure and happiness in activities and possessions, true Happiness exists only as a state of consciousness. So all of our dreaming, planning and working for what we would like to have to make our lives complete was an exercise in futility, a futility that made us look deeper. The satisfaction of desires has never led to Happiness. But since we believed it was possible, we continued to pursue goals as if the next one would surely make it happen. We ignored the entire unhappy history of the world and assumed that we were somehow going to do it better than ever before. It is amazing how an idea will continue to motivate otherwise rational minds even when all the evidence points to its absurdity. True Happiness is so rare in this world not because that is just the way it is and we have to make the best of it. True Happiness is not rare because we simply have not worked hard enough or because some mythical, malevolent being is keeping it from us. It is not the government's fault, or our parents or the nature of the Universe's fault. We have simply been looking in the wrong place.

We have been confusing the reflections of Light in the world for the Light itself. Like the inhabitants of Plato's cave, we have been mistaking shadows for the real objects. We have hit a dead end in this incredibly crazy three dimensional world. The insanity has reached its ultimate peak and we have explored to the depths every aspect of it in the vain search for the true Source. There is nothing we can take, nothing we can do, no place we can go that will give us the Joy that we seek. We have searched everywhere for everything and the only place left to look is within, and that is precisely where we find what we truly seek. What a magnificent scenario. To be at the end of all hope and in desperation to turn within asking for illumination, and to find everything we have been searching for all in the same place. What incredible drama! We can laugh hysterically at our past foolishness while rejoicing in the remarkable truth we have finally uncovered.

Now we get to use this Understanding to heal all aspects of our lives and our world. We can restructure the entire fabric of culture and human interaction, and share our Love with each other and with all other Life forms on this planet and beyond. And we get to experience the Happiness and Joy that we have always craved. At this very moment we begin Life anew as new Beings, born in the Light and nurtured by the Love that we are. This is the moment that we have all been waiting for, the flash of destiny that will allow us to become the creatures of intelligent Love and Light. Only this will satisfy us, because only then will we be who we intuitively know we are. Otherwise we are merely chasing goals that stretch into the future in an endless dance of dissatisfaction. In the Center we find the Source of true Contentment and Happiness.

In my own experience, goal pursuing took two forms; what I wanted to do with my time and a household that needed constant attention. It seems that as soon as one thing was taken care of there would be something that needed immediate fixing, and there was never enough time to attend to all needs, especially my own personal ones. Now, everything that needs to be attended to is taken care of in the natural flow of events. We do not have to be in control of what is going on, only aware of what is going on while at the same time allowing ourselves to be as bright as possible. It is sometimes difficult for Westerners to let go of the goals and drives associated with success. Yet as long as we believe these stresses and strivings are necessary, we will continue to have them. I would much rather concentrate my energies on love and expansion.

Releasing the Old Method

At first, releasing the old method can be tricky. We don't know how to release our drive or desires even if we are encouraged to do so. To put it another way, since allowing is really doing nothing, we don't know how to do nothing. We are so busy always making something happen that we don't know how to slow down and let it flow. But we are fast learners. We soon learn to focus on the Center and allow the Light to expand. It enlightens and heals all that needs to be healed so that we can grow. And as we grow and expand with our Light, we realize that we are Light, that we are suns, the Suns of God.

We are Light and only Light and when we fully realize this we only manifest Light. We can observe within our experiences, within our mind and emotions, how everything becomes Light. Thus we become positive and full of Love. We forget to worry or judge because we are too busy being positive. We know that all is well and going according to the larger scheme of things. Emotionally we begin to feel the Love flow, Love for all Life forms with which we are so intimately connected. As this Light flows through us it becomes Joy, and Joy becomes us. This Joy expresses itself as Contentment and Peace within. And we experience all of this and know it to be our true energy, Light expressing itself in Divine Celebration. We are weary of proving who we are and gladly let ourselves be all the wonderful expressions of Light and Love that we really are.

Encouragement

Today, I was thinking about the fact that we as humans need so much encouragement. To start a business or relationship or just to feel good about ourselves, we are always looking for signs or some kind of positive, outward demonstrations of love and respect. It must be because we don't trust ourselves or cannot trust the universe, so we are always looking for someone else's opinion. We learn to desperately need someone to tell us that everything is okay, that what we want to do is possible or that we are a good person. I suppose this kind of reassurance is necessary as long as we remain disconnected from our true Source within. These days, the opinion business is huge and everywhere you see shingles hung out professing accurate guidance and counseling on every imaginable subject. Even the spiritual movement has its share of ready experts who can be relied upon for accurate information, and psychic channelers who can access eternal truth for $2.99 a minute. Guidance can be helpful but is a poor substitute for self knowledge. Somewhere along the line of our evolution we gave up thinking for ourselves. We may have felt that we were not educated or bright enough to understand all the issues involved, but as long as we rely on someone else's judgment, we never will be. What we really need then, is not someone else we can rely on, but a reliable connection to our own Source of ultimate Understanding. We need to be able to reassure ourselves that all is well, and we can do that by going to the Center. There we will discover who we truly are and what is going on in our world so we do not need anyone else to tell us about it. We can directly perceive everything that is happening and make intelligent choices based on these observations. Our own informed observation is much more valuable than someone else's guess. And if someone else can help us by channeling information from our guides for us, then we can also learn to access that information for ourselves. We would do well to remove the hocus pocus aspects from the spiritual revolution and understand that no one is doing things that each of us are not also able to do. The healings and deep guidance that we apparently receive through others will at some point in our evolution be given to us directly. All healing comes from within and we can do any of this anytime we really allow it to happen. This involves a new way of structuring our perception of Life.

Structure

At the moment, most of our lives are structured by the mind. Its beliefs and desires determine the life's content. When we shift focus and see ourselves as Love and Light, then these become the structuring elements; Light as active and creative; Love as receptive and nurturing. These are the essence of the yang/yin model of cosmic cooperation which project themselves into manifestation when we allow them to do so. And this occurs automatically. We do not have to secure someone else's opinion about whether or not this will work for us. The very nature of Light is active, Love filled manifestation. By allowing these energies to manifest in our lives, we experience them and know them to be true. The paradox here is that once we do so, we will be showered with Love and affection everywhere that we go and experience much more joyfulness that we ever obtained by being assured by others, for now we will be loved because we know we are Love. Think of all the present absurdity we can then leave behind.

There are many groups on this earth who require initiates to perform many gruesome acts in order to be accepted as a member. I am thinking especially of organized gangs, military splinter and terrorist groups, and even some fraternities. If we can be made to commit acts of treachery merely to be accepted, then there is something deeply wrong with our need to be accepted. We need to find another, less manipulating way to get the acceptance and love that we crave. That can only happen when we return to the Source of Love within. As long as we rely on others for approval, then they will be able to tell us what we have to do to win that approval. This is far too much power entrusted in someone else's hands, and with all the disastrous results we witness in our lives and in the world today. Happily, the cure is easy and painless, immediate and eternal.

We only have to contact our own Source directly to initiate the change. We then experience a Life that is focused on the twin ideas at the Center of all existence. And we can experience a Life filled with Happiness and Joy rather than settling for one that supposedly leads in a happy direction. I seriously doubt whether any of us will ever find Happiness through the old methods and even if some of us do, it will be a very long time before we get there, maybe even not in this lifetime. It is too long to wait for too thin a promise. And yet we continue to hope that by adhering to a certain set of rules that we have been taught we will eventually succeed and understand it all by and by. I will exchange actual experience of Love and Joy for a future hope any day of the week. We get to surround ourselves with a halo of glorious Light and imbue that illumination with Love. And we do this by disconnecting from the mind and focusing on the Center, our Heart of Hearts. We leave behind the petty concerns of our conditioned thinking and embrace these more fulfilling ideas. It is a return to the simplicity of Life. We understand that we are simply these three dimensional transmitters of experience, an experience that can be anything we want it to be. It is the ultimate playground where we can participate in the creation of a joyful and fulfilling experience for everyone on the Earth.

Simplicity

The last time simplicity reared its gracious head was when this age began. The severity and complexity of the Roman Law was challenged by the simple teachings of Jesus. Now simplicity returns, replacing the incredibly complex system of laws and allegiances that make our life system so unwieldy. In our age, we took the ideas and precepts of Jesus and tried to force them on ourselves and others. We used severe conditioning along with punishment and guilt to help insure that we had heard and would never forget the message. Yet the original message was offered with gentleness and advised gentleness and patience, helping those in need from a position of deep Understanding. Because of our fear, we chose to be afraid of what might happen to us if we didn't follow these teachings rather than what we could gain if we did. This is fear, folks, fear that is inconsistent with perceived phenomena and totally opposite of the Truths Jesus was trying to convey. When we truly look within we see Love and we see Light, and these energies do not need to be forced. Prescribed behaviors or specific observances do not produce more Light and Love than gently allowing them to flow. Just as the Sun beams its lovely Light on everyone, so we also can allow our true brilliance to flow in all situations. Then our experiences begin to change and become aligned with these energies. Situations that we once found irksome become smoother, animosities turn into friendships, and Life becomes a tapestry of joyful experiences. Then we begin to attract others who wish to share them. We become students and teachers, learning and passing on what we know in an endlessly evolving cycle.

In the world this energy manifests as healing. All of the problems in the world that seem so insurmountable suddenly become easy. We only have to shine our Light and expand our Love, each of us, from the Center of our Being, and the world will heal. When we do this, all of the problems will melt away like snow in the spring sunlight. Our angers and lusts, confusions and dissatisfactions, our sadness and despair, will fade away like fog in the morning sky. Our anger then becomes appreciation for the lessons we have learned, our envy becomes joy at another's success, and our lusts become glorious relationships of spiritual intimacy. Instead of dissatisfaction with the past we are grateful for the lessons which have taught us the fallacies of our own thinking, fallacies which produced the confused feelings and erratic behaviors. To see our own foolishness, to say, "Yes, I see that all my problems have been caused by my anger, sadness and dissatisfaction" is a moment of supreme glory. It is up to us to change the thoughts that are ruining our enjoyment and driving us crazy. By observing these ideas as they manifest, we can allow them to release and change into more positive thought forms, becoming more and more filled with the wonderful projections of Love and Light.

This is the only method that will successfully help change take place. We will not be able to legislate kindness and joy any more than we have been able to legislate equality or justice. The last four decade's attempts at fixing problems from the governmental level have taught us clearly the ineffectiveness of this approach. Government has grown by over 400 % while the problems are worse than they ever were. We now have task forces and police forces for every conceivable problem yet each day witnesses increases in all of them. We cannot make people behave in kind or courteous ways by threatening them with punishment. Only when we help them to contact the Source of kindness within will the insanity stop. We now have the opportunity to expand our consciousness to include energies and powers of which we have never before been aware. It is this Consciousness and these Spiritual abilities that will transform our world.

It is our task as individuals to bring about this transformation within our selves, and then help others to do the same. As each of us becomes a Center of Love and Light, these energies expand and enlighten every aspect of our environment. Others we meet become affected by this new energy and become centers themselves. We need to shift our attention away from the top of the hierarchy of power, and realize that the true power to change everything lies within us and jumps to the rescue as soon as we allow it to flow.

The Masters tell us that when the student is ready, the teacher appears. By seeking first the Kingdom of Heaven within us, we gain access to both the Source of our energy and the Source of guidance and inspiration. Everything we need to know will be shown to us at the appropriate moment. How many times have we read or heard precisely what we needed to know, or run into just the right person at the right time? Intuition is the spiritual vehicle through which we perceive what is occurring on the levels of energy, and thus know how to respond to any given situation. Rather than trying to figure out with our mind what is happening, we can allow the guidance of intuition to show us what the particular experience is showing us about our self and about our projection of reality. We are interested in learning to become conscious creators of lives full of Love and Joy, and are leaving behind the old methods of acquisition and working for our heart's desire. Instead of trusting our memory and doubt to help us understand what we are experiencing, and thereby sentencing ourselves to a continual reliving of old tapes, we plug into our intuitive sense and begin to allow a new Life to form.

As we begin to observe the Light flowing, we perceive its glow and texture, and we see how it manifests into the reality around us. We can, for instance, watch it take all the energies in our physical bodies and imbue them with Light, making us strong and healthy, full of vitality and purpose. We have the ultimate purpose of participating in this transformation of our Being. It is an exciting and rewarding adventure for all of us to share. As our intuitive senses begin to open up, we see the beautiful colors of the aura and their interactions. We can see these energies and perceive how they affect the energies of others. This will bring about much positive change for each of us. Even if the circumstances do not change, our attitude, involvement and enjoyment of them will. And as we learn we become even more flowing and so our life experiences continue to become more wonderful. And this is accomplished by placing our attention on the Center of Love and Light. It is an amazingly simple change of focus which can be easily experienced through various forms of meditation.

Meditation is the placing of the attention on the Center. Most of us begin our spiritual journey by practicing meditation at some point during our day. At first, it is easier to quiet the mind by sitting in a relaxed position and then allowing the focus to drift away from the busy thoughts of the day to the calm Center where Peace and Contentment are found. We can focus on the breath as it moves in and out and imagine the Light doing the same, moving with the breath. Expanding and returning, the Light filled Love flows from within and surrounds us with its dazzling luminescence. When we see and feel these energies, then we realize that they are us and we can begin to let go of even more of our old, limiting thoughts. Our ideas of who we are and why we are here begin to change subtly, becoming focused in the Light and becoming infused with Love. In time, we can keep our focus in the Center throughout the day, knowing that this is the true Source from which our Life experiences flow. We learn to understand this as we become it. It is a continual process of growth and expansion in Understanding and experience.

We can also focus our attention on the Heart Center and see there our Light. We allow this Light to expand until it fills the heart area. As it does, we perceive the blood flowing from this Center moving wonderfully and easily, becoming filled with this Light and taking Its healing and invigorating energies to all parts of the body. We recognize that this energy is Love, the emotional aspect of Light. As Light expands, it condenses, first into the emotional realm as Love, and then into the physical aspect as creative experience. With each breath that we take, we become more and more this Love and Light that we are. With each breath we release the limitations of the past, let go of the hope and fear of the future, and embrace the Joy and Celebration of the present moment. It is all we really have anyway, and all that we really need.

Chapter 7
Moving Past The Future

The Past

I was thinking tonight about how our desires hang on over the long haul. For me there has been this desire to produce music since I was 15 years old. And there is much music I have produced over the years, both for my own enjoyment and for various dance, theatre and video productions when I attended the university. This desire leads periodically to a decision to create some music. Under the surface of this desire is a sincere hope of sharing and maybe helping. But there is also a need to prove myself by creating something wonderful, the old desire for specialness rearing its worried head above the sea of conformity. So the production of music is as much a validation of the ego as it is a desire to share and be involved in the musical scene. There lies the lesson, because anything that involves the ego to any great extent is colored by it, and anything colored by the ego leads us away from the Spiritual Path. The ego always wants isolated specialness while the Spiritual Path celebrates both our Oneness in the Light and an appreciation of our uniquely original expression of it. It is important to recognize our interconnections as Beings of Light before we tramp off to the fields of individual endeavor. Only if our endeavors are stamped with the Light of the Love within will we truly find Love and Joy for ourselves. This means that we find within us a totally different reason for expressing our uniqueness.

Rather than the tired parading of all we think makes us so different, which really only shows the depths of our low self-esteem, we become individuals brimming with the spirit of exploration. Instead of carefully crafted personalities designed to attract attention, we allow our true inner uniqueness to flow from us like water from a mountain spring. Instead of striving so hard to be different and thereby concentrate on things of little consequence like our looks or possessions, we become beings focused in the twin energies of Life itself. In the valiant attempts to find our individuality we often miss our true uniqueness. Our uniqueness lies in the way that we can create with energy. Our thoughts create a three dimensional reflection of their contents. Therefore, we can become conscious creators of our own movies rather than be at the mercy of the status quo. So far, we have been concentrating our efforts and attentions on the mere surface manifestations of this creative energy and feeling frustrated because we cannot find anything there of lasting value. Only by turning our attention to the Center will we ever find the value we seek so earnestly. And in that place we find our true creativity which can heal and allow us to grow into joyful beings of Love and Light instead of struggling, confused beings groping for meaning in the meaninglessness of surface appearances. We need to release the confused groping and the exhausting drive to succeed. Only then will we understand that we already have what we search for and already are what we are trying so desperately to become.

The Future is Now

I was thinking about tarot readings and I thought that the only reason they have been associated with the future is because the future is the only thing we have traditionally been interested in. The future has been our major concern and what we ask about most often. Now that we are becoming interested in the present, the tarot cards and other forms of divination can emerge into their true and much wider function. They can now be used to provide a sort of snapshot of where we are at this moment. They can reveal the assemblage of energies and intentions that we have initiated with our thinking and so help us to see what is going on inside us. This blueprint of our understandings and emotions can help us go on from here with more knowledge of who we are. The difference between this kind of reading and one which only tells us what is going to happen in the future are really quite different. This kind of reading helps to show the underlying forces at work in our lives, the forces that are produced by our thoughts and which in turn produce our three dimensional experiences. With this information, we are able to become part of the process of creation, true co-creators in our lives. And this is clearly already happening.

We are becoming aware that Life is much more than the mere day to day unfolding of events. As this consciousness grows we will become less and less interested in what happens and more interested in the underlying forces. Deep within us is where the real decisions are made and most of them presently without our conscious awareness. Going within allows us to participate in these formative meetings of ideas and forces. Rather than nervously waiting to see what is going to happen next we can have intimate knowledge of the direction our lives are taking. Yet this knowledge of ourselves need not include every detail. Once we know that our lives are only going to become more positive and more joyful, then we can release this old and impossible desire to know beforehand everything that is going to happen. Obsession with detail is only another aspect of fear of the future. Since all is Joy and Celebration, who cares about the details? Anyway, I would much rather be delightfully surprised at every turn than endure the boredom of knowing everything in advance. Like a movie that's totally predictable, our lives become dull and uninteresting without a sense of adventurous wonder.

We can achieve this sense of wonder by allowing ourselves to Trust. We have had great success in allowing ourselves to be fearful and our lives have been completely full of it. In our attempts to sidestep misfortune by controlling every detail we have plunged ourselves into a morass of confusion. If we can be so successful with fear and confusion, we should be equally successful with Trust. If fear can build the terrifying world we witness around us then Trust can just as easily build the joyful world we sense within us. The principles of creation always work and with any thought forms that we care to utilize. I choose to utilize only positive and joyful thoughts in the building of my world of experience. How about you?

Each of us will at some point reach this decision. When we are convinced that our present life direction is leading nowhere, we will turn around. When we become aware that the promises of the Path of Acquisition will never be fulfilled, we will look for a new path, one that leads more directly to the land of Joy and Happiness. That is why we are here. We must find the Source of Love and Joy within because only then will we stop our endless searching. In this search, we have encountered many remarkable obstacles.

Indeed, the history of man is the story of our struggle to achieve the right to pursue our own Happiness. The Founding Fathers of America threw off the chains of the kingdoms of Europe and proclaimed every person's freedom. It was a major step forward in human evolution and brought with it the tremendous growth and inventions of the American Legacy. For the first time in history, people were free to explore any and all aspects of themselves and build any kind of life they could manage. There have been many great success stories as well as countless abuses, but we have learned much of value about our capabilities and deepest desires. It is time now to move forward another step. For all freedom has done or us, it has not made us any happier than when we were at the mercy of ruthless monarchs. The dream of freedom is what kept the human spirit alive during the dark ages of religious persecution and political enslavement. To the eyes of the imprisoned, freedom seems like the answer to all prayers. Yet with our freedom we have only succeeded in building a world of greed and terror unequaled in the worst epochs of history. The problem was not in our desire for freedom, but in our assessment of the enemy. Fear has become the new monarch and has proven to be more ruthless than any of its human predecessors

In the past, there was always an enemy we could point to, the Kings, the infidels, the Church, the system, all those in powerful positions were responsible for keeping us down and their removal should remedy the situation. Yet as soon as one set of tyrants is removed, another set rises up from the ranks. If well meaning public servants can become tyrants as soon as they get power then either the system corrupts them or there is something fundamentally wrong with the way we, as humans, think. We have been changing systems since recorded history began with little effect, so the true enemy has to be the way we think. And this explains everything.

The reason no system is without corruption is because our thinking is full of selfishness. Selfish people in high places do not magically become unselfish, they become highly selfish. They may talk about helping the masses but are generally more interested in themselves because that is the way our minds have been trained to work. The reason that no system has succeeded in bringing Happiness to the masses is because we, the masses, have not been able to bring it to ourselves. To expect someone else to bring us Happiness is a mistake in judgment of the highest order. It's like expecting someone else to breathe for us. We are all responsible for ourselves and are becoming aware of the vast resources we have within. The old system is based on the belief that we need leaders to divide the riches of the country fairly among all of us. These riches are all outside the self and so up for grabs by whoever has the best access. Thus the problem with elected officials and others close to the pie. Yet by realizing that we are the Source of everything, that our pursuit of Happiness starts as a flow from the Center of each of us, then there is no longer anyone who has any power over us. The enemy has been us all along. It has been our lack of understanding of where our own Happiness and Joy comes from. It has been the erroneousness of our own thinking. We can change that. Just as we have been our own worst enemy, we now become our own best friend. This is the direction that we are going. We are learning to think positively, we are learning to be self reliant and we are learning to be focused in the Center where everything we are begins. Nothing can stop this growth because it is the next logical step in our evolution.

We can see this change everywhere if we but take a moment to look. Many of us are beginning to do things because of Love instead of selfishness because we understand how much more we gain when we allow our Love to expand. We have seen the Light and are replacing all of our former motivations, our greed and fear, our selfish schemes and worst nightmares with

Love. Understanding that all of these have not produced Happiness makes them easier to release than if they had been successful. My heart goes out to the celebrities and political personalities, to the corporate moguls and big time swindlers, because they have achieved some measure of success and even though their success has not brought any real Joy, it is enough to keep them running down the same path. They will never know the true joys of a Life lived from the Center because their focus is riveted on the external world of power and influence. Come to think of it, this is the first time in history that the little guys have the advantage. Because of most of our limited success in the current world system, we are enabled to look beyond it to a better way.

I remember in high school someone asked me if it wouldn't be wonderful to do what we love doing. I answered that it might be better to love whatever it is we do. I may not have understood this at the time, but I did try to practice it in my life, and that practice began to reveal the wonder of all things. Oh sure, I got caught up in the youth rebellion of the 60's, but that only further convinced me that anger and violence were not the best ways to facilitate change. There were too many involved who were merely angry without a shred of ethical or spiritual conviction. This was the latest rebellion party and all the thugs showed up to join in the fray. Meanwhile, there was at least an attempt by some to live for love and to love Life in all its aspects. So rather than try to arrange my life so that it only contains things that I love, I rather arrange my Love so that it shines on everything that occurs. This was an amazingly freeing realization. Whereas before I had been working towards the goal of satisfaction with all aspects of my life, I now had the key to satisfaction in my lap. Within my mind is where the decision is made to be happy or dissatisfied and I am taking full advantage of this at every opportunity.

As I watch my mind change I see my life change by itself. Activities that were once irksome are either joyful or absent. People who were royal pains are now friends and revered teachers. The Master said to Love our enemies and that is because they are showing us the most destructive aspects of ourselves. In understanding and appreciating those who have hurt us the most, we change from miserable and frustrated victims to mature and knowing beings. We know that everything that occurs in our lives is an accurate reflection of our thinking, so we welcome all as the opportunity to learn and grow. And our lesson in all Life situations is the same, to find the Joy. When we can do that, when we can see the grace in all things, when we can rise above all experiences, then our lives can become truly joyful. As long as we begrudge certain activities or bemoan certain situations, we will never know Joy and peace. We need only open up to the wonder of all and we will be shown that wonder. "Ask and it shall be given," we are told in the ancient writings, "seek and ye shall find." As long as we complain, we will never seek and never find. As long as we think things are hopeless then we will never ask and never receive. Because we are so sure that life is hopeless and nothing will get any better, we refuse to even ask to see a new possibility. This is only our own minds keeping us within its conditioned limitations. The only way out is to allow ourselves to think in a new and excitingly positive way.

In the world of psychology, staying centered means not going crazy, but in the spiritual world it means staying focused on the Source within. It means to keep our attention on the Center of Love and Light. We can only focus on one thing at a time, so if we are apprehensive about the future, we cannot be joyful in the present, if we are worried about money, we cannot enjoy Abundance. So I try to concentrate on positive ideas and aspects of living. I saw that I had been spending a lot of energy on ideas that were negative and destructive. This is what we have all traditionally done. By continually saying, "Boy, I hope things don't get worse" we are not only insuring that they will, but also that things cannot get any better. We are being foolish in the use of focus and are getting exactly what we think about. It's like driving the wrong way on the freeway and being surprised at the number of accidents we're having. This is how we learn. When we have enough accidents, we start to look for a cause. In this case, we discover that it is our own lack of focus that is causing all the problems. From here we can take the necessary steps to correct it.

The Control Issue

What is interesting about this change is the shift in the control issue. Whereas in the old system we tried to find ways to control everything, now we only have to control our focus. It should be a whole lot easier and usually is. The only real problem is that we have had so little practice that we don't know how to go about it. This is where meditation techniques come in because any of the various visualizations and affirmation techniques can help us learn to control what our mind is thinking about. And this is precisely what we are talking about. We are not interested in controlling our bodies or our money, or even our future, just our minds. Human history has been a story of minds out of control. We need to be able to keep our minds focused on one thing at a time and not let it continually go wherever it wants to go. The modern mind has been trained to have an incredibly short attention span and to be easily influenced by media and other inputs. We must reverse that trend. It is odd that while most of us would not allow another person to control our bodies, we think nothing of letting other people completely control our minds. In fact, most humans have no control over their minds at all and think whatever they are told to think. This is how the current system was put in our minds in the first place. Our parents and teachers opened us up and poured it in, then the media jumped in and completed the job. But this has been a tremendous, positive lesson for us.

Only by becoming completely programmed and controlled by external forces have we become aware of the game. Now we can take charge of what we think and learn to be the conscious creators of our own lives. We will be able to stop blaming everyone else for our misfortunes because we will see how we have allowed their creation. We will also see how easy it is to create lives of Love and Joy with the simple power of a focused mind.

Recognition

According to the present world's standards, one is only great if one accomplishes great things. The focus is on what we do and greatness is too easily subverted into fame or notoriety.

So the desire to be rich and famous takes the stage as the ultimate goal and substantiated proof of intrinsic value. Yet what we are willing to do to attain this fame or fortune, the lengths to which we will go to prove our greatness is usually the measure of our mediocre understanding. Because in the means we employ to succeed is our true wisdom displayed for all to see. I would rather be unknown and wise than famous for frivolity. I would rather experience the joys of conscious living than endure mediocrity for the sake of future profit. We are here to experience Life, not leave a legacy. We are here to expand and explore who we truly are, not make ourselves into a politically correct combination of traits for mass consumption. It makes me wonder why we are so afraid to quietly be who we are and instead noisily pretend to be someone else. Eventually we have to let another person close enough to see through the disguises. Perhaps our fear of intimacy is a device designed to somehow protect this cloak of image we wear like so much make-up and costuming. What a price to pay for theatrics. By giving up intimacy for showcasing our looks and talents, we give up one of the best sources of growth and Joy, relationships. We give up remaining in close harmony for the effect we can make in passing. I trust that soon we will all be able to be who we are and stop this insane pretense. Perhaps if we look closely at this strong desire for recognition, we will be able to perceive it for what it really is.

  We crave recognition from others for what we can do or what we appear to be, rather than for who we are. But this craving can be seen, not as a negative thing, but as a way of behaving that leads us towards the Spiritual Path. When we view it as a way of behaving, as a method for getting what we want, we begin to see the faults with it. We begin to perceive the drive and the fear, the inner insecurity and confusion that plague this approach to being a person. Then we recognize that the drive is a way to cover up the fear and confusion. We keep ourselves so busy going after what we think we need that we have no time to think about what we are doing, probably because we know the minute we stop, we will sink into confusion and doubt. We hate to be plagued by doubt or belittled by confusion. But is our constant running from our own thinking any answer?

We cannot hide forever behind a facade of outward confidence that covers the cavernous hole of our self-doubt. The lengths to which we will go, the depths of treachery and conceit that we will employ in the vain attempt to fill this inner void are remarkable in both their variety and ingenuity. They share a common drawback, however, they are all ultimately unsuccessful and usually destructive. Stress and fear take their toll on our health and cheerfulness. We have become known as a people who are unhappy and at the mercy of the forces of their own desires, an enemy within their own minds. In my own case, I was striving to become something that I could be proud of and that others would admire, yet my real self-image was quite barren even if I did occasionally receive some recognition. Usually, that little bit of recognition would spur me on to an ever more stressful drive to accomplish even more, in hopes of attaining more. The empty place within me was starved for affection and I would do almost anything to fill it, except, of course, look within to see what the problem really was.

At that time I was unaware that it was really an inside job. I was so focused on external accomplishment and recognition, that it never occurred to me that there might be an easier and better method to achieve what I was so sadly lacking. Finally, in utter exhaustion and despair, I gave up the insane drive for notoriety, and let the whole thing go. It was difficult to give up my dreams but I realized I could not keep them going any longer, so what the heck!

There was at first a period of dejection and hopelessness. I was a body going through the motions of living with some semblance of appropriate gesture and activity. Slowly some hope seeped back in to make my life tolerable, yet the promise of joy was gone and with it my life became a hollow routine. This all seems pretty melodramatic but is a fairly accurate description. It was during this time that I began to meditate because I couldn't think of anything else that would help. In those moments when I managed to forget what I was thinking and feel the flow of my breath, I experienced some ease and even moments of peace. I was able for a time to forget what I was missing, and began to see what I had. It is an addictive practice. So I began spending hours everyday in that relaxed space, working with various techniques and exercises like the Rainbow Bridge and the Course in Miracles, trying to surround myself with Light and release the blocks to my inner Contentment and peacefulness. In time, I began to relax and was able to enjoy my life more and things began to happen for me. I started a new business and began a new relationship. More importantly, I began to see that what was happening to me was a reflection of what I was thinking and feeling. The more I became positive and inwardly happy, the more Happiness and Joy I experienced. This was a gradual process of letting go of older, unproductive ideas and replacing them with the positive concepts of Love and Joy. It was learning to focus my attention in a new direction, a direction that made a positive difference in my life.

Learning to think positively produces excellent results and is used successfully in all kinds of therapy. First introduced by Bishop Sheen during the Great Depression, it has been used widely in business and sports, and is beginning to be respected as a sound psychological approach to change. But sometimes our negative thoughts are very strong and the attempt to make them positive becomes difficult. The mind, it seems, is so used to thinking negatively, that it views the positive approach with consummate skepticism. This skepticism in turn keeps any change from happening. In other cases, the very confusion in the mind eliminates any chance for enough concentration to affect a positive result. In these and many other cases, I have found that change is quicker and easier if the mind is bypassed altogether.

By focusing on the Center, by allowing our attention to drift to the Source within, we eliminate the tricky process of trying to change the mind while being surrounded by it. Attempting to see the big picture while being bombarded by disturbing details is trying, to say the least. By shifting our focus out of the mind, we allow ourselves the opportunity to view our experience from the perspective of Love and Light. It is this new awareness that we need and want if we are ever to make sense of all the conflicting thoughts and ideas that tumble through our minds every day. We can give ourselves the gift of quietness and peacefulness in meditation, and thus find a secure Understanding of who we are. And we can experience the flow of our Love and witness the brilliance of our Light within.

If extraneous thoughts or doubts should shift our attention back to the confused jungle of the mind, we can gently place our attention back to the Center. This is a process of training ourselves to focus within, of training ourselves to allow our inner Light to flow and thereby change all aspects of our experience as a Human Being. Older thoughts and feelings will surface to our attention as if asking, 'do you want to think about or feel me now?' And from this centered place we can answer, 'I wish to think of Love and Light now because I realize that then they will be my experience.' Every time these older ideas surface we can replace them with Love and Light, and pretty soon they will cease to surface because they are no longer perceived as necessary. And so our change continues through all the layers of our conditioned thinking and feelings. Gradually we release all undesirable aspects of our old self and replace them with a new self brimming with Joy and confidence, and a Life experience filled to the edges with Love and Celebration.

Getting Hurt

I was thinking about how a large part of our personalities are memories of past injuries. We get hurt then cover it up, thus insuring that we carry it with us forever. Instead of just feeling the hurt and dealing with it, we end up with several layers within us that will inevitably cause problems. Each layer will continue to radiate its upsetting energy and continue to manifest itself throughout the life of the host. This old way of dealing with hurt does not ease the pain, it only changes its nature, makes it three times as large and makes it last forever. The oddest part of this is that we were not really hurt at all, we merely imagined that we were. Life experiences are not designed to hurt, but only to teach. It is only our attachment to the results of our experiences which make us think we didn't get our money's worth. We had some kind of goal that was frustrated. So what we really suffered was a loss, a setback in our Life plan. When we release the drive to acquire, then we will never suffer loss and never be hurt again. This sense of loss is magnified in present times.

In the modern scene, we find millions demanding retribution for past hurts, as if Life is some kind of contract in which they have been wrongly treated. Our treatment is and has only been the consequence of our thinking. The treachery towards the Native Americans by early Whites was an exact reflection of their treatment of other tribes. It was also the Blacks in Africa who first sold their Black Brothers into slavery. These actions were all the result of selfish thinking on all sides.

When the idea of selfishness is extreme, the idea of Oneness cannot exist. How would it be possible to feel a Oneness with all Life and yet exploit others, or exploit the world's resources for profit? The very fact that men can exploit others shows that there is an idea of separateness expressed as 'I am I, you are you and the world is the world.' There is no connection between the two, there is no sense of Oneness. Early White Americans felt no Oneness with the Native Americans and greedily took their land and disrupted their culture. There was no sense of Oneness with Africans either so they were enslaved. But if hatred is instilled in young minds because of these historical events, if many are angry at these early perpetrators, then there is separateness. While the Native Americans may have believed in their Oneness with all of Nature, that Oneness did not extend to other humans, especially white ones. As long as there is one exception to Oneness then it does not truly exist. If we feel connected to all Life, then we Love all Life. If there is truly Love, then there is no room for hatred, no matter what the supposed justification might be. Hate and anger maintain separateness. The Native Americans continue to maintain their separateness from the White Man and in so doing show the limitation of their understanding. They do not really see the Oneness with all Life because the White Man is part of Life. They only feel a partial oneness, a oneness with only their own kind. In other words, their idea of oneness is selective, it is self centered, it is not Oneness.

While we may have great compassion for the suffering these people are experiencing, we must also understand that suffering is and has been an important aspect of their culture. Anything focused upon creates itself and thus their celebration of suffering had manifested in the extreme. Although the Native American concept of suffering 'for the people" implies self sacrifice for others, it still is firmly rooted in the belief that suffering is a necessary part of life, which, of course, creates it. Perhaps experiencing intense suffering and alienation is the only way these souls can learn what they need in order to evolve further. Let's support them in their learning so that they can emerge from this lesson with an even stronger Understanding of Oneness than they had before.

They are certainly not alone in this misunderstanding. All modern cultures are experiencing an intense amount of suffering and alienation, all caused by the same misguided focus. We must all learn Oneness now. Only by realizing the true mental causes of historical events will we ever move past this era. They were all caused by our collective selfish thinking. To seek justice for past wrongs is to limit the outcome to some token form of compensation, and to keep the focus on the past. This keeps emotional hurts painfully present and angers close to the surface, hardly a pleasant scenario for anyone involved. It also keeps the trustless system of acquisition going, a system which is at odds with most native traditions. Can an acquisition really make up for a perceived loss? By focusing on the hurts of the past we will never eliminate or rebalance them, but only guarantee their existence in the future. But with forgiveness, these hurts, angers and impossible struggles for restitution can be released and we can move on into a world of Peace and Joy.

If we can forgive and let go of our hurts, then we can let go of anything because these are the deepest wounds and the hardest to forgive. They are our test cases, challenging our Understanding to see if we can perceive the true path of forgiveness in the midst of age old pain. Eventually, we will all forgive everything because we will understand that all that baggage only weighs us down. They have been just lessons along the way towards perfection, lessons which are now blocking our progress. It is unimportant if they be compensated, it is only important that they be understood and released with Love.

Challenge

Another aspect of the current method that we encounter is the idea of challenge. It is all well and good to desire a happier life, but many of us feel we would miss the challenges of the present system. The idea of pitting ourselves against the forces of nature still holds its allure. In the inner cities, just staying alive is an adventure of mammoth proportions with all the excitement living on the edge is reputed to contain. Then there are all of the various causes for which humans are famous. Many spend their whole lives in pursuit of these and get from them both a feeling of purpose as well as pride in working for the betterment of their tribe or for their children's sake. It would be very difficult for those intimately involved in these kinds of challenges to forgo these adrenaline infused activities and be content just sitting around meditating or waiting for the Soul to manifest. Patience is rarely a virtue in any of us, let alone the overly driven who believe in the importance of their cause. But happily, there is not only more Love and Joy with the new method, there is also the ultimate in challenges.

We do not advocate forgetting about any of the injustices that need to be addressed, or ignoring the struggles and hardships in various parts of the world. On the contrary, we understand that the spread of Light and Love will heal all wounds regardless of their size, origin or nature. The challenge comes in perceiving all of these struggles clearly and then taking the most appropriate actions to heal them. It is a challenge to us of the utmost importance, coming at a time when correct perception and action is especially crucial. We are being asked to see beyond our own hurts and angers, to see beyond the petty squabbles we have manufactured in the name of culture or pride, and perceive the true glory of our Being. For only in seeing our amazing brotherhood, only in clearly perceiving the wondrousness of our true Essence, will we ever be able to let go of all the zillions of animosities and racial hatreds that so clearly mar our expression as the human race.

And this is simply and easily done. Just a few glimpses of the inner Light, just a few tastes of the ecstasy of our inner Love and we readily admit that the justice or retribution we were hoping to find in the outer world is shallow and cold in comparison. We understand that the issues that we felt to be so undeniably important in the past are as frivolous as the traumas of children who have misplaced a toy. We might feel compassion for the child but realize in our maturity that it is only a toy that was lost and not the end of the world. Now we are being asked to mature even further, and understand that the dreams and desires that we have considered so essential to our Happiness, the struggles and missions we have set ourselves to accomplish are pale in comparison to the incredible Abundance Life has to offer. We have been trying with all our might to fix a world that was only broken in our minds.

It's like we have been peeking through a keyhole at only one very small part of universal Abundance. We have seen just enough of it to desire it from the bottom of our hearts and have been prepared to do anything to get it. We have barely begun to taste the Joys of Life and we have not even begun to feel and express Love. We have been fighting over the beauties we could see just inside the door, unaware that there is a thousand times more if we look deeper, more than enough to satisfy everyone, everywhere, at every moment of their lives. This is what the Master meant when he said, "In my father's house there are many mansions." We have been fighting over hovels and that fighting has blinded us to the true castles that await us when the earth becomes the planet of Love and Light.

As we begin to realize this, we will release our struggles to forge new nations for ourselves, and instead accept the challenge to create them out of Love. For those who decide to remain with the present system, we can offer them our compassion for the fruitlessness of their mission. We can only hope that they will understand soon and join us in the building of the new planet Earth, the green planet, the planet of Love, Joy and Light.

Chapter 8
Goals and Growth

Punishment

Before I forget, I was thinking about punishment. Actually, I was releasing the idea of punishment. How pervasive it is throughout the current thought system. Not just the idea of eternal punishment, but the idea that life itself is a test during which we endure certain forms of limitation and loss in order to prove ourselves worthy of eternal reward. Somewhere, someone concocted the concept of punishment as a way to explain the human predicament, a concept also very useful in enforcing certain behavior patterns. It all started with the idea, and we've been punishing each other ever since. All with the best of intentions, of course. Punishment has become a necessary and expected part of our life experience. If someone is punished a lot he might feel abused, but normal. Others might feel equally neglected for not being punished. 'My parents didn't care enough about me to make me behave,' they say. So punishment becomes associated with love and is a part of life which must exist for there to be completeness. This even goes so far as in those who can't get enough of punishing themselves or others, or both. It is also a sign to some that they have successfully tasted the forbidden fruit. 'You don't get burned unless you walk on the edge,' the street saying goes, and the excitement of the edge is attractive for many. In some circles, one is not a man unless one pushes the membrane of acceptability, and getting into trouble is the measure of one's success. All of these are aspects of punishment. We are fearful of it, anxious for it, or proving something by suffering it. And we can see what it has produced in this world. This is a very powerful idea and one that needs to change.

Within the ideas that make up our self image, punishment sits like a jewel in the crown. 'For all have sinned and fallen short of the glory of God' the Christian Scriptures proclaim, and further explain that this is why we are being tested, that is, punished in this lifetime by the Supreme Being. He is testing our strength of character and the strength of our faith. It's a simple test of faith that has some very serious consequences, Joy and Bliss forever or, you guessed it, eternal punishment. Christians delight in going to great lengths to describe the horrors we might expect if we are unfortunate enough to be judged unworthy. No wonder we are so afraid of death, we suspect we are unworthy and fear we will have to suffer torments and damnation for the rest of Eternity. That's pretty heavy stuff with which to fill a small child's mind, and many of us are still recovering from the shock of seeing the immense wrath that awaits us at the hands of our 'Loving Father.' What a plight! When we finally see what this thought form is teaching us, we are on our way out of its grip.

We can begin by looking at the various layers this idea creates. There is punishment itself which is surrounded by fear. We all believe it to be a very real possibility so we consciously try to avoid it. And then we use the threat of it to get others to cooperate with our desires. We believe it, we fear it, we avoid it and we use it to get what we want. I think it is time we made up our mind about it and figured out what it really is, and what it isn't. Is it just a reality and we might as well use it to our benefit, or is it an insane idea manifesting its insanity in every corner of the globe? I'd vote for the insanity version, because the hurt and fear it causes makes us insane. Some of us get so insane with fear of it and with lack of love, that we welcome it as better than nothing. So it only produces its own misery. What's more, it completely blocks out any chance of seeing the Light within. We have become so accustomed to the darkness that the very idea of Light seems odd and out of place in our neat little world of struggle, suffering and woe. Finally, we tack guilt on top of all of this, the idea being that we wouldn't have to be punished if we hadn't been so bad in the first place.

Guilt really puts another thick layer on top of the almost unbearable load we already have. Guilt makes it legitimate and successfully removes any hope of it ever stopping. We are not even supposed to think about these things and we are taught to feel guilty if we do. So we are kept from even thinking about a life without punishment and fear because we feel guilty for even imagining that we might not deserve it. By adding guilt to the other layers, we end up with: we expect it, we fear it, we avoid it, we use it, and we deserve it. It is the idea of deserving which I think is the key to unlocking its grip.

We deserve punishment, the old saying goes, because we have sinned, we have done something wrong. This is some kind of original sin that our great and noble forefathers committed and we have to suffer the consequences of their actions. Eve tasted the apple and all men have been doomed ever since. In other words, we have to endure a life of deprivation and suffering to make up for their mistake. Of course, we keep adding to the debt with our own transgressions. This is not very promising. We can't escape it, we deserve it, we don't understand it and we're not allowed to think about it. A nice tidy little package perfectly suited to control our thinking and never allow any expansion of growth. It sounds like something the IRS would design, totally and deviously functional but quite insane. And the clincher is what usually constitutes our individual fall from grace, sexual interest.

The designers of this game knew they had to conclusively prove sinfulness so they chose the strongest urge that we have and made it sinful. What a brilliant idea. Just get the kids conditioned so that they think sex is bad, then when you ask them, 'You've been thinking about sex, haven't you,' all will guiltily confess. They could have used our desire for food but if we abstained from that too much, we would have disappeared. Sex was a much safer target and one guaranteed to work. And indeed, as Freud so astutly observed, the social history of our culture can be understood as our attempts to adjust to sexual behavior. Sexual satisfaction is a subject of as much concern as it is of misunderstanding and perversion. It is the subject of a vast amount of our literature and films. The uneasiness about sex has produced many sexual problems and an immense and lucrative industry. So it seems they picked a good one when they decided to black list sex. When we begin to know sexuality for what it truly is, all of its seedier aspects like pornography and perversions disappear in the brightness of true Understanding. Sex is simply a wonderful part of expressing Love, the Love within us all. It is a small fraction of the incredibly enlivening and sustaining power of Love. It doesn't have to be anything more than that! I think many of the current problems with sexuality come from our expecting it to be the fix all for every conceivable situation. It's supposed to take us to untold heights of passion and remarkable feelings of Oneness, and we're utterly disappointed when it doesn't. How can it when it is surrounded by all of this fear and guilt. Remove the bugaboos, and maybe we will begin to experience these higher aspects of sexual Love. But first, let's see that we have only been caught in this dark loop of fear and guilt to teach us something.

What we have been learning is the power of our own thinking, the intense power of ideas to completely and utterly influence every aspect of our lives. One look at the ramifications of sexuality should be enough to convince anyone that one idea, if misunderstood, twisted and exploited enough, can change the entire fabric of society. Now, imagine what will happen when we untwist this idea and allow it to become Love again, when we allow it to be a wonderful expression of our Oneness with a very special friend. Sexuality and all of its associated problems has been teaching us this as only it could. For only our desire for sexual union is strong enough for us to override our erroneous conditioning and finally see its true and intended beauty

What a wonderful lesson this has been for us! Being able to finally see through this facade of logic, seeing through the insanity of compounded layers of ideas, allows us to be free of them. Once we figure out how to get out of the dungeon, it is only a matter of time before we escape. We only have to trick the guards. Of course, this particular thought form has built in guards, guilt and fear. We are, in essence, outwitting our own guards. We are moving past the defenses we ourselves built to keep us in line, to hold us back from growth, to keep us where we have been. In recognizing these ideas and their interrelationships, we can release them and at the same time feel grateful that we have learned the major lessons of fear and guilt all at once. Now that we see the ruse, we can allow those ideas to evaporate in the bright Light of the Divinity within.

Really, it's probably a good thing we didn't discover the truth about thought energy before this time. Napoleon and Hitler were tyrants enough without this knowledge of how thoughts manifest. All they had was sustained drive and determination, the old way. But determination is not Love. Now is the perfect time for us to learn to be conscious creators because we have experimented enough with the old method to fully understand its severe limitations. There is very little doubt in our minds that the old way does not work, so we will not be tempted to try to utilize this new information to manipulate within the older system. Besides, it won't work anyway. There is no way we can force anything truly full of Light to flow, and without the flow, it cannot manifest. There are many things that can be forced but Love and Joy are not among them. Heaven knows, we have tried everything we can think of to do so. So the new method has its own built in defenses. We must Love before it will work for us. Those who are still dark and angry will not be able to experience the new way because their anger keeps them locked in the old way. Once we break out of the old way, our Understanding expands even more to see how fruitless the old way really is. It is another perfect growth step.

The Four Steps of Growth

There are four aspects to spiritual growth as it applies to ideas: 1) recognize the idea, 2) bless it for what it has taught us, 3) release it from the mind and 4) allow that space to be filled with new ideas based on Love and Light. As we focus on the Center, these older ideas surface to our attention so they can be released and replaced. The mind is cleared of all outworn ideas, and this process continues until all ideas are imbued with these brighter qualities. We can continue to think the old thoughts and create for ourselves the same old experiences, but in time we grow tired of this game. We say that need is the mother of invention, but in the case of these old ideas, uselessness is the mother of change.

In my own case, the ideas of punishment and its layers were a major issue which taught me most forcefully the full creative impact of my daily thinking. I have used that knowledge to create an experience based on the new trinity of Light, Love and Creative Physical Expression. In my experience of releasing, I have seen many instances in this life as well as previous incarnations where I suffered punishment. I imagine that within the collective subconscious, we all have experienced and can call up previous instances. It is now time for us to go past this kind of self torture and know that punishment has become a universal experience only because we have spent so much time thinking about it. If such negative and painful ideas can be so powerfully manifested, imagine what the even more powerful and positive ideas of Love and Light will accomplish. We should really enjoy the difference.

I was thinking about the idea for a section of this book called Growing Up Blind. The idea is that as we grow up, the only things we see are what everyone else sees. It's like we come in as children with wide open eyes but are taught to focus in on only certain very limited aspects of life. We are learning that the amount we have been blinded to far surpasses that which we see. We can see the trees and flowers and the skin of others, but we have yet to fully develop our ability to see within ourselves, or within other Life Forms. And it is within that the major energy exchanges take place. We have relied on the physical eyes so long that we have forgotten how to use our other, intuitive sight.

All of us, I am sure, have been outside in the dark and felt this kind of sensory expansion. If we pay attention to what is going on, we will notice that it is not even so much our peripheral vision but a different kind of sense, more like radar or psychic antennae. This is one of our intuitive senses. When we do perceive these other levels of energy, it's as if we had been blind but now we see. We remember the Master's words about the blindness he perceived in us. When we think about it, this new Understanding of who we are and why we are here is so totally beyond the comprehension of the old way of thinking, that we realize that the world is pretty blind right now. So many of us continue to doggedly pursue goals which have no hope of being fulfilled and driving ourselves to shore up self-images that will never be secure because we have been looking in the wrong place and with extremely limited vision. We have been truly blind, stumbling along in the darkness, looking vainly throughout the world for the Light that only exists within.

But now we are beginning to see clearly. It is a moment for intense rejoicing because we are on our way to creating this new wonder world of Love and Joy. We now know conclusively that there is nothing in the world that can make us any happier than we are right now. There is nothing that we can get, no place we can go, no pill that we can swallow that will make any lasting difference in our state of being. It may provide a momentary thrill or at least pass the time, but it has never satisfied our deepest longings and it never will. Those deepest needs can only be satisfied by being connected to the Source of Life itself. We want to feel energetic and exhilarated about being alive, not just for a few moments, but always. The Center is the home to those feelings of Bliss and Contentment. In the Center lies the connecting point to our true Source of Energy. We have only continued to pursue the path of desire and acquisition because we did not know of any other. Now that we do, the choice is clear.

Until we connect, our lives are actually just a playing out of our desires. It is a theatrical production, a dumb show with us as both actors and director. We get other people to play all the parts in our show as they get us to play the parts in theirs. And we all pretend that it is real and what we really want. But in our silent moments, in the moments when we are alone, we admit our confusion and wonder if this is really all there is.

I remember becoming an adult, well, turning twenty-one, and leaving the house to seek my fortune. I was going away to college and then to a brilliant career as a university professor, with some kids and a house in a nice neighborhood. But all the time I was thinking, is this it? Twenty years of study and all the seriousness about my responsibilities to God and country, and all for this ridiculous reality of 40 hour weeks, charge accounts and expensive vacations. About two months into the semester I began to see the ludicrousness of my situation. In two years, at the ripe old age of 23, I was going to impart the wisdom and philosophies of the ages to younger minds. I knew that I really didn't know anything about life myself which is probably why I studied philosophy in the first place. I could make a career of filling other minds with the contents of mine, but I was missing the point of it all. Why should I settle down now, and settle for the same lifestyle my parents had when they were not satisfied with it? They, of course, hoped I would do better and be happier than they had been and really could offer nothing else but what they had known. It seemed silly to settle for this when I hadn't even explored around the corner, let alone around the world or within myself. So I dropped out of this particular scenario to discover what life was all about so that, when it came time to teach, I would have something of value to share.

That was my intention, an intention which led me on an odyssey both without and within my mind. My parents would probably say most of my adventures were of the mindless variety and I'm sure it probably appeared so to them. Without a true Understanding of what is going on most of us are fairly mindless, as we can witness any night on the news. But all of this unrest and driven search for pleasure or identity is really just a simple quest for something of value. Somebody somewhere show me something that makes sense and makes me feel better, that makes me feel alive, loved and worthwhile! After searching through the worlds of rebellion and drugs, through education and career, through art and self-expression, I was finally led to the Center.

And there it was and still is, the Source I had been looking for all the time. The Truth of Existence, the Throne of Divinity, the Essence of Life itself. The end of my search for meaning became a dawning of Understanding. I turned in my seeker's hat for explorer's garb. Where I once looked for the secret of life, I now enjoy exploring all of its secrets and all of its wonders. In my blindness I thought I could somehow find the key and that would be it. Very Western thinking, to believe that if we achieve one thing, our fondest desire, then we will live happily ever after. We do live much more happily after discovering the Source of our Being, but that is only the very, very beginning of the journey.

Goals

The old way is filled with goals. As one desire is fulfilled, another comes up to take its place. As one thing is purchased, two more are added to the list. The goal keeps getting further away with each successful acquisition, and even further away with each failure. But either way, we never really arrive at the goal because the goal is to acquire. The goal is not so much to get a new couch as it is to acquire pieces of a lifestyle. The goal is not so much to make a lot of money as it is to feel more secure. The goal is not to have the perfect relationship but to have that relationship make us happy. Whereas one can go out and buy a couch, building a lifestyle is a project that can never be completed, and as for the feelings of security and happiness, they have been on the most wanted and least found list throughout our history as humans. I have been noticing this in my family. There never seems to be an end to what needs to be done, purchased, rearranged, etc. So we wish to involve ourselves in a process of simplification where much that is now perceived as so very necessary is allowed to flow in its own way. We wish to divorce ourselves from the responsibility to see to all of these minute items and rather view them as possibilities rather than necessities. It is amazing what can be released when this method is employed. The new house and car are suddenly not as important as time to meditate or spend with family or friends. The business opportunity that seemed so lucrative now appears as an interference with more important matters of the Spirit. It is a shift to thinking first of the

Kingdom of Heaven within, knowing that all will be provided. Interestingly enough, the new house and car soon appear and are more reasonable that we had originally thought. The various jobs that simply had to be completed are done without our worrying about them. Everything happens in its perfect time and effortlessly. This book which had been on my mind for several years but was always such a mammoth project was finished in a matter of months, and flowed easily and joyously like water dancing down a mountain stream. Everything that is really important and necessary still gets done, but with Joy and ease instead of stress and worry. We no longer have to run such a tight ship. We no longer need to exercise complete and total control over what is happening. We only have to be aware of what is going on and let it flow.

Identity

I was thinking about identity because I have been observing several of our close acquaintances, and seeing how their identity consumes such a large part of their daily efforts. For many of us, who we are, how we look and dress is an expression of our self-ness, and every moment is filled with decisions concerning who we believe we are and what we want other people to believe about us. In essence, we make ourselves an identity out of what we do, and what we do is how we plug our energy into the system to obtain certain rewards. If we choose to be a janitor we get far different rewards than if we choose to be a bank president. If we choose to follow the patterns of our parents we get a different experience than if we forge out on our own. So we decide to be an artist, salesman, politician or crook, all of which promise certain paybacks for our efforts. But none of these consciously plug into who we truly are, and by these decisions we limit ourselves to a life founded on these limiting ideas. We choose because of what can be gained rather than because of an inner desire to expand and grow. About as close to true expansion I ever got was during my 'artist' phase, that is, the artist whose desire is to express himself, though usually this is the small 'I,' the ego that demands such expression. It was fun and I Iearned a lot, but I cannot say that I was joyful. Busy? Yes. Happy? Only kind of, but it was a step in the right direction because at least I was doing something purely for what I was learning about myself with total disregard for what future monetary gains it might bring, or what anyone else thought about it. As long as we focus on what will be gained, we will continue to have millions of us doing things we really can't stand but feel we have to in order to get what we need. A life of dissatisfaction may be worse than none at all, and many of us choose to end the endless toil of a meaningless existence. All of this we get from focusing on what returns we would like to have. Yet it is those moments of serendipity, those flashes when we step out of our molds that we so cherish and point to as the turning points in our lives. Why, then, are we so afraid to step out if we enjoy them so much? It seems we only take a step forward when we are backed against the wall of no retreat.

One of the interesting things about the 60's was the influence of Zen thought on the youth culture. There was this mix of the Western 'make it happen' and the Eastern 'let it flow,' which produced a kind of hybrid philosophy of living. At first they seemed to be totally opposite understandings, but a closer look revealed that they were addressing different levels of reality. The ego makes it happen while it is the energies of the Soul which flow. This was the beginning of an understanding that the mind, by limiting its focus on the everyday, was really not capable of making important choices. It could decide what to eat for breakfast or what movie to see tonight, but when faced with anything of vital importance, often became lost in its own internal confusion.

Admittedly, a mechanism suited to simple decisions of yes or no, green or blue, today or tomorrow will have trouble understanding situations which are more involved, decisions which have both positive and negative aspects, many shades of possibilities and involve the rest of our lives. Our logical minds are simply not trained to handle such complex decisions and, indeed, we are often told to just let it happen. 'Que sera, sera' and 'its in God's hands' are common sayings. So we admit that we go to some other dimension for guidance during difficult decision times and yet afterwards maintain that we decided 'all by ourselves.' It is time to stop the ruse and realize that we have always resorted to letting it flow, eventually, so we might as well do it now rather than wait until we exhaust all of our energy working and thinking about it first, and then let go in the end anyway.

So this identity, this personality that we construct is nothing more than a catalog of our desires and self image stabilizers that we use to try and produce a life. It is a computer print out of our wants and the ways we have devised to get them. The worst problem with this system is the belief that we will not be happy until all of it happens. The result is that we have many who live boring, miserable lives in the midst of endless possibilities, who live in poverty of spirit in the midst of Abundance, and who search the world to find the secret which only lies within.

This situation occurs because our minds are confused. We are so busy focusing on the events of our lives and how they compare to our desired ends, that we really don't see what is happening at all, especially within us. If we are convinced that we are never going to be happy until all our goals are fulfilled, then we will never be happy. All of our activities will be spoiled before they even begin. We are projecting an aura of unhappiness in hopes of securing its opposite. This will never work, and rather than sentence ourselves to certain failure, perhaps we should invent a different approach.

We need to focus on the essence of what is happening instead of merely responding to the events themselves. It's as if we don't see anything beyond the information provided by the five senses. We are far more interested in our manufactured personalities than we are in the Essence of our very Being. We act as if we have no Source at all. We act as if the only thing that matters is what we want because we have control of this body and can make it do all kinds of things in our search for pleasure and happiness. We must believe that we are here to enjoy ourselves, but if so, why do we work so hard and enjoy so very little? These desire thoughts are all self-centered and produce the world we see, a world full of competition, full of driven goal seekers, full of egos seeking contentment, and full of those who have failed to procure even a modicum of survival. All of these control and identity games are aimed at acquiring what we need to define ourselves, yet our lives reflect not the Bliss we seek but the stress and suffering we experience in its pursuit. There are, to be sure, a few who succeed and they become our idols and supposedly spur us on to become like them. I would rather be One with all Life and see myself connected to the Source of Love and Light than be a member of any exclusive fraternity, no matter how cool or powerful.

The idea of identity being so central to the self effectively changes the Soul's agenda. If the Soul, for instance, needs to experience Love in order to grow, then a life spent trying to become a certain personality doesn't help produce that Love, it only produces things which are generally a poor substitute. There will probably be moments of Love but far less than if Love were the focus. We get what we focus on, so if we focus on things, whatever Love we get will be secondary to the main pursuit. So by focusing on identity, identity is all we produce. How much better to focus on the qualities we really want to experience, qualities like Love and Joy and Contentment. We will still have an identity, but it will be connected to our true Source. But there is another idea that operates within the concept of identity, and that is the belief that the three dimensional world is real.

The Real World

This belief states that we only have 70 years on this planet so we better go have as much fun as we can while we are here, because this is all we get. This lends an urgency to creating a lifestyle that will produce as much pleasure as possible. We are not enjoying our life experiences, we are trying to produce life experiences that will be enjoyable. This is stalling our enjoyment until some time in the future and this future of Joy never comes, which is what we continually complain about. We need to see that this is the fault of our thinking. As long as we think that Joy will come in the future, for whatever reasons, then it can never exist in the present. We should begin to insist that Joy exists now so that we can experience it now. Why work and wait and hope when we can have it immediately?

We can replace all of this old thinking with the Understanding that we are an expression of Love and Light flowing at this very moment, a flow which produces an environment that is full of radiant Joy and Contentment. This is the expression of our knowledge that we are connected to the Source of our Being which is Love and Joy. It is akin to the religious idea of being one of the chosen, but without the choosing by some distant deity. We are the choosers and we decide to choose a life full of these qualities. Of course, this implies that we believe we deserve to experience them.

Luckily, when we plug into the Center within, there is no longer any doubt about whether or not we deserve. In fact, the concept of deserving fades away in the Light of knowing who we truly are. We do not have to deserve what we already are. So this concept of deserving goes away with all the other useless thoughts of the negative self-image, all replaced with the firm knowledge of our Divine Essence. And so knowing who we are, we begin to share this with everyone we meet. We know that there is an Abundance of this energy within each of us and we try to help our Brothers and Sisters find the Source within them that we have found within us.

I was thinking about my desire system and how it so limited what I was able to experience. There were so many things to accomplish, so many old scores to settle, so much guilt to suffer endlessly, that there would not be any time to enjoy anything. It occurred to me that this was the person that I had built, one that wanted a lot of things if for no other reason than that they had never been experienced before. It was a list, a list of things and experiences that simply had to be fulfilled before I would be able to regard myself as successful. In letting go of these old desires, in tearing up this dreadful list, I permanently eliminated the old melodrama that had me in its tragic grip.

I no longer had to play any of these old games. These games may have been fairly realistic models of how the world worked 500 or 2000 years ago, but they certainly do not apply now. It's like we are still waiting for the old promises of long dead politicians to come true. This insane reverence for the past keeps us living there. I suppose this would be all right if things were better then, but they were definitely not better, and possibly worse. So I released all of them, or at least the ones I was aware of at that moment, and I have continued this releasing process every day. I could finally allow myself to become who I was within, and this was wonderful.

Before this time I had been stuck in the middle of a major conflict. While disliking the competitive, aggressive, me-first method, I nevertheless felt forced to play it because that was the way the world operated. I was accused often of being a romantic dreamer and that someday I would become a realist and understand that life is thus. I felt that I had to play some in order to survive, all the time wishing that things could be different. So discovering the Source within accomplished both a secure connection to Life Energy as well as the end of my fence walking. It is one thing to spout spirituality and another to live it. Finding the Center has allowed me to live it and to experience it daily, thus teaching me the ways of my own Soul. I could finally stop fighting with myself and learn to live in Peace, Contentment and Joy.

All of my disappointments could now be understood as misunderstandings, all of my hurts and fears as confused responses to life events that I now see as valuable lessons necessary for my growth. All of my desires are now seen as valiant yet misguided attempts to produce the Happiness I craved, the same Happiness I found waiting quietly within. I even let go of chastising myself for not having seen all of this sooner. I just let go because I was sick of fighting and tired of trying and being stressed about the future. 'Just let go and let it happen' became a kind of motto for every time I wanted to hang onto something, every time I wanted to go after some particular desire. So I realized what Paul meant when he said, 'I die daily,' because I experienced letting go of more and more of the old 'me' everyday. But rather than some kind of painful process, as death is generally perceived to be, letting go is a joyful, tremendous relief. By letting go of all the preconceived notions of who we think we have to be, we get to experience the Beings of Love and Light that we truly are.

Intimacy

It is an interesting situation I find myself in today. It is ridiculous and fills me with compassion for myself because I realize that I created it. Let me explain. Once upon a time I decided within my mind to be alone, to stay alone and never be intimate with anyone ever again. So I developed a mechanism which sooner or later forces people away. In my relationship with Ellyn, this has manifested as a desire to leave, citing various qualities that I feel she lacks, qualities that I feel are essential in order for me to be intimate with her. I am able to be kind and friendly and to care about her, but I cannot allow myself to Love her deeply. And I realize that all of my reasons are foolish and that I am really just afraid to open up, but I still can do nothing about it. The result is that she is leaving and I must watch helplessly with my mind split right down the middle. This split manifests because my ego wants her to leave to make room for someone better (prettier, richer, younger, any of the standard excuses) while my Higher Self very much wants me to open up to her. This is a major lesson for me and one I have always been able to skirt before. I have always before listened to my ego mind and ended the relationship before it had a chance to get close. So I thought this time that I would try to use all of the understandings that I have been discussing in this book to help solve this puzzle.

Intimacy is a common problem in our culture but I never thought it would turn up in me. After all, I had just successfully connected with my Center of Love and Light which should have cured any such malady within. What I couldn't see was that this very experience, this moment when I felt I was in danger of losing everything I wanted was the potential moment of healing.

It was here that I realized my fear of intimacy. It occurred because the stress of losing Ellyn knocked me out of my normal thinking mode. When I thought about my predicament I was not supporting my ego mind's decision but rather condemning it as foolish and without basis. The stress of this situation forced me to look past the mind to the Center I had so recently discovered. By allowing the Light to flow I was able to see what was truly going on. I saw in a flash of intuitive perception that my fear of intimacy was wrapped around me like a dark cloak, a cage composed of desires so specific and so unattainable that it guaranteed failure in all relationships forever. For 25 years I had been operating in the arena of these desires which I thought came from my heart but which really evolved from my fear. I was losing everything I really wanted not because I was doing something wrong, but because I was doing everything right. I was doing exactly what my thinking was telling me to do. It was an unsettling moment to realize that I was being my own worst enemy while thinking I was my one true friend. But this realization broke the spell.

By seeing the true picture in the Light I was able to let go of this fear and the result is more than I ever imagined possible. All of the qualities encased within this protective sheath of desires, which were designed to produce the perfect love, do not come close to the wondrous Love I have experienced by letting go of them. And I clearly saw that this fear of intimacy was but another of the old ways of thinking that I needed to release. It was a large one, a major lifelong thought form, but one which simply had to go if I was to be able to grow further. And what incredible growth. As the weight of this protective darkness faded away, it revealed more Light than I ever knew existed. It had only surfaced now because I was ready to understand and release it.

This realization is what led to the discovery of my personality as a manufactured entity. I suppose I had 'known' this before but had not truly experienced my personality as a self-destructive force. My personality had been acceptable before this time because I had only been aware of its more positive aspects. The kindness, humor, love of beauty and desire for Spiritual Understanding had eclipsed the sadness and grief deep within. The drive to succeed, while uncomfortable, seemed necessary and right within the personality system. But now that I had been confronted with a major negative aspect that was covering a deep fear, it occurred to me that the rest of it could also be covering something deeper. And looking deeper revealed more.

I had seen Light before but never as brilliant as this. Some of my old thinking had been in the way again. This time I realized I had been thinking, 'Well, I've seen it, now what,' as if one sighting should be enough to last for the rest of eternity. Of course, that is how the personality treats our desires. Like small children, as soon as we get something we throw it aside and grab for something else. So I had to substitute the concept of growing in the Light for the idea of finding it. We can only discover the Light for the first time once, but we can grow in it always, and in all ways.

I successfully stopped my personality from casting this relationship aside and going on to something theoretically better by opening up to the Source within. I had to admit that the Love that was flowing seemed more important than any of the ideas the personality had brought up for moving on. I began to see even more clearly that Love is the most important feeling we can share precisely because it is the one we have been looking for so long and which has seemed to be in such short supply. I had been looking only at the surface attributes of this relationship and not at its essence. On the surface it seemed that it would not be able to provide me with what I truly needed to grow, yet I was the only one who could allow the Love within me to flow. This is the oldest personality trick in the book, expecting others to make us happy, expecting others to somehow make up for all that we feel we lack. All someone else can really do is point to the Source within us and suggest that we find it our self. Yet how many years have all of us tried to bolster someone up, trying to comfort and soothe their misgivings and wounds, never realizing that all of these are self caused. It is tremendously freeing to realize that we are responsible for what we experience precisely because that means we have the ability to change it. And we change it by understanding what is really going on beneath the surface patterns of events.

Self Centeredness

To effectively change we must release another very cherished idea, and that is self-centeredness. Modern psychology works on the principle that if you change the thinking, you change the person and they expend all kinds of energy and time in the pursuit of more rational thinking. The problems with a violent client can be cured if he can be taught to think non-violently. But the problem is really deeper than that. It is not so much what we think as how we think. As long as we think self-centeredly, as long as 'I' begins every thought that we have, then we will never learn how to Love and share, the two things which make us truly happy. We can learn to trade, 'you give me that and I'll give you this,' but we never really share because we are always looking out for Number One. So our relationships become possible only if both people have the same goals, are going in the same direction and are willing to work together for those ends. This might be fine for some kind of contractual agreement, but it is certainly not true sharing, and without sharing there can be no Love, and without Love, well, there is close to nothing. We can never really share Love by being self-centered, because being self-centered focuses only on what we don't have.

Being self-centered is at the root of the desire system. We are the 'I' who is desiring. When we look at life selfishly, then we focus only on what we can get out of it. If we look at life with Love, then we want to make each situation as good as possible. The irony is that if we put the good of all concerned first in our minds, we get more Joy and Love than if we merely tried to get the most for us. Everybody wins and us most of all because we get the added joy of helping it to manifest. We infuse each life experience with as much Love as we can find and we get to share the bounty of Love this attitude creates.

We do this anyway, for it is only the Love that we give to our relationships and projects which really helps them happen. We have to Love what we are doing, or Love (at least like) what we get out of it in order to do anything. This new method is just making us consciously aware of what we do already and, hopefully, removing some of the ego-centric misconceptions we have built up during the time of our more limited understanding. If we look at all we have managed to produce when we have been focused on the self, when we have been relatively unaware of what is really happening, imagine what we can accomplish with focused, conscious awareness. We can produce a world that is so full of Love and Joy, that is so full of Light and Celebration, that the best descriptions of the Garden of Eden will seem pale by comparison.

Chapter 9

Aspects of the Self

The Ego

I was thinking about how in this series of lessons, this present lifetime, my Soul chose the ego as the means by which to get me to look within. I had to realize how destructive it is and how it relies on the ideas that everyone else believes rather than what comes from the deeper levels. What is interesting is that it was the search for my own uniqueness which led me in the search for wisdom. With wisdom I felt that I would be special, lovable, worthwhile, in other words, all the things that the ego in its weakness makes us strive to obtain. Yet the very quest for wisdom insured that my lessons would lead me in the spiritual direction, a direction that inevitably leads to the understanding and releasing of the ego. At some point along the Spiritual Path we run into the realization that the ego is not designed to run this vehicle. But it can be used to drive us towards the Gateway to the Soul In other words, the ego, in striving for uniqueness, discovered its Oneness with all Life, and thus the end of its own reign as king.

What is fascinating is that the Soul would decide to use the ego to promote its own growth. One would think that the Soul would eschew the ego and everything about it. Yet in reality, the ego is not bad, but only a vehicle to get us where we are going. As a motivating force, our egos can take us to the place where the Path of Spirituality can be seen, and where the transformation of the self can take place. The ego must be left behind at that point, but what a blessing to have arrived regardless of the means. This transformation lets us know that our true specialness is that we are like everyone else, full of Love and Light and boundless Creative Joy. What can be more special than that?

Our wonderful uniqueness as human beings is not all of the things we have been able to accomplish. It is not our music or books, our cities or scientific marvels, nor our halls of great learning. It is our amazing interconnectedness with all Life. Those of us who have spent lifetimes trying to prove our superiority over others have only succeeded in showing the rest of us what is possible. Our best composers, writers, inventors and film makers are only showing what we are all capable of when we let the Energy of Creation flow through us. By saying 'yes' to Life we allow our wonderful creative energy to flow out and manifest our intention.

We are discovering that we have these faulty mental systems and we are in the process of replacing them with better software. We focus on the Center instead of the mind, because the Center is a better connection point to the Source of all Life. The life of the mind has its charms but it cannot produce as good a Life experience as the Soul can. Why settle for houses made of mud when we can have golden ones? Why settle for dirty, diseased thinking when we can have thoughts that are infused with the Essence of Life Divine? So to focus on just the physical aspects of ourselves is absurd, insane, and destructive to our Happiness. It keeps us separate, and that is the source of our unhappiness.

Separateness

To be connected together is much better than trying to be separate with each of us pretending we are strong, independent, and willfully successful. How much easier to do everything together, to share our Love and Joy with everyone and so build a new world. Sharing with each other is much better than each of us struggling in solitude, trying to prove our independence or superiority. Those who are afraid to share what they have because they feel the present world is disintegrating, need no longer fear. It's very true, the world we now know is disintegrating, but that is a cause of celebration. Be grateful that we are releasing this valley of suffering and hardship for a world full of Love and Happiness. This older world will fade away the same way the older way of the Romans faded away. Each civilization builds upon the successes and eliminates the failures and misconceptions of the civilization before it. When Jesus showed up, we started dating events as before he came and after he came. We will talk the same way about this age, before and after Transformation.

We are finally beginning the Transformation Jesus initiated with his teachings. It is the biggest change that has happened since then, and one that is welcome. We are growing into Spiritual Beings of higher Understanding and purpose. But we are not becoming superior beings, we are becoming interconnected beings, intimately involved with all Life. Then we realize that everything is a projection of us as we are a projection of everything else

My fear of intimacy is a good example. I automatically created situations where intimacy was impossible in order to protect myself from what I feared. I was not in control of that situation even thought I was trying everything I knew to be in control of it. But what I was trying to control was the outcome when I should have been controlling my inner fear. My fear was in control, not me. So these guys that say, 'I'll never let a woman control my life' have no idea what control really is. We have to release the outcome and pay attention to the essence. If we are allowing fear to be the essence of us, if we are allowing anger or sadness to create their unfortunate scenarios, then we are allowing them to be in control. They become the Essence of our Being because they are the energies which we allow to manifest. We can just as easily allow Love and Joy to be our Essence and let them manifest.

In the beginning of this change, I thought that if I could release the mind and allow the Inner Light to manifest, it would take some time. It might be, who knows, several months or possibly even years. I didn't know. And yet I found that in just a few days I began feeling differently, better. In fact the very next day was wonderful, and all I had was a realization that I was afraid of intimacy, that fear was controlling my life experience and that this fear had taken the form of being judgmental.

I had been taught by my mother that no one was good enough for me. And I did believe that, I truly believed it and thus it manifested. No one was ever good enough, especially myself. So I developed a tremendous drive to be superior which we have already discussed. I think part of my mother's basic concept was that an inferior person would drag me down and keep me from my full potential. Whereas the truth is that the only way I could actually reach any real potential was to be interconnected with others. Eventually I understood the absurdity of the situation. I could be arrogant, superior and lonely, or I could be surrounded with Love and Joy.

I think one of the funny things about becoming wise to ourselves is to realize how foolish we have been. We can laugh at ourselves for the ultimate joke our minds have played on us, a joke that we used to be deadly serious about. I remember the old thinking that used to say, 'A man needs to be sure of himself, even if he's bluffing. He needs to act assured or no one will trust him.' Well, I wouldn't trust this guy. He's full of it: full of fears, full of confusion, full of himself, all of this 'be your own master' stuff. When we begin to make decisions spiritually, we change everything; our outlook, our methods, our attitudes and our emotional involvement. We do things only for Love or we learn how to Love what we are doing. We are just beginning to learn how to live spiritually, but that is enough.

To begin is enough because we can pay attention to the journey rather than the goal. We know we are living in a world of Love and Light so there is no longer any reason to worry about the goal. So we release the goal, which releases the future and brings our attention to the present moment. If we look at the search for love and power, we see them as the twin desires of wanting to share and needing to feel like we matter. If one is powerful, then, by definition, he matters. When we connect with everyone, when we become part of this larger humanity, we become instantly loved by everyone and we realize the true, incredible power that we have. After all, we have created the world the way that it is now.

There may be some who still believe that the earth is the way it is and we have merely adapted to it. But this is old thinking and neither accurate nor useful. If the earth is the way it is then there is nothing we can do about it. But when we realize that we create it, then to change it becomes easy. We only have to base our lives on different ideas, different emotions than the ones we have been using. It is so easy now that we know how, now that we have the inner Understanding of what is really going on and what we are truly creating in this world. Such Understanding insures success.

Success

Tonight, as I was playing music I was wondering, not whether the music was good or whether it was satisfying to hear, but whether it might be commercially viable. Whether or not I liked what I played depended more on my opinion of it rather than my enjoyment of it, rather than my flowing with it or seeing it as a wonderful expression of my deepest feelings. I was still trying to satisfy a judge and jury composed of aspects of my mind, aspects which demanded some sort of commercially successful direction before they would allow me the enjoyment of playing music.

When I was in the University it was alright to do something just for the creative fun of it, but in the real world it was not enough. I was not yet allowing my true inner brightness to shine but rather continually monitoring and censoring the contents of my life experiences. I used to agree with the monitoring part because that seemed like the observer, the part of us that sees what is going on with us. But monitoring implies some degree of anxious supervision (catching problems before they arise) that observing lacks. Observation is neutral and without bias, but the judgment/censoring part gives me pause.

Since I am a brilliant expression of Light, what am I worried about? I am not some kind of boiler that is going to blow if I don't keep myself under constant and unfailing surveillance. This is just another old idea from the depths of the

Old Thinking, the negative wastelands of my former mental and emotional existence. So it is time to replace the supervisor with the observer, a friendly guide who helps us see what is really going on within us.

This led me to the areas which the world considers great, the artist, dancer and poet routines. These are things that the world agrees show genius and which are rewarded with lots of praise and money. But there seemed to be something beyond art. It seemed to me that a true genius would be one who could invent a new reality on the Earth, a Happy and Joyful one. That would be the most wonderful creation of all and the one most greatly needed. There are plenty of books and movies and CD's but an apparent absence of rewarding lives. So we can dedicate ourselves to being spiritual people and combine our energies to create a joyful and loving experience for everyone. So I began to wonder why some of us, as artists, didn't create things that we would enjoy instead of concentrating on what others might purchase. We approach Life as a palette of activities, a series of creative enterprises that allow us to climb to the heights in our chosen field of endeavor. Success is still the goal. Why not elevate success and make it universal instead of so self-centered?

Creativity # 2

I am continually amazed at the outcome of creative energy. By sitting back and allowing it to flow, it does so with miraculous aplomb and direction. Once we disconnect the ego from the creative process and free it from all the problems of self esteem, it soars into previously unknown dimensions. Creativity is part of our growth. We no longer have to strive or hope to be creative, we are by our very nature. It is effortless and magical, full of promise for perfection and grace. We are all tremendously creative and in a much softer yet more powerful version than any present efforts being forced into existence. So to question our creativity is to question our very Essence within.

The reason we have historically striven for creativity in the first place is because we intuitively realized we are Creative

Beings and have been trying to find ways to express it. Our only problem has been that because we are so focused in the physical, we have insisted on physical expressions. The artist produces something and only then expresses the creative urge within. But a Love filled home or a joyous existence are equally good outlets for creativity, maybe even better and more satisfying. There is much more creativity that can be expressed in our lives than could ever be transferred to canvas or the silver screen. We are three dimensional interactive projectors with more potential than all of the latest creative tools put together. We need to change our focus from the three dimensional areas to the internal, spiritual ones. Let us use our creative powers to build a new world of Love and Joy. Together we can fulfill the prophesies of the ages and experience the Age of Joy. It is more important than art or career or self image, it the most important thing on Earth.

I began to think that true genius would be able to find a shorter path to this land of ultimate success for everyone. There had to be a quicker way, some sort of detour around the hard work and struggles to succeed, one that led more directly to the Source where Joy and Contentment reside, where the rainbow and the pot of gold meet. And there is. The trick is that we are all genius Children of Light, and the new world is produced by all of us having thoughts of Trust and Joy in our minds at all times, and the feelings of Love and Contentment in our hearts. This shift of focus creates this reality.

One of the more pervasive ideas says, 'I will become transformed when I see that it is to my best advantage.' The irony is that we can never understand its true impact without experiencing it. As long as we stay in the old mind, we can never experience the new mind. The old mind, for instance, says that one cannot be materially successful and still be holy. These are viewed as mutually exclusive realms where one has to give up the things of this world in order to become successful in the next. If one gives up the pursuit of wealth to become holy, what is it replaced with? And this is an excellent question. It can be replaced with a complete Understanding that there is tremendous Abundance of everything, for everyone, always.

Our striving for wealth is not only unnecessary, it actually interferes with the experience of Total Abundance.

We need to let go of the pursuit of wealth and its flawed Understanding of Life. It is based on the idea that there is not enough of everything out there so we had better get what we can while we can get it. And yet spiritual truth reveals that everything we need will be provided. The ancient teachings are full of references to this. 'Consider the lilies of the field' and 'seek ye first the kingdom of heaven and all else will be provided' are but two examples. Yet we continue to ignore these in favor of our other God, money.

In essence, because we believe in lack, we have invented money to show us lack in operation. There may be aisles and aisles of food at the market but without money, we cannot obtain it. There are thousands of acres of fertile land but we cannot live on it unless we pay. We can dream of owning practically anything but without money, they all remain dreams. There is not a shortage of anything on this earth. There is plenty of food, wide open spaces and plenty of wonderful people for us to have relationships with. There are lots of opportunities for adventure and learning, for expression and growth. There is only for many of us a shortage of money. And money is the only item on the list which is man-made. What does that tell us? It tells us that the perceived shortages are only in us and not in the Earth. In other words, we have manufactured these limitations and we can just as easily remove them.

We are involved in a process of growth and expansion where all the older ideas of limitation are no longer necessary. We are leaving behind the age of acquisition and entering the age of Spiritual Understanding. In observing myself I see my reality change. It is the end of the era of the over-worked, underpaid artist. It is the end of the seeker after truth and the lover of art and beauty. These traits still exist, but have been expanded with the insights of Spiritual Understanding. They thus gain in depth what they lose in shallow selfishness. The personality is giving way to the Soul. The old way of seeing life as a possession to do with what I please is being replaced with the knowledge that I am here to expand in the Light. I am no longer interested in my own self centered growth or expression, because the new world is an interconnected one where we grow through relationships rather than mass accumulations of goods. We become the masters of this Life rather than the slaves of our antiquated ideas.

Happiness

One of the more interesting ideas is our desire for Happiness. Most of the time, however, our despair at not being happy is the very block which makes happiness so elusive. When we focus on our Happiness, on how each day is filled with joyful events, then each day becomes filled with Happiness and Joy. All of a sudden we are experiencing Happiness. Everything becomes wonderful. The thank you card on the mantle, the way the light reflects off the mirror or the funny hat on the hook in the corner that you wore at Halloween. The lamp found at the garage sale and the new book that came in the mail can all be seen as a perfect manifestation of this wacky energy we call us. It's like a giant toy, we can manifest anything that we want in this three-dimensional energy system that we call Life. The soul can manifest, our minds can create, we can by force of will make anything we want happen. So far in this world we have been judging ourselves by how big a manifestation we have made. We all try to make our mark on the world and gauge our success thereby. We admire Carnegie and Rockefeller for the empire they built, and secretly I think we admire Hitler and Saddam Hussein for their strength and cunning. They were insane, of course, but so are we. They believed in conquest by force, we believe in conquest by manipulation or diplomacy, the differences are minimal. We are wanting to share and grow, we just don't know how. We are still working in hardware instead of software.

In hardware, we have to produce things manually and somehow distribute them to whoever needs them. And, of course, money has to change hands, so everything turns into a big deal. Almost half of the effort involved in any enterprise is moving the money around. That's really all we ever do with it, we move it around and mostly in number form. It really serves no purpose at all. If we allow our Souls to manifest and agree to allow our inner selves to expand then everything takes care of itself. We do not have to attend to all the tiny details but can rather focus on the larger picture. Like the Master Jesus who could feed the multitude from one basket of bread and a few fish, we have the ultimate power to create everything that we think about. We are so used to thinking that what we need is not there, that to even imagine Abundance seems alien. Jesus was only showing us how the energy works. We are now beginning to understand what he was trying to teach.

The Challenge of Change

It really seems to be in the practical application of these ideas that the greatest challenge lies. It is one thing to go within and see the Light and feel the Love, but it is quite another to live the truth of 'as we think, so we become.' To begin to change the way we approach existence is the next logical step in our evolution. As long as we remain ensconced in these old ways of living, the old tired world will continue to manifest. So we begin to approach Life with expectations of Joy and Abundance because we know that in doing so, we produce that very thing. We are constantly being challenged to overcome these old ideas. With Abundance, for instance, we have to deal with the idea that if you want more, you have to work more, sell more, or cheat more. The belief is that somehow we have to make a decision and a physical move of some kind in order to make the change we desire happen. The new idea, however, is that if we allow ourselves to expand, we naturally go in the best possible direction. As we let go of all preconceived desires and fears, the inner Self is freed to expand and manifest. In essence, we begin to treat our inner self like we treat most of the other things in our Life.

When we look at flowers, we do not worry about them becoming something other that what they are. A purple flower blossoms purple and a yellow one yellow. We do not wish for a mouse to be a dog or fear that a kitten will grow up and eat our children. And we look at our babies and just want them to grow up to be themselves because they are so beautiful. Yet, in time, we begin to treat our children and ourselves with all kinds of fears. We act as if we need to constantly keep ourselves in line to avoid disaster. Yet it is these very fears that make the disasters happen. There are no disasters lurking in our Heart of Hearts. Our Souls are not tainted by greed or violent tendencies. We condition ourselves to act in these ways precisely because we are so afraid of what will happen if we don't. We need to begin living by the truths we are discovering now, not the fear-filled guesses of ages long since decayed.

It is amazing to me how we think nothing of having reservations about our lives. Most of us like some parts of us and dislike other parts. We even detest some parts of us and consider this normal. But if we dislike something about our life, we fill it with negative energy which automatically creates more of it. Thinking dislike produces situations that we have to dislike, because we have filled them with dislike. Our life situations are like an artist's empty canvas. We can paint it any way that we choose. Anything we can imagine will manifest for us to experience. So we can experience Joy or a life we dislike. The choice is ours to make, but why fill each moment with dislike when we can fill it with Joy? Maybe because we didn't know any better until now. Life does not have be so full of judgments, we can just as easily accept it as a wonderful experience. It is what we imagine it to be, so let's imagine it full of Love and Joy. Why settle for anything else when we don't have to any longer?

We are involved in an amazing growth period. We are discovering our own absolute Perfection and allowing it to manifest in our experience. You might call it the perfection of the human form. We are becoming all that the human form is capable of becoming. It will be a period of continuous growth for us and will bring us prefect Love and perfect Joy if we just let it do its thing. When we experience this new form, when we see how easy and beautiful Life becomes, then we grow in our Understanding of how the universe works. It does not depend on our relationship to some King of the Heavens, it depends on us. It depends on our connections to the true Source of Life Energy. As long as we stay focused in the outer world, then the outer world will be our experience. By focusing on the inner world, a world that contains only Light and Love, that contains only Truth and Joy, we get to experience that. Even my ego has to admit that this sounds true and wonderful.

Ego can be our friend. It has gotten a pretty bad name in the last few decades because it was thought to be the source of all unhappiness and neurosis. As the supposed home of selfishness, it became an area of the self to keep down or at least keep quiet about. But the ego is not a real part of us at all. It is only the more or less peculiar collection of thoughts we have about our selves. The only time the ego causes trouble is when these thoughts convince us that we are the center of the Universe. Then the ego thinks it is the source of everything and becomes arrogant to cover its own confusion and fear. The ego is not the center of destructive impulses any more than it is the seat of selfishness. Selfishness and self-destruction are only concepts which have the power to influence ego-centered humans to behave like spoiled children. We do not chastise children for not knowing what they have not been taught, and we can just as graciously forgive ourselves for living by the only rules we knew at the time. And that includes our opinion of the ego.

I was thinking recently how lucky I was to be born with a huge ego. All my life I thought it was a asset rather than a liability. All this time I thought my ego was my friend and was getting for me everything that I really needed to be a successful person, and it has, in an odd way. My ego has been the cause of all of my failings as well as all my strivings and successes. It has been the source of all of my desires and the plans I laid in attempting to fulfill them. It has been the source of my confused self image and struggles to understand what I was supposed to do to be happy. The trouble is, it didn't handle any of this very well, and that is what launched me on my search for inner Strength and Understanding. So it is with relish that I now understand this ego of mine, truly understand not just its contents, but its structure and reason for Being.

The structure is very interesting. As a collections of ideas about the self, it is really nothing but words, and words get in the way of a more direct communication. It is a deep mire through which we drag ourselves in pursuit of dreams and flights of fancy. So to release this part of our thinking is both a tremendous relief and of immediate benefit. We are relieved of the necessity to play all of the games the current system demands of its successful members. This should be reward enough for the simple act of opening to the Higher Self, but there's more. We also get to experience remarkable Happiness and Joy as part of the Abundance of the Universe that is ours. I sometimes forget this for days and finally stumble upon myself lost in some idiomatic sense of ego self, far away from the Center and even unaware of its presence. Since it is no longer comfortable for me to feel lost and confused, I prefer to stay Centered most of the time. Since the ego is only ideas that have proven to be ineffective, we can improve our experience by making changes in the realm of ideas instead of the realm of flesh and earth. When we do so, the flesh and earth responds to intentions just as it does to our physical manipulation. So it is much easier to facilitate change on the mental level.

The ego is only one point of focus in the mind. It is the individual 'I am,' a spark of Light within the greater Light, the Divine 'I Am.' As such it can assume its true function as a point of focus through which Divine Energy flows. We can then switch our focus from the selfish ego to that part of us we call the observer.

The Observer

There is a part of us that is always there. When we think, it is the part that knows we are thinking. When we act, it is the part which watches the action take place. It is always observing and recording what is going on in our lives. An observer is neutral and clearly sees what is truly happening. It is not swayed by what has the best appearance or appeal, or seems the most familiar. What makes the most sense according to our minds, our emotions and intuition becomes truth. By focusing on the wise Observer rather than the self centered ego, we allow the Soul to have input into the Life system. With this centered sight, we can perceive clearly how forces are operating below the surface of sensory perceptions. We can understand how our mental concepts and our emotional responses create their characteristic feel and content. The self centered mind is too wrapped up in itself to see beyond itself. Only by becoming the observer can we see both sensory and solar dimensions of Life, and thus be able to make life changing decisions based on a fuller Understanding of what is really going on. Our ego then becomes a brilliant spark of Divine Consciousness within our minds. This attitude of acceptance for the ego allows it to reach its perfection as well so it can function within us in its own perfect balance.

So the ego takes on its true function as the individual point of consciousness within the mind. We no longer have to apologize for our lives. We no longer have to be ashamed of the shape our lives are in, or of the egocentrism which drove us to such desperate measures to be loved and appreciated. We can be content to allow our divine conscious spark to blaze into dazzling Light. This Light is us, as is the Love which infuses us with Joy and Bliss.

How much kinder to ourselves and others is this world we create with this new method of Being. We no longer have to be the bad guy in order to get ahead. We don't have to cheat or steal, or drive ourselves to exhaustion trying to get ahead. And best of all, we don't have to dream up something that makes us special, something we can do that no one else can do. We no longer have to prove ourselves in order to be worthwhile. Our Love and our Light are perfectly worthwhile, and we can allow them to manifest at any moment we choose. We can stop pretending and just be who we are. By doing so we all become filled with Love and Light, like the great Masters who came to show us the way, like Jesus of Nazareth.

Jesus was not only known for his wise words, he was famous for remarkable deeds with which he demonstrated the Truths that he was teaching. As we learn these Truths we, too, will become teachers because we will be able to guide others to the same Truth that we know. Of course, we have always been teachers, teaching every distorted view of life imaginable. But now we are becoming conscious teachers, those who know that they are teaching and know what to teach. Teachers and students we are, treading lightly now the path of Truth and Wisdom that leads to the experience of Love and Joy. We are learning and passing on that learning.

The teaching profession has been a little bogged down in the past because of its reliance on the teaching of facts, although that is now beginning to change. It's amazing how many facts we can learn and still know nothing about living. We take these young minds that can be taught anything and are open and curious about the world and we fill them full of information. These little bits of information are all neatly packaged into separate subjects and distilled into theories which supposedly will help us to make better decisions when we get older. But very few of these theories are based on Trust and even fewer attempt to illustrate the Oneness of all Life. There is a lot of fear and plenty of confusion for little minds to feed upon. Then we wonder why each new generation seems more confused and frustrated than the one before.

Each new generation appears to drift further from the truths most still pretend to believe because we ourselves have lost touch with them. The old truths have failed to produce the world they promised and we know that even though we might not admit it. We could wait until some future eternity to experience Love and Joy, or hope for some supreme being to come and rescue us from ourselves, but why bother when we know the secret to changing it ourselves. 'The Kingdom of Heaven is within us,' the Master said, and always has been. All we have to do is let it flow into manifestation. Like the lilies of the field, everything we ever need will be provided.

The World is ruled
by letting things
take their course.

LAO TZU

Chapter 10

Exploring a New Method

The rewards of this new method are intimate and immediate. We begin to feel more joyful right away. We begin to have more than hope for the future, we learn to Trust in the present. Who cares about the future if the present is hell? This method addresses the present so we become joyful now and feel this wonderful Life force flowing through us at this very moment. This is the feeling of exhilaration we have always wanted but now we do not have to produce something or be very lucky to experience it. We only have to allow it to manifest from our Center, we only have to allow it to grow. For that, we need an environment that is full of Love and Light instead of fear, anger and darkness. But this, too, is quite easily manifested from within.

This new environment we are creating gives us a lot more of what we wish we could have. It gives us Love and Joy, it gives us dynamic interaction with others and it gives us a sense of purpose which brings us all together in a common goal. We are working together to bring about a new community of Spiritual Beings. This eliminates the current problem of loneliness and isolation as well. It is the most marvelous thing to happen since we first began to speak in words.

Evolution Revisited

If we break human evolution into four phases we get 1) physical, 2) emotional, 3) intellectual and 4) spiritual. In the beginning, human existence was marked by physical maneuverings, alliances, acquisitions and activities. We worked very hard to survive and banded together for security and strength. If we imagine a trinity of qualities for this phase, they might be strength, agility and endurance. Here, the strongest would rule in a constant game of conflict and bravado. In the second phase, the emotions come into play and result in an additional trinity of hope, fear and desire. Most would feel powerless to control their destinies and would still ally themselves with whoever seemed to hold the most power. While physical strength would still be important, the rulers would also have to hold the key to happiness, whether in this world or the next, and be able to promise better times to come. In the third phase, the mind comes into play and becomes a controlling element. Brute force, although it is still admired, begins to become tempered with an attempt to use diplomacy and reason to build a better world. There are also the benefits of mechanization over manual labor, better transportation and marvelous ways of communication. Yet the overwhelming problems of the present world system persist in spite of reason. Fear continues to hold court and selfishness is still the god most humans bow to every morning. We begin to realize that we have some control over our destinies and so invent the additional stress of striving for personal fulfillment. Yet there is always something missing. The trinity here might be selfishness, ambition and confusion. But now we are entering the fourth phase, where we recognize our Oneness instead of our aggressive separateness. Instead of self centered actions and attitudes we employ Soul centered ones and with much greater positive results. This phase might be characterized by the trinity of compassion, creativity and Love.

This is what is happening now. It is during this phase that we achieve conscious control of ourselves and our world, a control based on an understanding of how the mind works rather than on fear of retaliation. We can have so much Understanding and Trust that we allow the Soul to influence the course of events in our lives. We understand that the Soul's perspective is vastly superior to the perceptions the logical mind is capable of having, and we have seen this mind's idea of a suitable world and find it fairly lacking in sanity, let alone Happiness or Joy. So we elect to allow the Soul to show us a better plan, to indicate a more positive direction, and to teach us to perceive the world as the interconnected system of energy that is truly is.

Some 500 years ago, when we began trying to become intelligent, rational beings, we hoped to put the petty squabbles and power testing conflicts of the world behind us. We hoped to create a world that would be safe and abundant. So we began to leave behind the reliance on strength and prowess and devote our energies to developing the mind's more rational influences. Yet we failed to eliminate the mental causes of violent and selfish tendencies so they continue to plague us. What good is a rational mind if it is only going to invent cleverer ways to be as selfish as we have always been? By going to the Soul level, we allow the mind to assume its true function as the organizational wizard while allowing the Soul to take its rightful place as our guide to perception and action.

With the Soul as guide, we can begin to create the world we have always known is possible, but we create it by allowing it to happen, not by forcing our own agenda. Yet it is amazing that when faced with the obvious truth of the new method, some of us still continue to think in the old way. Worse yet, many of us refuse to even consider a new direction even though we despise the present one. Why is this? The ego mind has been trained to keep tight control over all that happens, so it naturally has difficulty allowing control to be removed from its sphere of activity.

I noticed in my own case, I began by thinking these new thoughts and eventually understood them and believed them to be true. But it was still many months before I could let go of some of these strong mental habits. I was becoming a channel for information and was beginning to help others in their search for the new truth, but I had not yet opened up my Love energy. Whenever this was pointed out to me I would either deny it or insist that it was only the mind that needed to change, while yet remaining in complete control. Old habits, old ways of thinking. I was so used to tight control that a moment's relaxation was a major spiritual event, and I was so used to being unloving that what little love I allowed to flow seemed like a lot to me. It was a lot for me! Old habits! I had grown up in a house in which emotion was not demonstrated, so ordinary friendliness seemed like blatant affection to me. This misunderstanding made me misinterpret my own feelings for others as well as theirs for me, to the mutual confusion of everyone involved. This trickle of love was the level of emotional flow I was used to and so I did not notice that I wasn't loving. In fact, I was unloving and love starved at the same time and thus a prime target for the rushes of infatuation.

Infatuation

Infatuation is a strong rush, but it does not necessarily mean that the two people involved are 'meant for each other,' at least not forever. It more likely means that they both are afraid of intimacy and starve themselves for so long that they are catapulted past their defenses and into the open arms of flowing love. The only problem is that their defenses soon regain their grip and the affair ends in disaster and sadness. For me, the key was understanding that I had not been allowing my Love from within to flow, or only in limited amounts to certain people, and rectifying that situation. Through meditation and focus on the Center, I was able to open and allow the flow to begin, and it gets stronger everyday without the need for someone to 'bring it out of me.' This old fantasy has got to die before we all kill ourselves trying to make it come true. When we realize that the Source of our Love is within, then we can release the foolish search for Love outside of us and just allow our Inner Love to manifest. And it will manifest in absolutely every facet of our lives, with more strength and Joy than we have ever known even in our most magical moments of infatuation. It also lasts forever, which is a quality infatuations lack. Infatuations, however, do give us some idea of what is possible when we open up to Love. When we open up our true Source of Love within, we get to experience more Love than we ever dreamed possible and much, much more.

For one thing, we can have incredible connections with everyone that we meet. We no longer have to pine and wait for the 'one in the world' to someday save us from our lonely vigil. This does not mean we need to have sex with everyone, because Love and sex are not the same. Sex is the physical manifestation of Love for a certain person and is only one of the many amazing manifestations of Love. There are many other equally exciting and enjoyable aspects of Love that most of us have only just begun to experience, if at all. To think that sex is the ultimate expression of Love is to put a incredibly severe limitation on it. We used to think the world was flat and that the Earth was the center of the universe. Why do we suppose that our understanding of Love is somehow complete when our vision of the universe is just now crawling out from under a rock?

We are ready to pass beyond the present frustrated quest for affection and self-esteem (terms we suppose to be synonymous with Love) to an experience of perfect Love. We do not understand this broader Love because we have not yet experienced it, but we can experience it by opening up to our Center and allowing it to flow out unhampered by habitual ways of feeling. In the new world where there is an Abundance of everything, there is also an Abundance of Love, a Love that we cannot yet even imagine. It is about time we did imagine it, and create and experience it. We are moving beyond the days when a few brief moments of joy were all that we could expect out of Life. We now know that we can experience absolute, perfect Joy at all times. I'm game! It is as simple as deciding to be Beings of Light. It is fascinating to me that the way we get past all of our limitations is not by conquering them, but by releasing them. The way that we get to have Love and Joy in our lives is to release our desperateness for it and realize that it is and always has been our true Essence.

It is interesting to watch our old thought mechanisms wind down. They have been running on high speed for a very long time and now finally get to relax. Knowing that everything that is supposed to happen will happen in its own time is tremendously reassuring. We are feeling happy and joyous anyway so what's to worry about in the future? We no longer need to be concerned with our physical surroundings because we know they will change as we do, automatically. We can also forget about being critical of events in our life and begin to be who we are naturally and effortlessly. We can know that the Center within is the Source and knows everything. So we become knowledgeable about what is really happening in our lives, what is happening on the earth, why we are here and what we get to do while we're here. And what we get to do while we're here is the most amazing thing about this change. We get to do anything we want.

Some might say, 'well, that's obvious.' This has been the goal since time began, but look at all the trouble we go to now to prove we can do whatever we want. We rebel, we curse authority, we become arrogant, egotistical brats who do what we want sometimes just to prove that we can. What kind of intelligence is this? Of course we can, so why waste so much energy and cause so much distress to prove the obvious? Besides, if we are rebelling or proving something, then we are not really doing what we want but rather reacting to what someone else wants. It is a subtle but significant difference. We can relax and do whatever we want and leave the angry bombast in the past. It's as easy as allowing our True Self to manifest from within. And really, all we are trying to get is respect and Love anyway.

When we realize we are Love, we see that we have only been trying to achieve what we really are. We have been valiantly trying to prove the obvious truth, and this is good. Somewhere deep within us we knew we were Love or we would not be so driven to strive for it. We would not have expended so much energy looking for a Source of Love, whether in someone else or in our own creative efforts. We intuitively knew there was a Source somewhere. It was only a matter of time before we looked within and discovered it. So when we allow this Love to flow, everyone we meet responds to the Love which flows from us. Everyone respects Love. I don't doubt that the Master Jesus would receive immediate respect and recognition even in the midst of the darkest den of confusion and anger we could imagine. We can too!

Somewhere in our evolution we forgot that we are Love. We forgot that we have Love and Light in us, and so lost sight of it. Then we began to fear that it would not come back, that it was lost or that someone had taken it from us. And so began the mad search for the Holy Grail and Fountain of Youth. We found bits and pieces of Love and hoarded it all for ourselves in fear that we might lose it again. But these bits and pieces did not satisfy the hunger within, so we began to take whatever we could from others. If someone else seemed to be happy, we would devise a way to buy or steal what he had and thus have that Happiness for our self. We became self-centered egotists who frantically demanded everything and would do everything to get it. We became obsessed with anything that was even remotely related to Love and developed many substitutes, all in the vain attempt to fill the void within. Our prides and prejudices, our self-expressions and acquisitions, all of our plans and future dreams held onto like the useless bags of junk street people covet and fight about. We have been settling for the mere shadows of Love and fighting to the death to hold onto them while the bright, everlasting Love waited within to be found.

It has been a valiant quest and a grand story, but the ending was never quite satisfactory. It has been a story rife with disappointment and suffering, with sadness and misery, with ambition and only marginal success. Some of us began to doubt the existence of Love at all on this earth and so postulated its existence in some future afterlife. We knew it existed, it didn't seem to be here, so it must be somewhere else, in another dimension. And that is exactly true, it does exist in another dimension, the dimension of Spirit. Once we find it there, then it manifests in all other dimensions as well. The quest is over now. We have found the Source that legend and intuition tells about. So we can stop all of this fruitless searching outside of ourselves and relax in glory of the Love and Light within.

Exploration

We have fantasized about places like Hawaii and Tahiti and what it must have been like to live in paradise. No cares, no responsibilities, every day a plethora of sun, luscious fruits and innocence. The tales the sailors brought back created a myth of these places and a dissatisfaction for many with contemporary reality. Those stories planted the seed that led to the period of exploration. We scoured the globe for the perfect places and brought back the riches of these worlds to enrich our own. This helped some, but it never satisfied for very long. Then there sprang up the other myths of the Seven Cities of Gold and the Fountain of Youth. We hoped to find these things as well and bring them back to make life better, richer and more rewarding. We can turn that energy of exploration towards our Center now, and there find that for which we seek. We can begin the adventure by allowing the inner riches to flow. We can now create paradise everywhere that we are because we have finally learned how.

So we now understand the structure of the mind. We know that as we think in our heart of hearts, so we become. We see the former struggles to find Love outside of our self as the cosmic joke that it is. We thought we did not have Love and thinking so produced a reality without it. Then we began to look for Love everywhere but where it really was. Finally, we looked in the Center and found it again. Like a child with a lost toy we have been weeping and angry, yet the spirit of exploration has prevailed. We have persevered and are now reunited with the Source of our Being where Love and Light are ours once more. What is marvelous about this discovery is that we are conscious of it. It is not simply blind faith or adherence to the legends of our ancestors. We have observable proof that this is the truth of our Beingness, a truth which allows us to become conscious creators of our world. Instead of being at the mercy of fate where things just happen, we have complete Understanding of the rules by which the universe works. We no longer need control over the lives of others in order to feel in control of our own. We can now manifest all that we need together and effortlessly.

If we have suffered in our life, then the memories of suffering influence our thinking. Our thinking becomes infused with the suffering we have experienced along with the anger we feel for having been mistreated. This situation goes on indefinitely, recreating itself in endless cycles. Those who think anger is justified get to continually experience its energies. While it may give some sense of identity or purpose, it does so at the expense of blocking any vision beyond it. Yet the whole point of anger is that the person wants to move beyond the present experience, otherwise they would not be so angry about it. This is the paradox of the current method. The very mechanism that we believe will help us to change our experience is the very one which locks it in place. As long as we are angry, that will be our experience. Anger limits us to experiencing angry situations because it imbues every situation with anger. We are really only angry because we have not known how to be anything else until now. If we are truly looking for a way to change our lives and make them more positive and fulfilling, then anger is not the way to accomplish it. Any negative feeling automatically produces itself and effectively eliminates the possibility for anything else to exist. To change our lives we must change the content of our emotions and thinking. If we want to share Love and feel Joy, then we must begin to feel Love and see the Joy in our everyday events. 'Seek and ye shall find,' the Masters said. It is that simple. We are standing on the threshold of lives full of Joy and Celebration. The only thing holding us back is our old ideas and their emotional counterparts.

So let us begin by releasing these old ideas and emotions and replace them with the positive ideas of Love, Light and Joy. Where we see pain, promote healing. Where we detect sadness, infuse the situation with Love. For anger, substitute acceptance, and release dissatisfaction in favor of Happiness. There are many other ideas and emotions that will change as we allow our true self to emerge. One of these is our belief in goals.

Goals #2

There are no goals on the Spiritual Path. There are no statistics to which we have to adhere. There are neither guideposts nor any competitive measuring of our performance against the norm. We are embarking on the adventure of becoming who we truly are for which there are no road maps. We will each blossom into wonderfully unique expressions of the Divinity within us. Since all expressions of Light are positive, there is no need to worry about conformity or to be concerned about whether one is progressing correctly. All paths are perfect and lead to the same place. There is also no longer any hurry to get where we are going. We are no longer a human race, we are Human Beings experiencing growth in awareness. So things are much easier now, we merely have to be ourselves. This takes a lot of the pressure off being a human.

Right now the level of performance necessary to be a success is quite high and many of us fail the test or collapse under the strain. It demands more drive and will power than some of us can muster, especially given the low self-esteem that is the latest craze. As a result, large amounts of substances are taken to bolster this negative self-image and somehow deal with all the other thoughts in our heads which we call, for lack of a better word, our reality. Many of these problems are the direct result of the incredible demands that we put on ourselves. We sometimes wonder when we will be able to relax and enjoy a few moments in peace and contentment. We have been racing and, unfortunately, getting nowhere. But as Human Beings of Light, the entire scenario changes.

Firstly, we have no one to measure ourselves against. We recognize that we are wonderful sparks of Divine Energy so we need no longer feel inferior. There are acknowledged Masters, our great Teachers, who point the way, but we need not try to become like them. We have little reason to feel superior either because we recognize the incredible uniqueness of each of us as an expression of the Light. We are both beautifully unique expressions and completely connected in the One Light. In our present competitive system, there is only one best. In the Spiritual system, we are all completely wonderful. We are all totally successful and beautiful expressions of Divinity. And the beginnings of this change of awareness is learning to Trust.

When we understand that this is our true Essence, we are able to trust enough to open up to it and allow it to flow. This results in the inner Love and Light manifesting in our life. This positive feedback in turn encourages us to open up even more, and this cycle continues in ever increasing spirals of expansion into the Light. Growth is swift and sure. This is far different from the present system where any progress at all takes much determination and effort as well as a very long time. If we believe what we are taught, we are looking at 20 to 30 years before our life levels out and we can begin to enjoy the fruits of our labor. That's between 45 and 60 years old, a long time to wait for questionable rewards. Yet when we allow the Center of Love and Light to expand, the expansion is immediate and noticeable. It is also effortless, we only have to allow it to happen. There was a saying that was all the rage lately. It was on bumper stickers and said that a certain substance happens. But in fact, nothing just happens, everything occurs according to our plans and intentions. We are responsible for the events in our lives because we have programmed them into being with our thinking. We are three-dimensional, interactive holograms and our ideas and emotions are the lenses through which the Light is refracted into forms. As our awareness of this expands, our intentions shift emphasis.

We no longer have to worry about getting ahead nor do we fret about finding Love. We are living at the end of an era that has been marked by much learning and exploration. We are expanding that exploration and learning into the next level of Consciousness. The only aspects of this era we will leave behind us are those which are no longer necessary, no longer useful because they are more easily accomplished with the new method. We have been on a journey of separate paths that are now coming together. Like a prism, the One Light was split into all of our individual Lights which now shall recombine into the One Light again. And what a wonderful reflection that is on all of us.

Opportunities

I have noticed lately how many opportunities are presenting themselves. The opportunity to do this writing and to discuss this new direction with others, for example. This has taken an expansion of my trust to feel that I was now capable of performing this service. It makes me aware of all the opportunities in the past which I let slide because of doubt and low self-confidence. More than that, I realize even more possibilities that were undoubtedly presented and of which I was not even aware. Lost in my own limited thinking, I saw only the darkness of my doubt, only the shimmer of my own unrecognized potential. What a relief to finally emerge from behind that wall of illusion and false understanding. I really was exactly what I was thinking and quite a mess. By connecting to the Light within, I am able to expand and grow as we all are. And we can be of such help in the rebuilding of our lives and the world. Our hesitancy to begin is only a holdover from our previous doubt filled understanding.

I once had a teacher who told me the Secret of Life. "Do what you love," he said. In my life I have always done what I thought I needed to do, what I thought was necessary in order to survive and then, if there was time, what I wanted to do, provided I could still remember what it was. But I eventually understood more of what he was really trying to teach us. Love is the motivating force in our world. It is and always has been the reason we do anything. Love of luxury, self-preservation, love for others and for ourselves. Every other reason we give for our actions can be reduced to some form of love, even if it is a very twisted form like hatred. So when we do what we love, all the Love energy in the universe flows towards what we are doing. The entire project becomes filled with our Love and enthusiasm and we get to experience those, which is all we really want anyway. It is amazing that even with this knowledge I still continued to do what I thought I needed to for many years. I have finally begun to work past the limitations of my mind and allow my inner Love to flow into everything I do. So now I both love what I do and do what I love. This love is infectious and becomes a sharing of all that is the best in us with everyone that we meet.

When we function from the Center, all of our actions and thoughts will be filled with Love and be directed for the best of all concerned. There will eventually be no need for policemen and other forms of watchdogs because no one will be trying to take anything away from anyone else. With total Abundance and Love everywhere, why steal or harm? It is knowledge of this truth that will change our lives. It is the enthusiasm for spiritual growth that will heal our minds. It is the experience of absolute Love and Joy that will heal our hearts. It is this Understanding of the Oneness of all Life that will heal this planet.

Chapter 11

The Path of Service

The Missionary Tradition

I was thinking about the path of service and how in this culture, there are many who are trying to save others. The problem is that these missionaries and neighborhood do-gooders often appear to think they have a monopoly on the truth and believe it their god given duty to thrust it upon the unsuspecting. This is not the correct approach to serving God or any other positive force. From modern psychology we are learning that we cannot save anyone though we might be able to help them learn to save themselves. This is the basis of the spiritual principle of helping when asked, a method which both assures that the asking person is ready to receive and that the teacher is not overstepping the bounds of respect for another individual's present beliefs and choices. The old truth that when the student is ready, the teacher will appear again becomes acknowledged as accurate. Until then, we can have compassion for the many who are lost and confused, but we must also realize that we can do nothing until they realize their lost-ness. We can do nothing for those whose minds are filled with dark and cloudy thoughts or who bravely pretend to know where they are going when they really have no idea what is happening. When they are ready to learn they will be motivated to seek for answers just as we are now. So those of us who wish to help, who wish to serve the greater good would do well to

167

look within first and find there the truths of Light and Love. Then will come the opportunities to share these with others and to learn from them about what they have found. But we must be patient and allow the opportunities to teach and learn present themselves. We must release the desire to go out and tell the world for that is the very desire which has produced the legions of reformed whatevers who hammer on our doors and accost us in public places. It would be better if those with the complete truth in their minds wait until the world comes to them. For if they really do possess an Understanding of the Truth, the world will come just as sure as the light of day follows the darkest night.

Becoming a Center

I was thinking today about what I would most like to do as a person on this earth. The most important thing any of us can do is to help transform ourselves and the planet. I think that as we open up to the Light within, we will all become channels for this energy. We do not have to sit at home and wait for a Ram Dass or Wayne Dyer to come and tell us the secrets of Life, although contact with them or their books can be quite helpful. We really only need to open up our own sense of intuition and thereby see what we need to know for ourselves. Usually when we speak of channeling, we mean some information or other energy coming through someone from some other being outside of them rather than from within. This leads to the fallacy that these recognized experts are somehow privy to information and powers that we cannot access. These 'experts' may be a little further along in their Understanding, but we can all learn what they have learned and even more. This worship of experts is the same as traditional religion saying their saints could perform miracles because they were specially blessed by, or were the only begotten son of God (the term they use for the Light). We are all the Children of Light and we all can access all of these energies directly. So rather than wait around for the next lecture or workshop, let's instead open ourselves up as active channels for Divinity.

This will really help because rather than relying on a

couple of dozen international experts trying to reach millions with their words, we will have millions of local Centers of Light reaching millions with one on one sharing. It is like a resurrection of the gossip fence but for new reasons. One on one is always the best way to help someone else learn what they need to know, and at the same time, we learn what we need to know. One on one is the only way to help someone heal. So by thinking that we are willing to become Centers of Light, which is what we truly are anyway, we will become so. We don't have to get any funding to do this either. We do not need a building or any kind of equipment or gobs of money. We only have to open up to the possibility and allow it to happen and know that this is true creative living.

I suppose it is normal in Western culture to want to hear truth from some authority. After all, we have grown up in a culture which doesn't move without some authority's permission. Our minds were formed by millions of words, all quoted from recognized authorities. It is enlightening to realize that 'author' is the first section of the word authority. In other words, we believe that if they wrote the book, they must know what they are talking about. We were raised this way and initially believe everything we read, but we can change and allow ourselves to be our own authority on what we believe to be true. If it feels right to us then it must be right and we can work within those truths. We should stop worrying about who said what and whether they are really on the Spiritual Path or just talking. We can also stop worrying about whether we ourselves are on the Path and just relax and let it flow. We cannot not be on the Path because we are the Path and the Path is us. We only have to endeavor at all moments to be One with all Life. We only have to remain focused in our Center of Love and Light. We only have to desire to help and understand that in so intending, opportunities to be of help will present themselves.

And so begins the growth of a community of people interested in the expansion of the Self. It is a shift away from the focus on acquisition to a focus on learning and growth. We know that everything we need will be provided if we maintain this focus and attitude, and that every experience we need in order to grow will be presented. We are thus providing ourselves with the perfect environment. We will have Love and complete Abundance, Joyful expansion and Growth and a wonderful Celebration of Life.

It is sometimes a scary thing to contemplate the life of service. It's not that I'm afraid I might lose what I have worked so hard to get, but rather that I feel I may miss something. There is an emotional reluctance to leave this world of sadness and woe behind. Like an old friend at the crossroads, we meet with our old self before the new journey starts. As we stand, we gaze into the mists of our own minds for a moment to take in the enormity of the lessons we have learned. It is a moment of majesty and powerful grace when we step firmly onto the new path, and as we go our steps become lighter and fancy free. Like a dancer through time we transcend the ages with our enthusiastic cries of Love and Joy. Imagine in your mind the perfect environment. Place yourself in the midst of the Joy and Love you would like to experience. Now imagine it totally with all of your Being. Do this everyday as often as you can. In your meditations, in your moments of day dreaming, upon waking and going to sleep. Create in your minds the world you have always wanted to experience and know that as you think, so shall you become. If you should run into ideas that doubt this possibility, then they can be released and replaced with Trust and enthusiastic good will. This is a potent exercise in the process of purification.

Purification

One thing that all traditional religions stress is purification. It has always been understood that the mind is the source of our experience and that when we purify the mind, our experience becomes enlightened. Purification is the releasing of old ideas that block the growth of awareness. Purification is focusing the mind on positive ideas and allowing all older ideas to fade away. It is allowing the pure Light from within to expand and completely fill our Beings with its luminescence. And as it does, the world itself will purify and become the planet of Love and Joy. There is no reason why it can't now. All the old reasons about why the Earth is catapulting towards its own oblivion are shown to be misguided. The Earth, and everything else in the Universe, has really been moving towards its own perfection, we were just not aware of it. The belief that the world is falling apart has forced us to reevaluate our thinking and discover the true source of our dismay. It is the most incredible thing! All we have to do to survive this debacle is learn to control our minds. The only trick here is that we are not used to controlling our minds but are rather controlled by them. But we can learn how through the process of meditation.

By learning to quiet the mind, we begin to see it more clearly. We can then observe its many facets and learn to focus it where we want it to focus. Then we can focus it on the Center where all we really want resides. Love, Trust and the desire to grow are all that are necessary. It is so remarkably clear, so amazingly simple and obviously true. We are going to save ourselves by assuming control of our minds. We do no have to wait for some great teacher to return, but rather for the teaching they brought to take root in all of our minds. It is not necessary to implore some divine being to send his child to save us again because we are all the Children of Light and are capable of saving ourselves. It is the dawning of Divine Understanding within each of us, it is the birth of the Christ Consciousness within each of us, it is the beginning of the New Age of Heaven on this Earth.

It is a wonder to me that traditional religions do not understand this. They are still waiting for a physical Messiah to come and wave some kind of magic wand to save them. As long as they expect that to happen, they will be waiting in vain. Only when Divine Energy transforms each of us will the new millennium begin. All the signs of the New Age of man that are described in all the religious writings are coming to pass. The resurgence of interest in spiritual matters, people being healed all over the world, purification as a necessary beginning of the Spiritual Path are only a few of the exciting indications of change. That is what is happening right now and it is just incredible. Meanwhile, religions can continue to squabble about who has the corner on the truth market and thereby miss the real Transformation and all of its blessings entirely.

Self Expression

I was thinking about my former life as an aspiring artist. I felt frustrated because I did not have the means with which to produce the works that would express the beauty I saw within. I wanted to make films and show the world the incredible visions of Joy I had seen. I also wanted to impress everyone with the true genius I believed myself to be. Slowly I began to understand that this intense desire for self expression was covering very low self-esteem. If I really knew I was a genius Child of Light, then I would not be trying so hard to prove it. And who exactly was I trying to convince? It was only that part of me which was constantly telling me I was unworthy. Talk about a split personality! My entire desire system was pushing me to succeed in order to overcome these negative thoughts about myself while these negative thoughts by their very nature insured my continued failure at everything I tried. And I used to think, if only I could express myself fully, then I would be happy and things would be different. I thought my problem was that I was not expressing myself but the problem was precisely that I was expressing myself. My self image was expressing itself perfectly and every flaw was obvious, often a little too obvious for my comfort. When I realized that I needed only to change my self image and everything outside of myself would change, I began to become happier and more adjusted, less driven and more expressive. But rather than a frustrated and arrogant ego expressing itself, I was able to express the Love and Joy I had discovered within. It was a welcome change that continues to expand in every way.

We can all do this. We are all artists in the sense that we all continually express ourselves. We are always communicating in thought, word and deed precisely who we are. Everyone I meet is thinking about writing a book, changing careers, investigating inner transformation or moving to some other place, some kind of growth or change.

We all want to communicate our own unique expression of Divinity. For some this takes the more traditional forms of sports, fast cars and loose women, or the desire to be rich and powerful. For others it might be the accomplishment of some unique task or establishing a secure career. But beneath the form is always only the desire to be happy. For many of us today, the desire for Happiness takes the form of helping bring about this transformation of the human species. As we communicate this we help to heal ourselves and others. It becomes a calling, like a new career, but not a limited one like those at present which require the endless repetition of simple tasks. We will all get to help do whatever needs to be done. We can share everything, we can help each other heal, we can build what needs to be built and grow what needs to be grown. We can dance and sing and work and play to our heart's content. And so our lives become varied and fascinating. It's like every limitation of the present world system is lifted. Without competition there is no reason for each of us to concentrate on doing one thing very well. We can all do everything as well as we can. It is better to help each other fix a broken machine that to wait in line until some expert can get to it. It is also much better for all of us to join together and fix a broken world rather than wait for some governmental program to try as best it can. We do not need to wait any longer for anything.

This transformation is remarkably quick. As soon as we focus on the Light within we begin to see it. It is a joy to watch others open up to this new vision. It is like little children learning how to run. Each moment that we embrace our Oneness is a moment free of the cares and trials of the past. We realize that in this moment all is calm and good and we are functioning according to Divine Plan. We have been shown the keys to the kingdom and we will use them to transform it into the Kingdom of Earth, one that far surpasses our most wonderful and imaginative dreams.

Dreams

The idea for today is, as long as we continue to pursue our dreams, the most that we can hope for is that all of them will be fulfilled. So if at this moment we make a list of the things that will make us happy and joyful, we will see all that must be manifested before we can feel Happiness or Joy. The longer the list, the longer we will have to wait. The only apparent problem is that the list keeps getting longer and more exacting so never really ends, and so our Happiness and Joy never really arrives. Yet if we go to the Center and allow that Light to manifest, we get to experience it immediately. And we get something else.

If we were somehow to successfully obtain all that we have ever dreamed of having, if at one moment we could attain the perfection of all of our desires, then that moment would be filled with an incredible, joyful feeling of ultimate accomplishment. Yet the next moment would seem quite empty by comparison. We could, of course, remember the moment of our success and smile again, but that would only be a memory of joy, not joy itself. So, of course, we would quickly go about setting up more desires to be fulfilled in expectation of the rush of that marvelous moment of fulfillment. This is what we do. This is how our desire system works.

For the small percentage of us who are successful, we can look forward to a few moments of joy. A few moments, a half dozen minutes of triumph and accomplishment in 70 odd years of living. So it is really not the accomplishments we want after all but the feeling of joy and satisfaction we get from their attainment. We put the money in the bank, the trophy on the mantle and go back to striving for something else almost immediately. We're strung out on attaining things and we're always looking for a fix. Yet if we go within and connect directly to the Source, then we are filled with the ultimate Joy of Life flowing. And the next moment is filled as well, and the next and next, so that in a few moments we have experienced more Joy than is possible from a lifetime of accomplishments. This has been my experience and is reason enough to allow my focus to stay in the Center as much as possible. I am tired of working and waiting for a few precious moments of joyfulness, so I allow each day to fill with Joy completely.

When we are successful we gain a sense of accomplishment, of attainment. When we attain inner peace we have that sense at all times. This is accompanied by the observation that we are becoming more each moment than we were the moment before. Each moment has the sense of being beautifully perfect, perfect always. Yet even in this perfection there is growth because the universe is always evolving. It is always expanding its Light in all directions. And that's what we do with our focus in everyday situations, we expand our Light in all directions.

We can begin to view all situations from the viewpoint of 'what can I do to make this situation more wonderful than it already is, what can I do to help?' There are still activities, still challenges and much to be done. We are not being asked to sit around and do nothing. We can very actively participate in the healing and rebuilding of this planet. We do this most effectively if we view each day as perfect already. By seeing its perfection it becomes so, because the nature of energy is to manifest itself.

In my own case, I spent a lot of time focusing on the imperfection in my life, years, in fact. There was not enough money, enough time, enough friends, enough love, and so all of these qualities were perennially lacking. There was also not enough opportunities for growth or expression of the self (small self), and not enough spiritual progress being made. It's a wonder I had anything at all! All of these ideas are negative, focusing on what is missing, and naturally insures that everything never manifests. Everything is missing until we finally learn to focus on the perfection around and within us. So the only difference between my past situation and the present one is that I now have a positive attitude. I realized that all is perfect exactly the way it is at any given moment. And this is tremendous! From this point of perfection we can grow even more.

I think the first inkling of this came while working in the back yard garden planting seeds in the soil. In a couple of days they all popped out of the ground and I had to say, "My how beautiful you are." If I had looked at these bean plants with the same attitude that I looked at myself I would have said, "you're awfully small. You're really going to have to grow a lot before you will produce anything of real value." It struck me that this is what we do to ourselves and our children. We don't say, "Hello, how beautiful you are." Well, we do, but only for a few months or years. Then we say, "Well, we'll support you for now, but soon you're going to have to amount to something. You're going to have to earn your keep." And so it begins, the subtle conditioning that tells us we are not perfect the way we are, that tells us we are going to have to strive very hard to be worth anything, that teaches us to be self-centered and have stressful and negative attitudes about ourselves.

A Positive Attitude

When I realized all of this, I began to adopt the attitude towards myself that I was doing well, that Life was wonderful and there was Joy in all moments. With these ideas in place, I began to notice these things manifesting, and I was able to pull my attention away from the fallacies of the suffering and hardships I had believed in before, and instead focus on and find the true wondrousness of existence. It was here that I first understood that I was here to discover the Joy of each moment, not try to build a life that would produce it. Anyway, if my life was not joyful, what could I possibly do to change it on the outside? My Happiness is an inner attitude, not a response to outward circumstances. I began to feel trusting towards my life and the feedback of feeling better about things only added to my Trust. There were days when I lost this new Trust and days when I despaired, but the overriding experience has been positive. At times it felt like the proverbial uphill struggle with all of my old, negative thinking doing its best to hold me back. Yet each day saw progress as I focused more and more on the Center of Light and less and less on my old gloomy attitudes. And there came a time when I knew I was more positive than negative. It felt like I had crested the high hill of my endeavor to become positive and saw the valley of Love and Joy reaching out before me in a glorious vista. This has been the experience of many of our friends as well. Time and time again they are discouraged at the apparent enormity of the change they are attempting. Time after time they feel like they will never be able to get away from the grip of these old ideas. But one day it's easy. One day they realize the progress they have made and how much better they feel about themselves and their life situations. Then the old attitude of impatience to improve gets replaced with a fascination with the journey they are taking. That is the day of their rebirth.

From then on they find that they focus on the positive most of the time. There are occasional set backs when the old ideas weave their tales of negativity for an hour or two, but these soon pass away. The more we are positive, the more we see how positive our lives become. This wonderful feedback system teaches us very quickly. It is amazing how fast this transformation can occur. Looking back a few months or even weeks shows us the remarkable changes that have taken place. We change from people immersed in confusion and pain to Beings manifesting Love and Joy. And indeed, this is part of the ancient prophecy, that this transformation will happen 'in the twinkling of an eye.' But perhaps it is more accurate to say it is in the blinking of the 'I,' because true growth occurs in those moments when we let our egos take a rest. If we look at our modern culture, we can see the change everywhere.

In the past ten years many marvelous things have happened. Ten years ago alternative medicine was a rare phenomenon, books on the best seller list had nothing to do with spirituality and talk show guests rarely talked about reincarnation or taking responsibility for one's own life. If we go back 25 years, we can trace a sort of remarkable beginning of this whole movement in the 60's summer of love. This was when the idea of Spirituality first became a popular subject in the youth culture of the time. It was the introduction of Eastern religious thought into mainstream American culture as well as the beginning of the concepts of non-violence and that we are Love. The media, of course, helped focus attention on the rebellion, lack of cleanliness and more sensational sexual aspects of the movement, but a spiritual revolution had begun nonetheless.

This was also the beginning of the various psychological purification rights. EST, Primal Scream and other therapies swept the nation with their claims of instant release from deep, life inhibiting traumas. We began to understand that there could be deposits of memory within us that were causing problems with our happiness and sense of well being. The history of self-help tapes and books can also be traced to this era and their continued appeal is evidence enough that the time of transformation is upon us. Even traditional religious prophecy cites the year 2000 AD as a time of spiritual revolution, a time also in line with the astrological shift to the age of Aquarius.

If there can be such amazing change and progress in Spiritual Understanding in such a short time, imagine what will transpire in the next 10 and 25 years, especially considering the momentum this movement has now. It is estimated that at least 20 per cent of Americans are interested and actively participating in some form of spiritual growth through study and meditation. I'm sure it is the same in many other countries as well. This is far different from the late 60's when the mere mention of Eastern meditation would bring shouts of un-American and unaccepting ridicule. I remember in my religious studies how Jesus said he came not to bring peace, but the sword. The sword is the esoteric symbol of swift change, not the slow evolution of normal culture. This present change is swift yet completely non-violent. It is the perfection of the human soul which will totally transform each of us and our world in our lifetime. We are focusing more on who we are as intelligent, feeling human beings and less on what we own. It is a wonderful time to be alive, when the true magnificence of the human species is finally beginning to manifest.

Chapter 12

The Problem with Problems

The Inner City Puzzle

I was thinking this morning about the troubles in the inner cities. I was reading a magazine which was lamenting the fact that there is uncontrolled violence in many places. What struck me about this was not that it is taking place, but that there could be the possibility of 'controlled violence.' How can one attempt to control violence when violence itself is the result of being uncontrolled? The absurdity of the situation becomes apparent. Both those perpetrating and those trying to control them are on the wrong track. Violence is the result of uncontrolled thinking and can only be stopped within the mind, and the mind can only be controlled by allowing it to expand to a Higher Understanding.

Enforcers (force is violence) are not trying to control thinking, but rather focus their energies in trying to control actions. Actions can never be controlled when thinking is as off-center as it is now. In fact, the entire system of trying to stop certain actions is off the mark. Only when off-center thinking stops will its inevitable manifestations cease. Only when those involved understand that they can have everything they want without all the conniving and bloodshed will they be willing to forgo it. They are caught within the opposite of Abundance. As long as we believe in limitations of anything there will be those who will bend their energies in unlawful acquisi-

179

tion. And really, they are not doing anything that the government or large corporations are not doing. We all see the carrot and some of us reach for it with all that we are worth. The problem is not in the reaching, but in the belief that only a limited number of carrots exist. Until that concept changes, we will continue on the present path. The current problems with unrest and greed everywhere are forcing us to find a solution, a path which inevitably leads to the true source of the problem.

Drugs are another example. The massive programs seem to focus their attention on getting youth to 'say no,' as if this is the brunt of the matter. The true thinking behind drugs is much deeper than willfully saying yes or no. It goes back to the human desire to feel pleasure and some form of joy at all moments. Drugs give that feeling of calm euphoria that is so incredibly lacking in most modern cultures. We have no real rites to celebrate life, no gatherings to express the joys of being who we are, and this has to be made up someplace. The problem with the current official programs is that they have no idea how to substitute some other form of Joy for the one they want to remove. The scare tactics of what will happen to one strung out is often times not enough to deter use. After all, these people are also suffering from incredibly low self-esteem as well. The answer has to include both a positive sense of self and some promise of Joy. And it has to happen fast.

These people are not going to be able to wait years to feel better nor are they going to be able to expend large amounts of energy to attain feelings of Joy that drugs produce instantly. Once one has felt this way, it is difficult to settle for less. Promises of future Happiness or trips to theme parks are not going to get it. It is our nature to seek a state of continuous Happiness. It is our nature! The answer has to be universally effective and easy to obtain. Meditation is the only possible candidate for the job and indeed is starting to be used in some places experimentally. It will also have to be used by those administering these programs so that they know what they are talking about. It is the only hope, but fortunately, the perfect choice.

Inner Joy

Like any other aspect of culture, drugs are only showing us what is possible. Drugs cannot make something happen within us that is outside our range of possibilities. They only open up potentials for feeling and vision and as such are showing us what we can experience with a little training in meditation. It is troublesome to tell addicts that they will just have to give up these feelings of Joy and Contentment because it may hurt their bodies in the long run. To many, a short time of euphoria is better than a lifetime of dull aches. And in many ways, the short euphoric period drugs give is no shorter than the brief moments of Joy most of us hope to encounter in the present cultural system. If we are to truly be of help, we need to demonstrate that through contact with the Center, not only are the feelings of Joy and Contentment possible, they can also become permanent as well as being absolutely free for the asking.

This also points up a fundamental error in the way we approach problems. We approach them negatively. In fact, the only reason we pay any attention to anything at all is if it causes us trouble. We learn as children that necessity is the mother of invention from which one deduces that without it nothing much would ever be done. This is incredibly negative thinking! To believe that we have to have problems before we will put forth the effort to evolve past them stifles our desire to grow and limits our ability to learn. We become problem solvers rather than explorers. We focus all of our law enforcement efforts in trying to stop aberrant behaviors rather than trying to understand and encourage positive ones. "If it isn't broken, why fix it," we say? Well fortunately for us, it is very broken at the moment and we must fix it, now! But let's do it from a positive point of view. Rather than lamenting the state of the world and resenting all of the time and effort we have to muster to make it better, let's see this as an opportunity to grow beyond our wildest imagination.

We are what we think, so by concentrating so hard on all the problems we are only making them worse. The legacy of Lyndon Johnson's Great Society should have taught us all we need to know about massive government programs and their effectiveness in fighting poverty or any other kind of 'problem.' The problems these and all programs attempt to cure have only continued to worsen as government becomes only larger and more inept. Somewhere along this line we must realize that the reason for the failure is not human nature, but our limited understanding. Negative focus produces negative results and the victim mentality is the result of making being a victim so rewarding. If instead we focus on the opportunity to expand our awareness of the Light within, if instead we focus all of our attentions on letting this Light filled Love shine its healing rays on every situation we encounter, then the result cannot help but be positive. We have to admit that the current thrust of programs are hopeless failures, so much so that government funding is being cut. They are failures because they create more problems with their focus than they can ever solve.

As long as we continue to focus on stopping aberrant behavior, we will never have any real progress. Only by seeing the Joy in every situation will Joy ever be produced. Only by seeing the healing in every moment will healing take place. Only by overcoming problems with Love and Understanding will they, like riddles, ever be solved. We are to the point of unraveling the riddles of Life and Energy. Let's try not to get bogged down in the old way of dealing with 'problems' and step out into the light of brilliant opportunities for growth. When problems become opportunities, then we will all want to help each other learn about them and grow in understanding instead of recoiling from the unfortunate and demanding that somebody else do something about it.

We see this kind of service being done by people like Mother Teresa who demonstrates in her life both the method and the work that needs to be done. And rather than exhibit the toil worn face of one who is suffering in order to help others, she presents the radiant countenance of one who has found Joy in doing what she can to make things better for all of us.

A Brief Moment of Doubt

We are remarkably conditioned. I am always amazed at the ideas I encounter in my meditations and how they try to limit me. No matter what I tell myself that I can do in my affirmations and in deepest moments, there is at times a part of my mind which tries to make me doubt it. When I work on the idea that I am in the process of creating my most perfect life, I sometimes encounter the opposite idea. And this is good, because without conscious meditation on this positive idea of growth, I would never encounter this limited thinking so deep within my subconscious mind. I find myself doubting that I will be able to achieve such perfection or that there will not be enough time to manifest this Higher Truth in my life. And seeing these ideas come forth from the depths of my conditioning allows me to release yet another layer and know that it is gone forever. We have friends who are also involved in this process of purification who call often, chagrined by the surfacing of these old ideas. It is an inevitable part of growing. In order to go past the limited thinking we have been taught, we must encounter and release these old ideas. It's like cleaning out an old closet full of useless articles. But rather than being a nuisance or interference with forward growth, it should be viewed as the miracle that it is. Without becoming aware of these old ideas, no matter how many times they surface or in how many forms, we would never grow in our awareness. This is what awareness is! I suppose some friends would rather take some kind of pill and wake up a transformed Being, but then, where would the awareness come from? Only by becoming conscious of these old thoughts and joyfully replacing them with new, positive thoughts do we truly become conscious creators. This type of change requires a different kind of focus.

It is characteristic of Western culture that we look for the larger project. Rather than focus on the opportunities for day to day growth we concentrate on the future goal and feel frustrated that we are not yet there. But the Spiritual Path is characterized by focusing on the now moment. It is not as important for us to get to the top of the Mountain of Transformation as to enjoy each moment of the journey. It is not as important to write a book or attend a series of workshops about meditation as to experience it ourselves. And for some of our friends, they are already seeing themselves in positions of influence and on talk shows before they have even begun.

Personally, I tend to shy away from such imaginings. To be an authority on spiritual matters would be more than I sometimes think I could handle. I am more interested in having my quiet transformation and experiencing a Life of Love and Joy, and leaving the hoopla to those who seem to thrive on it. Yet here I am writing this book in order to share what I am experiencing in hopes that it will encourage someone to explore Inner Transformation themselves. But as I grow, I get another voice which says that all will be provided when it is necessary. And, indeed, my experience with doing readings and healings is that whatever needs to be done is accomplished if I just get myself out of the way and let the inner energies manifest themselves.

What is interesting about this is the two opposing ideas I see within Western thinking, namely, that of feeling we are not capable of doing anything and yet wanting to do it all. Teenagers don't just want to learn to play the guitar, they want to be rock stars, and yet the pressure of wanting to be a star often thwarts true exploration of the instrument. By deciding on a direction before experiencing the instrument, they severely limit themselves to what they will be able to learn. It seems that it's not okay to just play the guitar, soon we are asked, "Well, what are you going to do with it?" This is part of the immense idea of acquisition. When we see something, we immediately try to imagine what use we can make of it, as if simple enjoyment is not enough! We have the silly idea of making everything, every moment count. The opposite of this is wasting time, perhaps the worst thing a Western human can be caught doing, that is, doing nothing. What is this teaching us about Life?

For one thing it almost totally eliminates being in the now moment. How can we enjoy the present moment when we only pass through it on our way somewhere? We are so used to actively going somewhere that even our leisure time is structured and full of goals. This presents a real obstacle to meditation and an even bigger one for Transformation. Meditation is doing nothing, consciously. In my own case, it was very difficult at first to sit still for 20 or 30 minutes, let alone let go of all the things I had planned for the rest of the evening. My mind would race from thought to thought as I anxiously waited for the meditation time to be over. It took some determination, patience and practice before I could actually relax and enjoy this quiet time. Once I did I began to experience the joys of our true inner nature, but at first I only felt dumb and confused. My mind kept asking, "Shouldn't you be doing something?"

Transformation is leaving the world of doing behind us and embracing the world of Being. When we focus all of our attentions on what we are doing then we never develop the necessary focus to go within and allow ourselves to Be, let alone be transformed. And since we are so consumed with doing in order to express our personality, transformation implies a different sense of self as well. We must allow ourselves to be who we truly are within and stop pretending to be our made up personalities. What little pleasure our personalities give us is more than made up for by the wealth of Joy and Love we find within our Heart of Hearts. Only by becoming quiet, only by allowing the mind to focus on the Center will we ever know that this incredible part of us exists. Until that time we are only chasing reflections of who we are and pursuing dreams that have little chance of producing any lasting Happiness.

Desire, Accomplishment and Failure

We have nothing to prove. We are perfect just as we are, we just don't know it yet. By releasing the twin ideas of accomplishment and failure, we reach a state beyond them where everything just is. This produces a change in our desire system. Instead of desiring individual things or experiences, we begin to desire growth and expansion. There are some schools that teach the goal of desirelessness, but the main stumbling block is really only our attachment to the things we desire rather than the things themselves. Instead of trying to subdue desire and eliminate it from our consciousness, focusing on expansion and growth expands our desire to include the experience of Spirituality. In this way, our present desire/goal system can help get us going in this new direction. By providing an impetus to meditate and seek the Source Within, our desire system can propel us forward as much as it now holds us back. In time, we will release all desire and be totally unconcerned with what happens to us at any given moment. But at first, desire infuses our inner adventure with energy and purpose. And really, the rewards of Transformation are enough to motivate most of us. In a country where physical starvation is fairly rare, Joy starvation is on the rampage. The starvation for goods, for luxuries and for opportunities are every bit as pathetic as the starving children of Calcutta, and the source is the same.

As long as we believe in lack, as long as we think that we have to continually get more and more, then no matter how much we have, we will always be hungry. We are as hungry for position and power as we were for food 1000 years ago. We are still trying to get what we need from outside of us and the long history of wanting so much for so long makes us continue to walk the fine line between accomplishment and failure. When will we understand that this is only conditioned thinking? Surely the foolish clamoring for more from those who have so very much can teach us to look beneath the surface of our wants and see the real culprit, attachment. If we were not so attached to our fear of want, we would not be so full of rampant desires. As long as we believe in this kind of desire, we will always desire and nothing on this earth will satisfy our hunger. This is a simple fact of thoughts manifesting themselves. So we need to replace this rampant desire with acceptance. Accepting the Abundance of the Universe is the fulfillment of all desire. We can replace our dissatisfaction with our life achievement by finding the Joy in each moment and in every situation. Only by thinking, feeling and being joyful will we ever know what all of our desires are sent out to find, Joy. Joy is an inner feeling, not an outer acquisition. If we can release the idea of acquisition, we are also freed from another mainstay of Western Culture, misery.

When we live within the realm of desire fulfillment, there are three possible paths we will follow, 1) we can go after desires and be successful, 2) we can go after them and fail, or 3) we can decide not to go after them at all, usually because we are afraid of failure. If we follow this third path and forgo the chase entirely, it is because we feel that we do not really deserve to succeed so why bother trying, we are sure to fail anyway. We also get to feast ourselves on endless self recriminations for not having the strength to even try. If we go after our desires and still fail, then we get to live with a weakened self image. This failure only further damages an already weak self image and makes our desires loom ever more luminous in the dark sky of our dreams. We can chastise ourselves for doing whatever it was we did wrong and/or for being so stupid as to try in the first place. Both of these are very popular and do wonders for self confidence. The final choice is success. At last, we succeed, we are on top of the world and bathe our self in the glow of our accomplishment. The trouble is, it only lasts a few moments and then we are right back in the stew again, running after the next goal that is sure to do it for us. All three tactics lead to actual failure because we never really arrive at the goal of Happiness. This is like asking the prisoner if he would rather be shot, hanged or drown. We are all the prisoners of our own desires. It is a prison with a long history and many legends, but few happy endings. The only way out is to dig ourselves out. We must tunnel to the Center of the Castle where the key to escape can be found. From the Center, we will find another way to go, a way of freedom and Happiness, the Happiness and Joy our desires were supposed to create for us, but never did. It is the only way.

One of the most interesting things about our desire system is the small amount of time we actually spend doing anything about them. We spend an enormous amount of time thinking about what we want and then an even longer time deciding whether or not we should have them, if we deserve them, whether they are good enough for us, what other people will think of us if we go after these things, and on and on. Our budding rock star could be a good example. He can spend oodles of time deciding what instrument he wants to play and fantasizing about how cool that will be, what style of music and what that says about him as a person, what kind of clothes he will get to wear, how much he will get to travel, how much money he could make and meanwhile, no music is being made. They say that producing something is 1 percent inspiration and 99 percent work, but this sounds more like daydreaming. The point is, while we are deciding and judging and making up our minds, the time for action may be past.

If he were to just start playing music he might be surprised at what comes through without all of the preliminary mental exercises. And so we see that the goal actually gets in the way of its own accomplishment. We focus so much on the outcome that we lose sight entirely of the process. We are thinking so very much about every aspect of Life that no living is actually taking place. We need to reintroduce ourselves to the process, to the flow of Life as it creates our experiences. We need to forget about the outcome and let the Life force flow through us into joyful manifestation.

The whole reason this discussion came about was because I was feeling the enormity of the task of writing this book and the music that will at some point accompany it. Then I began to see that I did not have to do all of it. I could start with one part, and so the writing began with the rest to follow when the time is right. And really, I began to see that what I was actually trying to accomplish was to make a joyful life for myself. The book and music were only desires I thought would bring the experience of Joy that I wanted. As it turned out, the book and music were only excuses I could give my ego to allow me to delve within and find the Source of Love and Light. What my ego didn't know was that I would undergo a transformation in the process that would be the end of its total control of me.

And how this message spreads. As we decide to become Spiritual Beings, we place ourselves on the path that leads to Spiritual Transformation. It is automatic just as the path of desire leads to a life spent chasing desires. When we make this decision, the Universe within cooperates by sending us the precise situations that will allow us to grow the most. If we focus our entire attention on understanding these situations and on the growth and expansion we are experiencing through them, then we will become more aware of who we truly are. We leave behind the tired ideas of this age, the fear, the victory and defeat and the vain and lonely quest for satisfaction. All of those elements within the present system are totally unnecessary and must be replaced.

Competition

We traditionally respect competition in business or between national ideologies, but abhor it in relationships. Yet when we believe in competition and conflict in one area, it naturally manifests in all others. As long as we see the world in terms of black and white, male and female, good and evil, then our life will be a competition between these opposites. It is the idea of opposites which has created the world of opposites that we perceive. If we compare the Eastern concept of Yin/Yang with the Western concept of male/female as opposites, we are immediately struck by the profound difference. Where the Western thought structure insures competition, the battle of the sexes, the Eastern structure implies complementary co-existence. Where the Western man might say "You can't live with 'em and you can't live without 'em," the Eastern mind would be respectful and appreciative of the subtle differences between men and women. Eastern cultures are by no means ideal, but we can learn much from the concept of Yin and Yang. Just to ease the tensions between men and women in Western culture would be a blessing, not to mention easing the tension associated with all other forms of prejudice which are based on this same idea of competition. When we eliminate competition from our minds, we begin to cure most of the world's ailments immediately. Of course, we have to give up the supposed 'joys' of aggressive behaviors like sports and conquest of new markets, but that can only be viewed as another very positive benefit of this mental change of course. If we look at competition and all of its aspects, violence, rebellion, greed and corruption, we get a pretty good idea of all that it has done for us.

The western thought system says two things about competition; 1) it encourages the adventurous to seek out new markets and new products (and keeps prices down, of course) and, 2) it helps us define ourselves by comparison with others. The first of these we can thank for all the wars, the broken treaties, the rape of the environment and the greed and corruption we have come to know and love. As long as we continue to compete, we will always find excuses to steal and harm others to get what they have. As long as we believe that there are limited markets and resources, we will always attempt to get whatever we think we need by any means we can conjure.

The second is responsible for all the self image problems from macho to milk toast in men, and from wall flower to man eater in women. We define ourselves by how we fit into the norm or by how we appear to others. This is not being connected to any strength within, this is living at the whim of the latest fashion or worse, staying the same person we were raised to be. While this might insure some kind of conformity and the continuation of the culture our grandfathers fought and died for, it certainly doesn't point in the direction of growth or the expansion of consciousness. And that's the point. As long as we continue to believe and behave as if this concept is valuable, we will continue to experience the same world we do now. For those who like the modern world of stress and fear I suppose this is fine, but for those who dream of a better world, for those who know this is not the best we can do, the present thought system only spells disaster. So, these concepts of life and self image that surround the idea of competition have done much for us. They have produced a world that is a perfect reflection of their arrogant and aggressive ignorance. Now that we see what these ideas are capable of producing, it's obvious that some new thoughts are in order. To be able now to see this clearly, to be able to understand that it is our thoughts manifesting is indeed a blessing. We are now not only ready to try out some more positive ideas, we know beyond a shadow of a doubt that these positive ideas will manifest a new and better world. This new Trust replaces the old idea of fear.

Fear

In the old system, fear was the real reason we did anything. Competition is really only a response to fear, fear of starvation, fear of being harmed, fear of what others think of us and fear of the future. Fear is based upon an understanding of life which states that we can never know what is going to happen next so we had better be well prepared. So, we have developed elaborate systems of insurance and military might to guard against every conceivable kind of future mishap. But what have we really done?

Since the future is a direct projection of our present thinking, these thoughts have projected their reality onto the world. So, rather than protecting us from the future, all of our investments in security and espionage have only served to make the world a more fearful place. We have believed that strife and violence were the games humans played so we all have played with everything that we are worth, and for everything that we have. We need only change the game and the world will change with it. Imagine a world in which everyone shares. Since we know that our true Source is within and that it is limitless, there is no longer any reason to horde anything for ourselves. In fact, the more we give, the more there is, just like traditional religious thought tells us. What is interesting is that many who know, study and teach these truths have not been able to discern the gap between their religious minds and their practical living. These 'truths' are fine for Sunday morning, but come Monday, a different set of rules has always applied. The separation of church and state has served to accentuate the gap between what we have said we believe, and what our actions have shown we truly believe. And really, this has been good.

Only by taking these ideas of lack and self centeredness to their extremes have we finally been able to see how erroneous they are. By allowing these ideas to manifest to their logical absurdity, we have understood their true nature. Any idea that will not stand up under all circumstances is not a true idea. Any idea that can be subjected to abuse in any form is not a consistent truth. So we see that Western culture has been laboring under two very different sets of beliefs that are in direct conflict with each other. This is but another aspect of the conflict and competition that has been the foundation of our life experiences up to this point.

I, for one, am tired of competition, of conflict and all its manifestations. Why should we have to live in a world full of stress and bitter struggles? There is no spiritual reason for this. Only our limited understanding has made us believe there is no other way. And thus we have forced ourselves to live like aggressive animals because we thought we could not do otherwise.

We have behaved like self-centered brats in an international battle for acquisitions because we were greedy to have more than our fair share. We have been so afraid of not having enough that we have taken what little other countries have to satisfy our unending thirst for riches and luxuries. And so have we molded the world into a system to supply us with our desires in the vain pursuit of our own happiness, a happiness which never arrives because we have not had the faintest idea what happiness truly is. Yet through this aggressive, self-centered and hopelessly misguided process we have at last discovered the true Source of our Happiness, of our Joy, and of our Love and Being. They were all within us all the time just waiting to be allowed to manifest in our lives.

Just think how incredible this journey has been and how much we have learned by taking it. We have proven that we can do anything we want. There are still many who doubt their abilities, but the major truth we have come to know is that if we can imagine it, we can become it. Our world is full of incredible success stories of people who overcame tremendous odds to succeed. We attribute this to the strength of the human spirit, a spirit revealed in the truth of 'as we think, so we become.' To have learned this is worth any price because it allows us to evolve past the state of living like animals at the mercy of our own ignorance. And to learn that we are here to learn, to expand and to grow is the greatest gift of all.

We have been so serious for so long about this thing called Life that we have all but lost our capacity to enjoy it. Life is the greatest game of all because it is our game and we can play it anyway that we like. And if we include the new Understanding that we all can have everything that we want, then we eliminate the conflict and competition that have caused all of the problems in the past. Like the Phoenix, we emerge from the ashes of the present darkness and soar towards the central sun of Unity and Love.

Adventure

In place of competition we substitute the idea of adventure, the challenge and adventure of becoming Beings of Light.

We can still symbolize this aspect of life by the Knight in armor, but instead of engaging in battle for fame and fortune, this Knight searches out the Secrets of Life itself. He still seeks the Holy Grail but is no longer concerned with fighting for his Lady's honor. It is time to put honor and prejudice behind us and yet continue to embrace the spirit of exploration and adventure for which the last few centuries have been famous. But let us take this adventurous spirit within where the true riches reside instead of scratching and digging in the earth or in each other's pockets in hopes of finding something of value. But here lies perhaps the most difficult part of this journey.

Western culture is rife with the tales and exploits of the most adventurous. From the Reader's Digest to tabloid 'true stories,' from fairy tales to the latest blockbuster film, the stories of dangerous exploits fill our minds as children with dreams of romance and far off places. It is what our most popular books and cherished legends are about, and there are many dare devils and a multitudes of macho types who profess their lust for conquest and adventure. Yet when faced with the amazing adventure of going within, many quail at the thought. You would think that the monsters of the deep or unearthly beings on other planets are as nothing when compared to the terrors in our own souls. How did we become people who are more afraid of what's inside than what's outside? All of a sudden, the strongest among us cowers in the corner as if in the presence of death itself. It is very easily explained, we have been taught to fear.

But these fears are unfounded. There is no reason to recoil from what's inside of us and most of us experience them only in nightmares or now, thanks to the luxury of modern special effects, in the privacy of our televisioned living rooms. Our fascination with fear exists because we have grown up in an inner and outer environment filled to the brim with it. And this fear has manifested almost everywhere that we look, within our inner cities and in international skirmishes. Yet the greatest fear is of the unknown.

Our greatest adventurousness is actually just bravado in the face of our deep inner fear. We thrust ourselves into the fray to prove that we are not afraid, and by so foolishly thrusting give testament to the seething fears within. We only fear what is within because we are mostly ignorant of what is truly there, and have a legendary history of wild tales and vivid imaginings of what might exist within our darkest recesses. It is enough for most that we can feel pain within or that we know there are buried memories of lack of love or abuse. It is also enough that almost everyone else fears the within as well. This only serves to strengthen our fears as we all share the universal camaraderie of eternal dread. I agree that we need to share, but why must it be something so destructive to the self as fear of the very part of us that will set us free? By fearing our inner selves, we sentence ourselves to living within the life of fear and quasi hope we have experienced up until now.

When you think about it, something unknown can just as easily be better than what we know as worse. So the secret is not that we do not know what is inside, but rather than we have the habit of fearing everything new regardless of where it comes from. That is why most outer space movies show dangerous aliens instead of potential teachers and friends. We enjoy danger, especially armchair danger, only because it reinforces the fear we feel within. And we only feel this fear of what lies within because we have been taught that evil lurks there. This was not always our understanding.

The Devil Created

Prior to 660 BC, the concept to the Devil was unknown, at least in writing. It was in that year that Zoroaster penned his theory of life as a conflict between the forces of good and evil. Before that time, the heavens were filled with many gods, each with a unique character. There was Jupiter, God of Expansion and Saturn, the God of Limitation. There was Neptune of the Oceans and Pluto of the Underworld while Diana ruled the Moon and Apollo the Sun. So the Devil became the focal point for all gods with harmful intent, those responsible for thunder, floods, drought and death, and God became the sum total of all the positive influences like sunshine, rain, vegetation and children. It is not a coincidence that God is only Good with an 'o' removed and Devil is evil with a 'D' (and 'lived' spelled backwards because Evil is destructive or backwards towards Life). With the invention of the Devil came also the story of his hold on humans, his grip on the very Soul of man. Life, then, became a struggle where these two immense forces battled for the souls of men. One supposes that whoever got the most souls won the contest and some form of reward like eternal adoration or some such.

In our recent world history this conflict played itself out as America versus Communism where America was the perfect manifestation of God's Will on Earth and Communism was the den of selfish, atheistic child eating monsters. This is a cute little story but hardly anywhere near the truth. It is amazing that otherwise intelligent, thinking adults would harbor such an archaic fairy tale as the explanation of what Life is all about, and be completely unaware of how that fantasy manifests in international politics. As if Life could be a mere game board on which a larger drama was being played with us as hapless pawns. It is time, it is past time to move beyond fairy tales and embrace knowledge. But this knowledge is only available to those who will go within. We must realize that our fears of what's inside us are unfounded and so grow past them and allow our attention to focus on the Center. It may seem like a risk, but it is well worth the trouble to try to understand and overcome these ancient prejudices against our inner Selves.

Risk

The idea of risk taking is another concept that gets transferred to the Spiritual Path. But risk is only another form of fear and completely out of line with the concepts of Abundance and Love. So the question becomes, where is the risk if everything is provided? The answer is simple, the risk is all in our minds. It is only our lack of understanding and belief that makes any enterprise a risk. It's what we don't know that fools us every time, and we will never stop being fools until we become intuitively aware. To have only the perceptions of the five senses to guide us is like living with only one eye open. It is playing with only three suits of a possible four. 'In the valley of the blind, the one eyed man is king,' the old saying goes. But in the valley of intelligence the two eyed man is lost because he does not even begin to see all that is really there. And as he blindly follows the edicts of the masses in hopes of that bright future, every once in while he might take a risk.

On the Spiritual Path, risk becomes nonsense. Since we know nothing of any harm will come to us by our positive and inquisitive actions, we freely release ourselves to explore these realms of spiritual energy and learn their secrets. We are moving past the limitations of three dimensional living and have crossed the border into the fourth, the dimension of Spirit.

Striving

I was thinking about the idea of pressure within. I have been feeling an inner pressure to keep going, to look for opportunities, to be ready to take advantage of what is presented. It's like an edge, an aggressive projection of energy designed to get things done and desires accomplished. By relaxing this tension, I was able to feel its cause, the fear of failure. I realized that it had been a huge desire to be successful that had played such a large role in my self image. Of course, the fallacy of this approach is that we are always successful. Success is the norm because all things are possible and imminently perfect. The Masters have always told us this, yet we continue to doubt the words of Truth. We prefer to remain locked in the prison of our own misgivings instead of expanding into the realms of Joy where we truly belong. So, the first step in our growth out of the failure syndrome is to realize that we have kept ourselves there by our erroneous thinking. The second step is to forgive ourselves for being so blind.

This is very important. Once we understand that we have been responsible for all of our past miseries, it is remarkably easy to fall into the trap of blaming ourselves for the problems. After all, if we hadn't been so stupid we could have seen this sooner and saved ourselves all of this grief and discontent. But this is only another example of the same kind of negative thinking. Blaming ourselves doesn't produce anything except more grief and is based entirely on old ideas, the very ideas we are trying to outgrow. Blame is based on the idea that life is a game that we are supposed to win. Therefore, failure of any kind is seen as defeat which, by definition, is someone's fault. But we just decided that life is not a game but an adventure, and one of the steps in this adventure is realizing that our thoughts make a difference in our experiences. To blame ourselves is once again to allow a negative thought to produce its negative effects, the very thing our new Understanding is designed to prevent.

To force ourselves along, to develop an inner pressure to get things done is negative as well, because it can only be based on a belief that we will not get anywhere unless we press on and persevere. Both of these, creating a pressure and blaming ourselves for past failures, are injurious to the present growth and need to be released from the conscious mind. As long as we continue to focus on these ideas, we are not focusing on our growth. We are, instead, getting stuck in the past. In blaming we are both wallowing in the past and keeping the present from manifesting. But by forcing we are getting stuck in something even more interesting.

The whole thrust of the new method is to allow the inner energies to manifest. As long as we continue to force, then we are not allowing. As long as we force, then only the old forms will manifest, the forms that forcing can produce. This is interesting because we are so used to forcing, so used to going after what we want that the first thing we do when we decide to approach the Spiritual Path is to try to force it to happen quickly. But, of course, we cannot force what can only happen by allowing. Forcing is really only a fear anyway, the fear that we have to hurry up because there isn't enough time. By allowing, on the other hand, things can happen very quickly. We need to release the idea of keeping up this outward pressure before we can experience anything else. And when we release it, our entire organism feels a wonderful sense of relaxation the like of which we have never known.

I know I need to be here now, but I can't seem to find the time.

ZEN DUDE

Chapter 13
Time and Eternity

The Clock Ticks On

realized the other night that as I have become older, I have become more concerned with time. Of course we all grew up with the belief that there are only seventy years or so and only fifty of them really active. We were also constantly bombarded with the limitations of time like being late, growing old and letting our life slip between our fingers. What interests me is not that I am concerned, because we all are, but rather just how pervasive this idea is within our thinking. It's as if every thought we think relates in some way to time. We are always either in a hurry, sitting bored with time on our hands or impatient at our life's clock ticking away as we accomplish very little. Add to this all of the thoughts about the future and the past, and we have a real winner here. Time is very, very important to us right now. It is a major player in the present world system, and we are forever worrying about the ever advancing specter of Death, the apparent end of it all, the end of Time as we know it. These last few words are very important because the way we understand Time has a huge effect on our Life Experience.

When we replace the idea of time with the concept of eternity, all the other thoughts in our minds begin to change accordingly. Impatience, worry and all of its children no longer play in our inner gardens. Our minds are released from all aspects of fear and are freed to ponder more positive things or, better yet, not to think at all. What a blessing to finally be able to turn this thing off, this mind that drives us crazy and worries us to death. We have been following the rules of this time based system and reaping its rewards, rewards which are small in comparison to what is to be experienced on the Spiritual Path. There is nothing that the present understanding of life produces for us that cannot be extended a hundred fold by an increase in Spiritual Understanding. Love, Trust, Abundance and Joy are in ample supply within our Heart of Hearts. Within our Center lies the Source of all that we are, and all that we can experience.

So we can see that the pressure we thought was so necessary in order to insure survival or happiness was actually a result of our fear of death. It takes real courage to Trust, a courage based on an acute understanding of how the universe of energy is structured. This Trust is not the hope filled faith of traditional religion which uses the carrot of eternal life to persuade its denizens to follow the prescribed path. This Trust is based on actual, scientifically proven knowledge of how energy in this universe works. We know for a fact that we are Light and that this Light manifests as Light unless we instruct it to do otherwise. We also know that it is our thinking that constitutes these instructions. It is as simple and as profound as that. Our task, our challenge, our adventure is to use this knowledge to transform our minds, our emotions and our life experiences into reflections of this new Understanding. So instead of pressure or forcing, we substitute the idea of focus.

Focus

When we focus on something, when we place our attention on anything, it begins to manifest. It has long been recognized that concentration is the key to accomplishing anything. We were taught and cajoled since we were little to concentrate on what we were doing at all times. Of course, concentration has some aspects of forcing. We were actually taught to put on our thinking caps and try to come up with the answers, as if by trying hard we could force our minds to think better. Eventually, hopefully, we learn that forcing does not produce but rather blocks. We usually have to think of something else and then the answer pops in our heads. This is allowing! We are merely using the trick of thinking of something else to allow our minds time to produce the required information. So, really, we have always known this but were not consciously aware of what we were doing. And that's the point, to become consciously aware of what we are doing. We do not need to employ tricks or magic or lucky socks to make our dreams come true. We do not have to scheme or push or keep up the pressure to make things happen. We only have to consciously understand what we are doing and how the energy works. That is what we are learning by going Within.

We can relax on the pressure. We can allow the inner qualities of Love and Light to manifest. And if we decide to manifest a change in our lives, we only have to say 'yes' to that change and it will happen. If we wish to become a Center of Light so that we can help ourselves and others attain a more joyful life, we only have to understand that it is possible and allow it to happen. We have a choice here! We can be totally open and allow our inner selves to manifest, whatever that might be, or we can be totally active and use our ego minds to project a specific reality that we think will make us happy. We can even do both. We can use the conscious mind to observe what is gong on within and make suggestions as to possible courses of action. Each of us must experiment with our energy and determine what works best for us. In any event, our lives will become more positive, our outlook more promising and our experience full of Joy. We will cease to be selfish because we will recognize the true creative joys of sharing. We will cease to be greedy because we understand that there is an Abundance of everything for everyone. And we will forget about having to worry about the past or the future because we will be too busy celebrating the present moment.

Being and Becoming

One of the key concepts in our minds that helps us in this transformation into Beings of Light is to realize that we already are these Beings of Light. This may sound simplistic or naively obvious, but it is based on observation of many who go through this process of change. A major thought form in the old system is that of becoming. We never really achieve anything, we are always working towards it. We never really arrive at our destination of happiness, we are just trying to get there. We are generally not even for one moment standing still in peace and contentment, but are rather always moving towards some goal. We are in the process of becoming in the old system. In the new system we are Being. We can say that we are becoming Beings but that is only an unfortunate linguistic twist, a sort of transitional phrase in our Understanding. The becoming part takes place only in our awareness. We are becoming aware that we are Light and Love. We are becoming aware of what we truly are and have always been. This opens up a new interpretation of the big bang theory.

When we imagine all of the energy of the universe compressed in the size of a pin head, we can interpret that in any number of ways. It could be a literal piece of matter waiting to explode, but it is more likely a tiny speck of Light beginning to expand. Like a pin hole in the fabric of Eternity, this Light leaked into Space and created our Universe and everything we know. This speck of Light can be viewed as the Center from which all Life as we know it began. Within us there is a matching speck of Light, a matching hole through which Light flows and creates us. At the Center of all manifested forms there exists this place, a passageway for Light to enter and manifest itself. We call this passageway the Soul, and we call this Light that seeps through by many names, all of which indicate some sort of greater Being of which everything we know and all that we can imagine is a part. There is a sense of awe and calm peacefulness in contemplating this larger Being whose major attribute is Light. Makes one wonder how so many humans can limit themselves to only thinking about their individual needs and wants. It's like hanging out in a dark corner of the world when the entire realm of creation is at our disposal. What is more amazing is that so many will not even listen to another explanation, though they will eventually.

Changing Beliefs

Many I have known seem welded to their belief systems just as I once was. Even to think for a moment that there might be another way of looking at life fills them with misgivings. As a result, they judge what we say before we say anything. Their attitude is to refute anything anyone else believes automatically. It's a perfect example of the extremes a shaky consciousness will employ in order to protect its own vulnerability. Some humans possess a very precarious self image which holds onto beliefs like rafts in the misty sea of doubt. For them, just the act of thinking about what they believe puts at risk what little mental security they have. So they disregard other belief systems in order to protect their own 'purity' of mind. Many traditional belief systems encourage close mindedness as a way to insure their continued survival. This is a fascinating control mechanism started by early kings and clerics.

What better way to insure that others will be faithful to you than by demanding their acceptance of your way as the best, and then making even thinking about some other way a sin. It is a perfect system and has kept us effectively enslaved for centuries. Surely we can allow ourselves to follow our own best intuition when it comes to the subject of what we believe, rather than submit to some older way of thinking merely because we have been conditioned to believe we have to. This sense of honoring our fathers and their fathers before them needs to be reevaluated. To believe because it makes sense to us is one thing, but to believe because we feel we don't have any choice is something else again. We need not allow our minds to be controlled from the outside by someone else's thoughts, no matter how ancient or venerated. We can rely on our own intuitive Understanding to guide us always. This will even help open up our intuitive awareness to the levels of energy going on around us. In fact, it is the best and only way to learn to be intuitive. We merely need to become aware of these intuitive perceptions that we are already, at all times, receiving. It is a process of tuning into this other level of manifested energy. We cannot be aware of our body or what we are thinking unless we concentrate on those areas, the same is true of the intuition. Only by focusing on the intuition will we become aware of it. This is part of the adventure, the exploration of intuitive realms. These realms are just as real as those perceived by the five senses. They only differ in the level of their manifestation.

Work and Freedom

I was thinking about the idea that if we play, then someone else has to do the work. This is a fairly common thought in the working class, a kind of resentment that they do all the work and the politicians, lawyers and salesmen make all the profit. But it is also the very deep idea that there is a certain amount of work that needs to be done in order for us to survive. The very reason the industrial revolution was so welcomed is that it promised that machines would do a lot of the work that humans had to do. So the promise of freedom lured us into developing the machines which have transformed our lives so much already, and continue to do so. Still, it is widely believed that we each have to pull our own weight, a metaphor left over from the dark ages of animal powered transportation. We all do need to be responsible for our lives, but there are many new concepts that now apply.

For instance, since we are what we think we are, then we only need to work very hard to pull our own weight if we think that we do. There is nothing wrong with devising new, easier ways to produce goods and foods that do not involve so much manual labor. Yet there is a pride in being physically working that makes it hard to break the older pattern, and so limits exploration in new directions. Thinking that the world is a real place where we have to do real work to make anything happen limits us to functioning on that plane of reality. Jesus, among others, was able to manifest all kinds of things, food, water and healings, for instance, from nothing and without apparent effort. Most of us cannot do what he could, but perhaps we can learn how. But we can only learn something this miraculous if we admit to its possibility, and for that we must let go of some older ways of thinking. Making ourselves responsible for getting the work done is one of those ideas.

The point is not that we no longer need to be responsible for ourselves. Just the opposite! With our new Understanding that we are what we think, we are more than ever totally responsible for what we experience in this life. Yet, it is the way in which we are responsible that is up for review. Being responsible by working hard is only one way of keeping that contract. We can also become wise and learn to manifest directly from the Center of our Being. If there is physical work to be done, as in the growing of food and the manufacture of goods, then we can join in joyously as we are able.

An interesting aside to this idea is the disdain with which we presently treat farmers. We do not reward them for their efforts, in fact they have, by and large, been relegated a mean existence for the work which produces all the food for the rest of us. This is insane behavior. If anything we should thank them for their efforts to sustain us and allow them to make a decent living from their efforts. And this attitude of gratefulness will increase productivity more surely than some new wonder fertilizer or farm subsidy. A positive attitude will insure even more success than we already enjoy. Yet the overriding paradox of this issue is that we both enshrine hard work and disdain those who do it.

There is almost an arrogance surrounding many who perform pleasant, dignified, work as opposed to getting their hands dirty. I suppose it's okay to work hard as long as it's dignified and/or profitable, yet I would question the idea of hard work altogether. For one thing, the very fact that we think of it as hard makes it hard. The word work, as well, prevents us from viewing how we spend a third of our life with anything but begrudging resignation. Why can't we view our labors as physical activities that are necessary and joyful instead of filled with drudgery and boredom? This is some more exploration we can do. We can explore the true nature of our jobs and thereby discover the hidden joys they contain. This positive attitude will almost certainly add a new level of interest and reward us in every way we can imagine. I would much rather have an activity that fills me with joy as it fills my pockets than one I detest and only do because I don't know what else to do. And each of us can discover these aspects in everything that we do.

One of two things will happen when our attitudes and motivations remain positive; either our present activities will change, or we will discover new, more rewarding aspects of what we are presently doing. Those are the only two options if we are positive and truly seek the joy of each moment, even while at our jobs. This is a wonderful method for improving half of our waking hours with very little real effort. All of the change happens within and quite easily if we allow it, yet the results are absolutely stupendous. I have always shied away from major change because of the effort involved. In other words, I believed that it took a lot of hard work to make changes happen. Even if part of me wanted to change, it just seemed like too much trouble. Now I know differently. It is effortless and magically effective as well as immediate.

The whole idea of not having to work so hard is well founded. We do not really have to struggle and fight in order to survive. In fact, the findings of the Global Conference in Buenos Aires indicated that if we spent two percent of the world military budget on food, clothing, shelter and health care, everyone on this earth would be healthy and prosperous. Two percent! That's how close we are to the doorway that leads to Abundance. And really, what we are talking about it Love. It is Love which feeds and clothes us, which keeps us warm and cares about our health and happiness. So if we increased our Love by two percent, everything would be considerably better than it is right now. And we can do that quite easily by focusing two percent more of our energy on Love than we do now.

That's a little over a minute every hour. If we are the angry type, that's one less tantrum. For others, it's a few kind words where we usually criticize, a few moments of patience or understanding where we habitually feel anxious or disdainful. And we can add to this our time of daily meditation, 15 or 20 minutes of focusing on the Center of Light and Love within, which is enough to allow these energies to manifest in our lives and in the lives of those around us. That's all it will take! If we create these energies in our lives, then they will naturally expand into the larger world and provide the impetus necessary to feed, clothe, house and heal everyone on the planet. This would accomplish a lot.

Without poverty in the world, many warring groups would have little reason to fight and even inner cities would relax if the necessities of life were more readily available. This would free up even more of us to become positive and add to the growing expansion of Light. The irony is that all of this conflict and aggression is designed to produce some kind of security or happiness anyway. Happiness and security, in other words, food, clothing, housing, health and contentment. There are, to be sure, some who crave power or are fighting to settle old grudges, but most would undoubtedly be satisfied with these basic essentials. And if two percent would produce all that everyone now needs, imagine what 10 per cent would create, or 20. Sounds to me like the old way is totally out of touch with reality. Looks like the old way of conflict and greed and violence is actually counterproductive, although destructive is a better word. And what else could it be?

By the nature of energy, using destructive tools can only produce destruction. To use warfare in the attempt to secure peace is absurd. To use aggression to try and secure a homeland dooms that homeland to a violent end. As the Persian poet Omar Khayyam wrote some 900 years ago, "Those who put their faith in fire, in fire their faith shall be repaid." It is high time we started putting our faith in something other than violence and fear. How about Love?

I remember growing up in Church and watching my

father put ten percent of his check in the offering plate every Sunday morning as the Pastor reminded us how good it was to return a portion of what we were given to the Source. It's kind of like priming the Universal Pump. But I can see now that it is all Love, and when we give Love, it primes everything and helps it to flow more strongly. Surely we can do that. Surely we can give a kind word, help a neighbor or just keep a positive, Love filled attitude ten percent of the time. That's six minutes out of every hour, six minutes that will increase our Love, Joy and Contentment and everyone else's by 500 percent. Those are pretty good odds. This is what we are talking about, this is what we are doing. We are using the creative power of our thoughts to change our world. And it is as easy and beneficial as this. If the Love we share can accomplish all that we now enjoy, I'd like to see what ten or twenty per cent more could do, wouldn't you?

When we change this way, the world will change with us, and this will bring about many interesting transformations. For one thing, if all of these aggressive and warring people quit fighting tomorrow, then they could help the rest of us build a new world where everyone could enjoy peace and prosperity. Everyone would include all of these warriors, too, and they might find that, this way, they actually get to enjoy the prosperity they are supposedly fighting for instead of it always being somewhere in the future after the final victory. There is already plenty of food and we could easily produce the rest of the necessary goods and services, especially considering the fact that we would have a work force much larger than its present size. We are even beginning to see this happening as America's emphasis begins to shift from defense spending to areas like ecology and new, friendly sources of energy. New sources of energy, that's what the Light within is and this inner expansion is being mirrored by our interest in solar and other kinds of power. Of course, the current money game might slow things down a bit because we would have to figure out a way to pay wages to everyone who stopped warring and to finance all the new projects and their distribution.

But perhaps we don't need money any longer either. After all, what does it really accomplish for us?

Money

If money is a game, then it is a wasteful one. It is estimated that 40 percent of the work force deals with money. In other words, 40 percent of the work is merely keeping track of who bought what and what they paid for it. This is only perceived to be necessary because of the importance we put on ownership, and ownership itself is founded on the old idea that 'there is only so much of everything.' This is not Abundance, it is scarcity and the money only serves to compound the problems. How many times have you or I wanted to help someone in need but did not have the money? How many times has there been an international emergency but the logistics of getting the necessary funding and arranging for transportation made helping impossible. Most of the world at present is in dire need of food, clothing and shelter, yet they remain have-nots because there are not funds available.

For most of us, the world would not change very much if money went away. We would find ourselves in pretty much the same shape we are now. We would have the same house and friends and probably work the same job, and would probably continue to do so like the million dollar lottery winners who continue to put in forty hours at the transmission factory. Most of us need to keep busy doing something, so we would continue to perform some kind of job. But if money disappeared there would be forty percent more of us to do the jobs that need to be done. If we add this to the previous reductions by eliminating warfare, then we have about 20 times as many of us to do what needs to be done. That leaves even more free space to explore ourselves and rebuild the planet. There is not a shortage of goods or food or services, but only a shortage of money. Money is obviously a severely limiting concept. In fact, it is the manifestation of our belief in lack.

An interesting situation occurred with our decision to find a new house. We realized that we needed a larger house because of all the guests we have and all of the people who live here. So we marked a few prospects and went out looking. What struck us immediately was the shabbiness of the neighborhoods we drove through, where the lack of care and consequent lack of self esteem were quite evident. The houses themselves all seemed to need a lot of work and we realized that we were looking at large but not very livable buildings in questionable neighborhoods. When we returned home we looked again in the book of listings and found that we were only looking at the houses we thought we could afford. Ellyn asked me if I had seen the five bedroom with two acres and I said I hadn't. Of course I hadn't, it hadn't been in our projected range! So we were limiting ourselves by imagining what we thought we could afford. If we were allowing this house to manifest from the Center, then these kinds of limitations would not surface. The perfect house would show up, and without a lot of searching through lists or endless contacts with real estate agents. The perfect house could even be offered as a gift or some kind of live-in arrangement, options which were not even considered with the tunnel vision we had on how much money we could afford. And we realized how often we do this. It is one thing to believe that we are always provided with what we need, yet it is quite another to actually live it.

If we dare to dream of something better how often we immediately limit our dreams to what experiences we have known. It's like we choose the colors for our newest painting from the palette we have used before and then complain that it ends up looking the same. So the best approach we decided was to go ahead and read even the very expensive listings and know that if we really needed to go in that direction, a way would be presented. So we have let go of the whole project and are allowing the Universe to manifest what we truly need. This is a wonderful approach that is much easier and equally successful. We don't have to do anything to make it happen, and in the long run the results will be better because we will not be limiting ourselves to what we think we might need, what we believe we can honestly afford, or what we perceive to be the true direction we are going. Our Souls understand much more than we do and should be allowed to manifest the best possible situation. And so it shall be.

In deciding to let our souls manifest we accomplished two very important things, 1) we insured that the best possible result will happen and, 2) we reversed the old training that merely remanifests what it already knows (and is obviously unsatisfactory or we wouldn't be trying to change). Letting the Soul control this situation will manifest a new house, but letting go of the old way of thinking will manifest an entirely new and more joyful existence.

These are some other ideas that played into this scenario. The old way of thinking says that 'you get what you pay for' which implies that the more expensive it is, the better it is. It also insists that we are all paid what we are worth. The new way states that you always get what you think you deserve both in terms of wages and acquisitions. So the old way insists on making money and then using it to trade for the goods we need and want, with all of the crippling self esteem issues we have come to know only too well. The new way goes past all of this mental maneuvering and simply allows the Soul to manifest what we need when we need it. The old idea of being paid for what we produce is giving way to always getting what we need in accordance with our Understanding.

So if we do things for the benefit we see coming to us, then we only will accomplish those bare essentials. We will manifest what we think we need, which is never enough. But if we decide to live and work for the good of all concerned, if we do things in the spirit of sharing and nurturing ourselves and the planet, then everything we need will be provided. And what is provided will be so much more than the limited essentials we imagined when we were only concerned with our own selves.

When we open up to the energies of the universe, the universe sends us all that it has. We are the prodigal children returning after a long sojourn in the world of selfish woes. The universe is waiting to give us the wealth it has been holding in Trust until we were ready to understand and accept it. We are becoming ready now. We are learning and growing at a fantastic rate, at the speed of light. We are becoming the beings of Light that we have always been but are just now realizing we are.

Chapter 14

Transformation

Intention

As we grow in awareness, we will begin to initiate all of our actions from the viewpoint of Love. This is the era in the evolution of human consciousness when we all become saints, when we all become healers and helpers and the entire world benefits immensely. Instead of self centered egos competing to carve up the world for their own security issues, we have humanity as a whole consciously cooperating to build a world full of Joy and Love. Instead of disrupting the world order to demand our fair share, we know that we naturally get everything we need by working together. This new kind of activity will transform the planet in a very short time, in the time it takes to change our minds.

It is the nature of our minds to change. Sometimes we lament this propensity in others, but the fact remains that our minds change often and sometimes dramatically. How many of us have not had experiences where in an instant we saw a vision of our lives unfolding? Meeting a life mate, finding the perfect job, or merely gazing at the night sky and feeling inspired by the beauty and immensity of the Universe, these moments mark turning points in our lives and we often experience dramatic changes seemingly overnight. Later, we might talk about 'before my experience' and 'after my experience', reinforcing the fact that we recognize we have grown. Most traditional religions have some kind of salvation moment when one sees the Light or is born again, and nothing is ever the same afterwards. Inner transformation is one of these moments.

When our minds change from self centeredness to world centeredness, an immense change has occurred. Most individuals describe a vision or feeling of remarkable clarity or purpose. It doesn't matter that their life situation has not changed because something much more fundamental has changed which the surface life circumstances will soon reflect. For most, it is the beginning of a new life, and a beginning is enough. When we allow ourselves to truly experience the majesty of existence, then we are ever after different Beings. Some describe a feeling of having an immense burden lifted from their shoulders as the weight of their worries and fears falls away. Others describe amazing opportunities which present themselves, the kind that used to be called the chances of a lifetime, but are now every week, or every day, occurrences. Still others describe how this initial rush of positive feeling and vigor combine to produce wonderful new feelings of Love and Joy. A minor change, a simple growth of perspective, but one which fills our lives with many varied experiences of happiness and the challenge of continued inner exploration. This is not merely the thrilling moment of acquisition of some long cherished goal that brings a fleeting sense of happiness, but the beginning of a whole lifetime of joyful moments in continuous and amazing manifestation.

In my own experience, I notice the difference from how I used to work to how I work now. Whenever I would think about writing before, I would always be filled with questions about what to write and how to get it published. In my set design business I would live from contract to contract always hopeful that new business would arrive, but still plagued by small doubts about the future. The idea of taking a few weeks off to do some writing was not possible because of these inner fears. When I finally understood that this new direction would allow me to share more with others as well as learn and grow the most myself, then I quietly asked for the opportunity to make this book a finished document. I soon found myself with two months fairly free of business obligations and with plenty of money in the bank to pay all necessary bills. I had manifested my request and I used that opportunity to produce the initial manuscript. The same procedure applies to all aspects of our lives. The most important single attribute of this kind of expansion is motivation.

Motivation and Growth

In my case, I was no longer interested in becoming rich and famous by becoming an author, I was only interested in growing and sharing this chronicle of growth so that we all might have more joyous lives. I felt that we all need to help this transformational process in the best way we can. Since I had a long history of writing, study and meditation on this very subject, I volunteered to go for it. I had no idea it would involve all that has transpired in these pages. My imagination stopped at producing a book about my Understanding of Life at the time I started writing. Little did I realize the depth of the change I had initiated by saying 'yes' to this project. I think this is always the case. All of my theatre experiences involved much more than I anticipated. I would volunteer to play a part in a play or choreograph a dance and be amazed at what came out of it. I would always learn so much about myself and about theatre that I was propelled to volunteer often and for almost any kind of project. So I had a history of excitement in doing projects yet was continually blown away by the finished result. It is like this for everyone. As soon as we say 'yes' to our Heart of Hearts, as soon as we allow our Soul to manifest the best possible experiences for us to learn and grow through, we are always amazed at the difference it makes in our lives. Most of us are also amazed at ourselves for not allowing these things to happen sooner and clearly see how our old thinking had limited us in so many ways. All it takes is saying 'yes' once, then the positive feedback will insure that we want the flow to continue.

I was thinking today about this question of flow. In attempting to produce some music as a companion to this book, I am again running into doubt. This doubt takes two forms; doubt of ability and doubt of the music coming through me.

They are both negative. One questions whether I have the skills while the other doubts the whole process of creative flow. This is an old attitude of mine that has always been in the way. I have always forced myself past this block and been successful in producing anything I chose to try. But this time, I would rather understand and release these ideas than keep up the forcing. I often spend many hours in thought about whether or not I will be able to complete the task. This is all time that could be used to work on the project that I have historically wasted on useless doubt. So, once and for all I wish to understand these negative ideas completely so that I will no longer be bothered by their destructive presence. The most amazing thing about these ideas is that they ignore the total success I have had in the past. From listening to the ceaseless banter within, one would think that I had always been a complete and total failure in anything I had ever attempted.

This is remarkable because it points to the very nature of these ideas. Negative ideas have no foundation in fact. They may have a history in the life experiences or they may not, it really has no bearing on the idea itself. This is because the idea dwells in that very deep part of our minds we call beliefs. As long as self doubt remains there, then no amount of material success will remove it from its position of influence. It's like a large corporation where the supervisor is a spiteful jerk. No matter how good a worker we are or how fair and honest our big boss might be, we will always be treated with disdain by the negative minded manager. But unlike a large corporation, we can easily change the managers of our mind. The first step is to realize that these negative ideas are unfounded and then replace then with positive ones. Since we are what we think we are, there is no longer any decent reason to be negative about ourselves, regardless of our personal or cultural history.

In my case, just seeing this truth clearly allowed me to release these negative ideas. Then my next job was to forgive myself for having believed such nonsense for such a long time, and also forgive myself for all of the failures these old beliefs had caused. My feelings of being unworthy had caused me to make many choices where I did not receive what the other part of me thought I should receive. I was struck by the consistent pattern of my striving and failing in many areas of my life. Where I was always successful in theatre, video or work projects, I was consistently lacking in personal affairs like money, relationships and joy. All of this negative mentality surrounded the idea of unworthiness, which was clearly a major belief. On the Spiritual Path, all are worthy. In fact, the idea of worthiness does not even come up. It is a non-issue. A Human Being who is unworthy is a contradiction in terms, like trying to describe a star which doesn't shine. This is one of the most important lessons we, as humans, are engaged in learning.

When we begin to enter the realms of Trust and Truth, we are met at the gate with our habitual worry about the future. This feeling is only caused by long association and in no way impinges upon the quality of the Human Being experiencing it. We must understand that though we will experience exactly what we think, we are not our thoughts any more than we are our bodies. Our bodies are merely the vehicles through which our Souls are experiencing being Human and our thoughts are merely the filters through which Life Energy passes on its way into this Human manifestation. We have traditionally identified with our bodies and our thinking, and this has led to all the misunderstandings, conflicts and adherences to false doctrines which have plagued our entire history. We are Light which is manifesting through these vehicles of physical, emotional and physical forms. We are three dimensional, interactive holograms. We are the Light which projects through while our thoughts and emotions determine the character of the projection. This projection is our experience that manifests in a three dimensional energy matrix. It is a very simple process and easily understood with this model.

The Energy Matrix

Our thoughts expand into this matrix much like the way a balloon expands into the space around it. Our thoughts flow out and anchor themselves in this universal stuff physicists call the space-time continuum. There they create an existence that can be experienced by the mind and its senses. What we project out is what we become. Most of us now are a combination of personality, body stance and conscious understanding that we call a person. And we relate to each other as persons rather than as Souls. Yet we actually are Souls expressing themselves through personalities, not personalities that happen to have Souls. Why do we not acknowledge this more often? It must be that we do not understand what it means to be a Soul having a three dimensional experience. We have learned how to be physical bodies and how to feel emotions. Some of us have learned to think and even do it well, but very few of us know what it means to be a living Soul, and thus we are unable to relate to each other as such. What this means is that we continue to interact with each other as mere surface personalities, personalities that are filled with self centered misunderstandings, negative self images and fear. And then we wonder why we can't seem to get along together. As long as we strive to be uniquely different and separate personalities on the earth's surface, we will never understand our true Brotherhood. We will never understand our Oneness because we are concentrating all of our attention on our differences. In other words, we are seeing ourselves as people, individual people competing for happiness rather than Souls united here for learning. It's true that we learn through the vehicle of the personality, but we are not the personality. We are something far beyond it. We can now expand our Understanding and allow the Soul's energies to manifest in a personality rather than trying to project a personality solely from the ego mind. This leads to an appreciation of the similarities of all cultures on the earth.

Cultures differ in their thoughts, but are identical in the way in which these thoughts manifest. The American, for instance, actively projects desires into the matrix whereas the Zen Buddhist would patiently allow the inner self to manifest in its own time and own way. The traditionally religious ask God to provide what they need while the very devout ask the Priest or Medicine Man to ask God on their behalf. There are a myriad of methods between complete allowing and total active forcing, a range that runs from total acceptance to complete and ruthless manipulation. All of us are operating somewhere in between these extremes of need/control and loving/allowing, both of which aim towards the single goal of Happiness.

Happiness

I was thinking about happiness and how we need to get past this idea. As long as we are focused on our own happiness then we will be driven to do things to make this happiness occur. Happiness contains within it the connotation that it can be pursued, the idea that one can go out into the world and find it, when in fact, Happiness must be allowed to rise up from its Source within. Happiness can never be created out of the sorrow and frustrations of deep need and pursuit. These can only reproduce themselves and never come near the assumed goal. So the pursuit of Happiness is the very thing which keeps it always just out of reach. We must learn to be happy with what is going on now in our lives. All the pursuit of happiness creates is drive and frustrated desires. This is because our desires are focused on the small goal of happiness rather than the larger goal of conscious awareness. We are here to grow and only through growth will we ever become happy. Growth is very important to all forms of life on the earth, us included. Recognizing that this is the reason we are here allows us to shift our focus from the acquisition of happiness to awareness of our growth in Understanding.

Interestingly enough, I noticed aspects of this in my physical body. I have historically had a very upright posture which is both the result of dance training and also from our culture's insistence on standing straight, tall and proud. Many of us are taught to hold ourselves very erect. I suppose the extreme is the exaggerated posture of the military, but the point is that this is a conscious decision. So I wondered how my ideas of posture and holding myself were changing, and I related it to the difference between classical dance and martial arts. In ballet, one lifts up to produce a kind of lightness which is the reason dancers can leap so effortlessly. In martial arts, the Ki flows from the Center and provides more of a buoyancy from within. Both provide support, but whereas ballet is a conscious arrangement of tense muscles, buoyancy flows effortlessly from the Center.

So I have begun to feel this inner buoyancy along with a sense of peacefulness. My mind seems at ease most of the time, curious about what is happening, but not really concerned about outcome. This is in stark contrast to my former self which all but demanded to know the contents of every moment and how that might affect the future. This may very well be what I have done for my forty odd years of life. I have, in one way or another, demanded everything that I wanted. This was not an outward demanding of others, but an inward demanding of myself. I simply had to prove once and for all to myself that I was capable of producing wonderful things, as well as being good, kind and generous. I found that I could be joyful and creative and full of Love, and I suppose that at first I sort of demanded of the universe itself that I learn to be this way. Like daring eternity itself to surface and reveal its secrets and taking the risk of not being able to understand what is being shown. We all have the opportunity to be incredible, fearless and loving people. If one of us can do it, then we all can.

I have been using this kind of thinking and find that it keeps me from doubting what is possible. So many have come to show the way and have always told us that someday we would be following. Now we are walking in the footsteps of the Masters and learning what they have learned before us. All of our lessons of fear and ego attachment, of doubt and disillusion are falling behind us, and we are expanding into the Universe of Spirit which has always surrounded us. This involves understanding and utilizing the concept of Acceptance.

Acceptance

Acceptance of all things as they are is the only way we will ever be able to let them expand. If we view them as deficient, they naturally wither like plants without sunlight. But when we embrace our selves and our lives as the perfect expression of our Highest Being, then we open the door and allow all our beauty, grace and natural genius to come out. If we like ourselves now, imagine how we'll feel when we see our deeper Essence. And if we don't like ourselves yet, then each of us will experience enough of our true Inner Essence to change our minds so that we do. Once we are comfortable with who we are now, then we can continue the expansion by opening further. Like the flow of inner buoyancy, our Soul Energies expand and support us in this, our new growth as humans.

If I am accomplishing anything for myself by writing this running commentary on Transformation, it is in allowing myself the opportunity to get the inner flow moving continuously. This is easily done by anyone who wishes. How much different this is from the present system where only those with talent, luck and incredible determination succeed in accomplishing anything. The Spiritual Path needs none of these attributes. On this path, all are fully qualified simply because we are Human Beings. On this path, the only determination we need is to allow the flow to begin. And the faith we require is really Trust in the divinity of our true inner selves, a Trust based on a secure knowledge of who we really are rather than legends scribbled in some ancient book. It is looking up and seeing the sun. It is so easy that any child can do it, and in fact they always do.

If we would only watch the children we would see this. I don't mean to watch them the way we watch them now, which is to make sure they are not doing anything wrong. But if we would actually observe how they interact with life. We can learn much from the Joy they experience in all things, about the careless abandon they exhibit in their exploration of the new dimension in which they find themselves.

When we do, we begin to notice how nice this way of looking at things is. Instead of worry there is enthusiasm, instead of boredom, interest and excitement. If we allow ourselves to see Life as through a child's eye, we begin to discover the true beauty and fascination it contains. As parents, we do this all the time and generally remark how wonderful it is to share with a young child. Everything is new to them, we say, that is why they are so fascinated. We call these the magic years and lament their passing. We imply that nothing is new to us and that is why we are now so bored. But perhaps if we took a moment and looked beneath the bare surface of things, we might see more of what the child sees. If for one moment we could suspend all of our thinking and look with new eyes, we might be amazed at what we would find. Just because we have experienced a few years of three dimensional living doesn't mean we've seen it all! But many of us are too busy trying to be who we think we are to even try to see things differently, let alone see something new and exciting. Thus we sentence ourselves to a life of endless repetition. And what is it we repeat?

We repeat the thoughts in our heads and the emotions in our hearts. We relive all of our old memories and fears and continually drive ourselves to secure impossible dreams. And all the time we are responding from the middle of an incredibly mutilated self image. What a strain this is upon the mind and emotional system. Even a little bit of failure is enough to send some of us over the edge into all sorts of complicated defense mechanisms. All of this stress, all of this confusion and questioning and inner anger combine to produce lives of suffering and misery with only occasional glimpses of joy. Yet the world continues to be beautiful with all of this negativity going on within us. In spite of our pitiful self images and misguided intentions, and in spite of many of us not wanting to be here in the first place, we still manage to enjoy some parts of life. Imagine what it will be like when we have only truly positive motivations.

Just for one minute imagine what the possibilities would be if we could remain positive and trusting for a day, if for one day we could experience the absolute happy, joyful and perfect life. Then take these possibilities and make them what we think about every moment of everyday. Let's fill our minds with only the best and most positive thoughts we can muster. If we think this way, so shall we become. We are in the process of retraining the mind to think and feel what we would like to experience. Then, when we begin to feel depressed or think negatively again, we can stop ourselves, gently, and encourage ourselves to think and feel positively again. We can imagine that the world is a wonderful place full of Love and Joy, a place full of sharing and caring and transforming Humans coming together in a state of higher consciousness. The world is a place where Celebration is the rule of the day, where suffering, anxiety and fear are viewed as the artifacts of some past civilization, artifacts that were useful then, but are no longer employed. We would not for a moment try to do work today with ancient stone tools, so why do we continue to think today with stone age thoughts? We are using outworn ideas in a modern world. More precisely, we are using physically based, ego controlled ideas in a world that is actually based on Spirit. We are changing the very foundation of the way we think and the essence of how we feel. And we are doing this consciously. We are allowing the Love and Light deep within us to manifest into our existence. And as we do, we leave these older ideas, these old tools behind us. Future generations may unearth them and put them in museums to study, but for us it is only important to leave them beside the road as we pass by. They are nothing more than the utensils we have used to cook up our present life experiences. And what crude tools they have been, creating a reality all but unfit for human consumption. And yet they have been the very concepts that have enabled us to at last understand the nature of our thinking. Without all of this modern alienation and suffering, we might not have searched for a better way, a way that is leading us to a higher state of Consciousness. We are finally beginning to study the way that we think and, like anthropologists, are amazed at some of the cultural oddities we are finding. We look at aboriginal cultures and remark on their innocence and apparent peacefulness. In some minds, aboriginal societies are beginning to look much better than they did before.

It is interesting that at this point in human history, missionary zeal is taking a new twist. The passion for spreading modern religion and culture to poor natives has been replaced in some countries by a policy of protection. They have clearly recognized the destructive nature of modern Western culture and wish to spare these primitive cultures from being ravaged. We are trying to protect their innocence because we fear that once it is lost, like ours, it can never be regained. What kind of thinking is this? To imagine that the future cannot be more wonderful than the past is to put too much energy into historical theories. The past was not better than it is now and returning to the past is not a solution to any present problems. If these older cultures were so enlightened why did they not survive? Every culture on the earth has its day and then passes away for the next, and each cycle improves on the old to build a continually evolving world. This hearkening back to olden times is reactionary, unenlightened and ultimately destructive. It is propagated by people who did not live during those times so really have no idea what they are talking about. It is time we moved forward into the Light, not back into the dark ages of savagery and ignorance that masquerade in our memories as innocent blessedness.

In the recent American past, one of the golden eras is the late Forties and early Fifties. Perhaps what was better about this era was not the circumstances themselves, but the attitudes of the people at that time. I remember my father and friends talking about the period after World War II when baseball was king and new cars came out with automatic transmissions and power steering. They had just defeated the ultimate foe in Germany and were riding high in a culture infused with enthusiasm for rebuilding and expansion. This period was marked by many advances in products for the consumer and by television and entertainments. Life was truly good. So, what was it that makes the attitudes so different today? All of the same products are here and more. We have television and entertainments like they would hardly believe, and more gadgets than sense, but we are missing something, something fundamental to our zest for life. Perhaps what is missing is the American Dream, a dream that never really materialized. It was a lovely dream but was based on a faith in old ideas, and old ideas can only produce the same cycles of Recession and Warfare that they always have. The Dream expected modern Medicine and Science to somehow make life better, but they really only succeeded in making it more complicated. It is time we put aside hopes and dreams and replaced them with Knowledge.

Chapter 15

The Freedom of Knowing

The Truth Shall Set Us Free

The first thing we need to become knowledgeable about are the basic ideas in our minds, the ones we have been discussing since page one. These are the fundamental beliefs about Life on which our cultures are built. We need to understand that today's leaders, like the rest of us, are doing the very best they can within the present belief system, so we can stop clamoring for them to somehow do more. They can only respond within the cultural framework of their respective countries. To expect enlightenment and peace from countries who pride themselves on military might is absurd. And almost all countries are based on this concept of self protection, so warfare is the game that is played. Only when cultures become based on Love and Light will we see a change in this scenario. Going back in time does not help because these same aggressive, warlike concepts were in full operation then and even less understood than they are now. We must go forward into our new Understanding.

We are moving to a new level of reality, a new level of functioning as Humans. The only way for us to learn how to function this way is to do so. By the time we could get together and pass some kind of comprehensive legislation designed to promote this change, we could have produced it several times over. Any energy we might spend trying to make something happen within the present system only results in friction, more expensive government and general failure to produce any perceivable results. Fortunately, we can become Centers of Light quite easily without any help from the big guys. We are like children who are being given an entirely new world to live in, and we hold the key to its creation within our Heart of Hearts.

This is wonderfully freeing. It's not like we are being given a choice between fulfilling this desire or that one, we can have everything we really want. We are opening up to a reality in which not only our wildest dreams can come true, but so much more that I can't even begin to tell you. I can't even begin to tell myself because there are realities waiting to be manifested that even the most vivid imaginations have not yet touched. For a world that seems to many to be on the brink of disaster, this is the Vision of the Promised Land. We have not even started to explore this new world yet it already surpasses anything that has been experienced at any time in our history except by a handful of Enlightened Masters.

All we need to see are the wondrous possibilities. All that matters is the joy and enthusiasm we feel for the new emotions we are expressing and the new Understandings within our awareness. I feel such pleasure to be involved with so many wonderful people and to help and be helped in this quest for Love and Joy. To share in this flowering of the human spirit is reward enough. For those who feel afraid to take the first step towards total Joy, I have compassion, for I was once one of those who doubted his ability to understand what is really going on. I once felt inadequate and undeserving of Joy and Love. I didn't feel up to the task of being human, let alone being able to walk where angels walk and know the Truths the Masters know. But now I know that we are all sparks of Divine Light and that everything I have been able to do is as nothing compared to what others will be able to accomplish. If I can rise from the depths of depression and despair and see the Light within, then everyone else can, too, and more. We are all equal in the sight of God because we are all made of the same Essence. If this book is anything, it is a testament to the spirit of Love and Light that dwells within each of us.

All of us will eventually take the first step on the Spiritual

Path, and that first step is realizing that we are Spiritual Beings in human form. It is knowing that we are the Children of Light. It is our nature, it is our heritage, our Essence and what we now get to experience.

The Signs of Growth

I was thinking about what this project is doing for me. Because this book is manifesting before my eyes, it provides instant feedback on the changes in my Understanding. I can see its growth and progress which helps refute the part of me which wonders if I might not be better off going in a different direction. To think that I should bypass this project for something else is to severely limit myself. When I get back from these detours into the realms of habitual doubt, I again see the wonderfulness of Life and its manifestations. What does it matter if every one of us who goes through this transformation writes a book about it, or writes a song or a symphony? What would it hurt? It could only help in solidifying the concepts in each of our minds and also help those who read it gain another perspective on the process. In any case, it would be preferable to the shrieks of anger and disdain that often pass for songs these days, or the epistles of sex and violence that masquerade as books or films. We have these media and massive systems of distribution and it would benefit us to utilize them as much as possible in a more positive way. And if we do not produce anything other than a happier and more contented life, is that not wonderful and enough impetus to take the risk of that first step? The only possible hesitation each of us might have is the naked fear of doing something that we have not done before. Surely we will not let this stand in our way.

Fear

The remarkable thing about fear is that it will continue to hold on long after there is a verifiable reason for it. Even when we begin to live within the Light and experience Joy these fears still surface from time to time. This allows us the opportunity to look at them again. In a culture in which men are not supposed to be afraid, men cover their fear with bravado. Women can be a little more honest about their feelings, but at some point, we all have to admit that we are afraid of death and, in many ways, of Life itself. From the inner observation point, the feeling of fear appears far differently than when we allow the emotion of fear to take control of us.

By becoming quiet and just experiencing fear without emotional involvement, it can be sensed as a constriction around the heart area. It is a holding in of energy because of the perceived danger of expanding outward, like cowering behind closed doors. So our fear is what limits us, yet within our heart is the Source of Love that wants to come out. This is the modern dilemma we face, how to expand into Living yet do so safely. The answer is not to pretend to be brave or to purchase massive amounts of insurance or security devices, but to eliminate fear from our energy system. Since fear is the cause of this constriction, it has to go.

By concentrating on the heart area, we can relax and allow these held in energies to expand. With the mind quiet, these tensions melt away and we feel an easy and comfortable sensation within. For myself, this was one of the first times in my life that I had ever relaxed this area, at least consciously. Just by allowing the Light to expand and permeate this area, it quickly relaxed from its usual tense state. It sometimes takes longer than others to find this relaxation, but it always happens if we focus on finding it. This is the relaxed state I try to maintain throughout the day.

When I reached this state of total relaxation I noticed another pressure. It was like a force holding me upright. Like the one previously mentioned, it was not a gentle buoyancy flowing from the Center but more like a sheer force of will shooting up my spine. We even talk admiringly about someone with a strong will or about another losing their will to live, as if will is the most important attribute of life. Will is desire, so it's like saying that the only reason we stay alive is because we desire it so very much. Thus the adage that the only way to get anything is to really desire it and latch onto it. Yet we only latch onto it because we fear we might lose it. So here we are again, stuck between desiring and fearing at the same time. With our new Understanding, we can let go of this older, stiffer model of living. Instead of this harsh, rigid and unchanging will we have the easy flow of Love and Light. We are replacing will power with Soul power. When we release our will to survive or to succeed, then we can allow ourselves to become the expanded Beings that we are meant to be. As long as we are focused on the will's agenda, we will never know what we might become if we just let go and Trust. As long as we are focused on goals, we will never learn how to enjoy the incredible journey.

All of our resistance to growing in the spiritual direction can be attributed to fear of change and fear of what we might find inside of us. It is a habit of the most conditioned and apparently normal kind, yet totally lacking in truth. There are no natural monsters inside of us, but rather only shadows of ones that we have created. Since all of them have been created when we were still small children, it seems like now would be a good time to look at them again. It amazes me that we, as mature, thinking adults can be so terrified of memories. Memories are only words and pictures like fairy tales lodged in our minds, yet many of us would rather spend a lifetime in the utmost pain and suffering than face a moment's confrontation with the past. But what was frightening as a small child can be easily understood as an adult. Our parents no longer tower over us and we are no longer dependent on their good will for our survival. It really should not matter what they or anyone else thought of us in some ancient memory, yet we seem to be more easily wounded by another's opinion of us than we are by all the physical hardships known to man. And we hold onto these wounds as if our lives depended on them, and indeed, they are the source of our major personality issues. When you think about it, how can a simple unkind word ruin our day? It is only a word spoken by someone else who may be quite unbalanced. But we have grown up in a culture which values a good name and thus prizes what others think. This is most blatantly demonstrated by some celebrities who expend incredible effort to secure national recognition. They have taken this idea of public opinion to the ultimate absurdity. It is time for us to grow up and realize that the only monsters inside of us are thoughts, thoughts which are easily understood and changed from an adult perspective.

So when these scary thoughts show up in our consciousness, we can release them with Love and replace them with positive thoughts. They may come back time and again, but each time they will be weaker because each time we will have replaced them with Love. In time, they will disappear altogether and our minds will be full of the beautiful, positive and uplifting aspects of Divine Energy. As such, we will be concerned only with being the best and most wonderful people we can be rather than striving to overcome all the stuff we have in our memory banks. And so shall we become true Human Beings on the planet Earth.

Of all creatures on the earth, how can we as humans think it is not our nature to grow and change? The flowers and trees, the animals and seasons all change and grow. Are not we the crown of creation, or so we tell ourselves? So to think that we are somehow left out of the Divine picture of evolution is insane. Just because we have the ability to think that we cannot grow or change is no reason to believe it. We are able to think anything that we want, but why would we want to think so negatively? Why do we think so negatively when we do not have to? Habits and more habits, these curses of self consciousness that make us afraid to be embarrassed, make us feel the fool for past mistakes and leave us cowering in the corner when faced with almost anything new. If there have been misunderstandings in the past, we need to change them into accurate knowledge, not chastise ourselves for having been foolish or ignorant in some former time. If we have done things wrong at some point in our life or lives, then it is time to forgive and forget, and get on with the present growth.

The current method teaches us to weigh the good we have done with the bad and somehow arrive at an accurate picture of who we are. But we are not what we have done nor are we what we have believed. We are Light which has been manifesting in these events and in these beliefs. To continuously rehash old events is to deny the Divinity of the present. All of these ideas we have about ourselves are only so much newsprint. All that matters is whether they are positive or negative. There is not a perfect self-image on the planet so why keep pretending that we have one? All of this worrying about who we are and whether we are a worthwhile person is a meaningless exercise. It's like looking at the sun and arguing with someone else about whether or not it is bright. We know ourselves to be these Beings of Light and yet debate about whether or not it is true. We say with traditional religion that we are made in the image of God who is Light, and then argue that if we are Light, where does all this darkness come from? Why are there wars and greed and suffering? The traditional answer has been that within us is darkness or evil, but the truth is that we have only been manifesting dark, erroneous thoughts about who we are. We need to stop this, now! We need to replace these old ideas with new ones, and transform our lives into expressions of Love and Joy.

By seeking the Kingdom of Heaven within us, we create it on the earth. This old system of fear and its siblings has finally and irrevocably proved itself to be inadequate to the task of creating a life worth living. This antiquated thought and belief structure has shown itself to be full of holes and misunderstandings. And this is good. At the time when we need most to move on we are able to because our Understanding has grown.

The reason we want a joyful Life so badly is because intuitively we know it is possible, not only possible, but probable, not only probable, but the very nature of who we are. We are learning now that all of the things we have done throughout recorded history has been a learning experience. We have done everything wrong in our minds that is humanly possible as well as much that has been beneficial to our growth. We have thought ourselves into being who we are not and have lived within the erroneous concept of fear, anger and vengeance when what we really wanted to experience was Love. We have done this because we didn't know any better. There is no one we can blame for this. It's not anyone's fault that we have not truly understood until now what Life is all about. There is only the wonderful opportunity to change it by changing the way that we think. There is no reason to rally against the forces that have ruined our past, to chastise our leaders or ask for redress for what our people have suffered at the hands of former members of some society. If we all did this, we would be taking Rome to court for all the slavery the Roman Empire instituted against everyone. We could also sue any country in the earth for the damage their wars caused to our country and our world, and thereby insure that we would be in court for the next ten thousand years accomplishing absolutely nothing. We could go all the way back to Cain hitting Abel on the head if we wanted to, but it will not accomplish what we really want. It is time that all be forgiven and left beside the road we are traveling. All of this angry baggage only weighs us down and makes it more difficult for everyone, especially those who carry the bags.

Anger and Love

Anger and hatred are not as strong as Love, they are weaker. They are weaker because they come from a lesser and weaker understanding. They can only exist in a mind that believes itself to be something different than what it is. When we have the Source of Strength within, there is no reason to put anyone else down to make ourselves feel better. Only if we trot out all of our old ways of thinking will we be able to see how erroneous they are. Many areas of the world are releasing their present political structures and unearthing age old animosities that are exploding from the bowels of cultures everywhere. Why is this happening? Because these old animosities have never been understood and released. Like the old fears within our own minds, these racial ideas are surfacing again for our learning. They have always been squelched before by some stronger force. By stringent laws and the threat of nuclear weapons we have tried to bring these ancient broiling hatreds under control. But they can never be controlled, they can only be understood, forgiven and released with healing Love.

The real point here is that we have been convinced that hatreds and wars were just a part of human nature and somehow needed to be controlled. By thinking that these things were part of our nature, we have insured their continued existence. Every Jordanian is raised with a deep hatred of most of its neighbors and thinks nothing of it. There are many in the Western world who still hold prejudices against minority groups. And many of these are well on their way to producing their own backlash hatreds. All of this only degrades the life experience of everyone involved and produces nothing of any real value. As long as we continue to believe that we have this barbarian thread within us, there will be those who attempt to find it, and in the attempt, will be successful. As long as we believe we have evil within us, we will continue to project it in the vain attempt to secure the power and pleasure that it is purported to hold. Face it, we have glorified evil to the point where anyone with any adventurousness at all is dying for the chance to explore its supposed wonders and taste its forbidden fruits. If there were ever an idea that needs to change, this is it. It is at the very core of our belief system and is the reason for all our troubles.

Superstition and Evil

We talked earlier about the Devil and his debut in Western thought, but he was really just the consolidation of all the old superstitions since the first man became frightened on a moonless night. This simple beginning compounded millions of times has created the present fascination with the dark side of life. But what we are actually showing ourselves through the experience of world debauchery and violence is just how powerful our creative energies are. They are creating negatively, but creating nonetheless. The fact that we are learning this, the fact that we are becoming aware that we are Creative Beings is cause for the most opulent celebration. We are emerging from the darkness of our long struggle with Superstition and Fate and are realizing that we are in control of what goes on here. All of the present turmoil and selfishness is not a sign that the world is coming to an end, but is rather a graphic demonstration of our creative abilities. When we have understood this fully we can begin to create a positive experience for ourselves and then the present world system will end. But this ending will not be the disaster so many traditional religions foretell, but rather the quiet emergence of a world built upon a new foundation of Love and Light. Rather than cringe in fear at the inevitable doom, or rail at the present turmoil, we can open up to the joyful opportunities of what we can create by thinking positively and by feeling Love in all situations.

Love is much stronger than any other emotion. All emotions are Love, or some negative perversions of it. Anger and hatred are only Love in disguise, Love with a dark filter covering and hiding most of the Light. At times, this covering seems so dark that we cannot recognize the Love underneath. Some Life force gets through, just enough to create a semblance of feeling, a feeling that for many is the only sense of being alive that they have. What a sad commentary on the human spirit, to have come so far away from our true Essence of Love that we will settle for anger or hatred. But if we can create such mountains of hatred and anger with a filter that only lets a small portion of the Light through, imagine what we can create when the filter is removed. The Light will pour out full strength and create a world like the Universe has never before witnessed. All we have to do is remove these filters and let the Light shine forth. These filters are the thoughts that we have about ourselves and about the world.

When we meditate on this Light and feel its brilliance flow through us, we feel encouraged about the transformation we are experiencing. We feel so wonderful and have such visions of a world full of Peace and Joy. The feeling reminds me of early church meetings I used to attend as a child. I remember the mood of hope and thankfulness when the preacher would talk about how things were going to be different. Christ was going to return and make the world better and, in the world after this, there would be so much Joy and Love as to make the little bit of suffering we endured on this earth unimportant. I remember the vision that rose like a silver cloud above the congregation, each one of us filled with Trust for the future and gratefulness to God for being one of the chosen.

I remember feeling the encouragement and Trust, but also feeling that this would not be for a very long time. So this fragile hope was tinged with the despair of endless waiting for the time of testing to be over. This was also a situation over which we had zero control. We were the pawns in this supernatural game that we were forced to play without our apparent consent. If we were good enough, our heavenly Father would give us an eternal piece of candy. But now we are learning what is actually happening here. The encouragement we feel now is based not on some kind of blind faith or brief glimpse of future bliss, but on the knowledge of how Life Energy works. And we know we do not have to play a waiting game until some grand being comes down to rescue us from our self created mishaps.

We have the key to change this world any way that we want. We have the Source of all Love and Light within us and it will manifest the instant we allow it to do so. Now that's real encouragement! It is more than a vague promise for some future time in some other dimension. It is a reality we can experience right here, this very moment simply by opening our hearts to the energies within.

When I first began to entertain thoughts of writing this book, my mind was filled with doubts and misgivings. In order to make myself begin, I had to get my ego behind it to give me a sort of push to overcome these fears. I also thought how much easier it would be to access these fears directly and decide if they had any validity. By thinking and meditating about this I saw that I was even afraid of leaving the fears behind, as if I had some kind of allegiance to negative energy. And, indeed, that is the definition of a black magician, a person who, like Faust, makes some sort of commitment to negative energy, the proverbial pact with the Devil.

Over long centuries of superstition and fear, we have become accustomed to treating negative energy as if it were a real part of life that can be cajoled into cooperating with our desire. This can be as simple as telling ourselves that we do not care what happens to anyone else as long as we get what we need, or as involved as wholesale racketeering. It's crossing the line to where things matter more than people. There is a confusion of levels here where power, money or fame becomes more important than relationships and Love. The fearful ego forces us to take the darker path. Keeping the self separate from others protects the fragile ego mechanism from having to expand beyond its limited sphere of knowledge, and so retain control.

A Choice Is Presented

I remember coming into my maturity as a man and seeing the choices that this culture had to offer. There was the career choice with all of its strivings and acquisitions or its opposite, the bum strategy with its reliance on working the system. There was the alternative artist thing with its theatrical approach or the university approach which seemed to be merely more of the same useless bits of information for a mind already full of such trivia. So my response to the choices was to choose none of the above, thank you. I could have left town to travel the world with a friend of mine, but there was really no place that seemed to offer anything of value. I would have liked to have a relationship and possibly children and that did seem like a way to plug into a Source of Love. But most of my friends who tried that ended up single parents or embroiled in the endless routines of stressful living. Everything seemed to be lacking in some unnamable, essential something. Life was alright but certainly nothing to write home about and I had not met anyone who felt very differently.

My traditional religious upbringing had presented faith in God as the connection point, but this God was located outside the self in some distant place with no real apparent contact. It seemed too vague, too far away and too surrounded by mythical dogmas and rituals for my taste. There had to be something closer and more immediate than the promises of some omnipotent intervention on our behalf. It was many years before I found something that supplied the kind of connection I had always missed. That was when I began to meditate and discovered the Center within. The Light is real and can be seen and the Love can be felt as it flows.

This was the beginning of perceiving myself as a Child of Light, as a human Being expressing this Light on Earth with Joy and Celebration. It was the end of my self concept as some form of animal boldly clinging to the surface of a spinning ball of mud in a small corner of the Milky Way galaxy. This was the beginning of the new world I had always dreamed was possible and needed so very much to find.

Need

This started me thinking about need. I really needed to find this Source within, but what was this need I felt? I encountered this idea as I was driving home from visiting a friend. It came to me that we only need what we think we need. When we put that in the light of the fact that everything is provided, then it becomes an idea without foundation. Need becomes just another idea on which we choose to focus our attention, and as long as we focus on what we need we will always need something. No matter how much we have there will always be something lacking because the idea of need in our minds produces a constant condition of neediness. Need is an unnecessary mechanism. It's like needing the sun to shine everyday when it already does, but with one very important addition. With the idea of need firmly in place, the sun will never shine brightly enough to satisfy our need for it to do so.

The idea of need is the source of discontent, and our discontent is the source of all of our misery. This is a vicious cycle of amazing depth. The idea of need covers up the truth that we already have everything, everything that we think we need. The concept of need is a major thought form of present human consciousness but a completely unnecessary one. The idea of need is even counterproductive, producing needs where none actually exist. This is one of the major blinders we have and only by removing its negative influence will we ever see the true Light of Abundance. As long as this concept is in place, we will never progress past our present state of experience. Let's see what the idea of need has produced.

It doesn't matter whether it is children starving on the streets of Bombay or young Americans sitting in a hot tub complaining about how they are barely able to make the payments. Everyone is trying to get what they need and so needs become endless. We all have huge lists of needs that must be satisfied before we can be happy, all of which insures that Happiness never arrives. How much easier to let Abundance flow.

I remember thinking in my youth how traditional religion teaches that God will supply all our needs while secular education stresses going after them. No one ever seemed to see any contradiction in these two opposing approaches. But they both focus on needs and so spur us on to create our lists. Needs translate into desires and desire becomes the driving force of our lives, completely ignoring the deeper issues involved. It's like we skate on the surface looking for satisfaction without ever knowing that true satisfaction lies in the depths. It is time we eliminated neediness from our vocabulary and instead understood that everything will be provided to all who focus on growth and expansion of the Light within. But to do this, we must eliminate another old idea.

Emptiness

We are taught that we are empty vessels that need to be filled. Our mouths need to be filled with food, our hearts with Love, our minds with thoughts and our lives with activities. We become these ravenous automatons who consume everything in sight. And indeed, we have been trained to be consumers. All of this striving for fulfillment is based on the idea of emptiness. What if the idea that we are empty is false? What if there is another explanation for the hole we feel within?

I think the feeling of emptiness is caused by our not being aware of the Love and Light within. We have been taught to believe that there is nothing but darkness within, an unspeakable void that will cause eternal death if we are not filled with God's benevolent Grace. Perhaps that is why we are so afraid of it, because it appears to be a void like death. Yet if we would just take a look we would see that this apparent hole is already filled with Light. Like a black hole, it might appear to be surrounded by impenetrable darkness, but that is only because we have been trained to surround it with exactly those qualities. A single look is all that is necessary to dispel this false notion. A single glance within with openness and Trust can reverse years of fearful conditioning because it shows us the true nature of our inner selves.

So the emptiness we feel within is only our fear that we are empty, a fear which keeps us from looking and seeing the Light and which keeps us living in fear and dread of the omnipresent darkness. What is interesting is how this idea feeds upon itself. We believe we are empty which creates the appearance of emptiness. This erroneous belief blocks our own vision of the truth and then we get afraid because we cannot see the Light we need to sustain us. But the Light is always there, we have just trained ourselves not to see it. We can easily retrain ourselves to stay immersed in the Light at all times. We only have to practice our meditations. Remaining in the Light fills us with Love and Joy and we no longer feel empty, and the absurdity of all of this old, foolish thinking is clearly revealed.

Thereafter we are no longer driven to consume everything we can get our hands on nor do we utilize all of our energies in the vain attempt to satisfy our deepest cravings. To satisfy our desire for Love and Light it is only necessary to go within to the Source of these Energies and there find them in Abundance. This Center that is filled with all that we will ever need is a far cry from the emptiness we have been taught that we are. It is time that we realize the truth about ourselves and become these beings of effervescent Light and Love. To see ourselves as fountains of energy, to see ourselves connected to every other Life form on the planet and in our universe, is to see ourselves as we truly are. Rather than fragile personalities that we become so easily bored with, we realize that we are magnificent beings engaged in constant growth and expansion. We not only realize it, we see, feel and become these incredible beings, and all of our past frustrations, futile strivings and mutilated self images become like wispy memories of places we have passed through on our way to the truth. We become, as many scriptures tell us, new beings 'reborn in the Spirit.' And it all begins when we see ourselves not as empty vessels needing to be filled, but as vessels full to overflowing with marvelous things to share. One simple change of focus to the Center unlocks all the secrets of this inner Transformation. We release the idea of emptiness and need and replace them with Acceptance, acceptance of the Abundance of Universal Light.

Abundance

When we accept Abundance, we open the gates that have kept it from us for all of these hundreds of thousands of years. We have always accepted scarcity and thus we have always experienced it. We can just as easily accept Abundance so why don't we see how well it works? We have nothing but scarcity to lose as well as all of the problems associated with it. We only have to think Abundance and it will be so. We only need to imagine the joys of an Abundant Life and it will be ours. We can take the deepest aspirations within us and envision ourselves in that situation, act as if we are already enjoying these experiences and they will begin to manifest as surely as the new day. Since what we all really want is a Life full of Love and Joyfulness, these aspirations will be for the good of all concerned. Every one of us who experiences Joy increases the joyfulness of the entire human family.

So I looked at my own growth in this new light of Understanding, at my various projects like producing this book and getting it finished and published, and I realized how much easier it would have been if I had just allowed the process of Transformation to happen instead of spending all of this time trying to figure it out mentally. But for my particular makeup it was very important to understand these concepts in the mind and how they interact before I would be able to let the mind go and just allow the Love and Light within to expand. All of these older ideas were so firmly in the way of any new approach to living that they needed to be understood and released before anything else could happen. This has been a worthwhile exercise and I am grateful for the opportunity to learn and share it.

All of these older ideas were scattered throughout the mental realms. None of them were connected to the Center. Every time we think about fear we are thinking about something outside of ourselves. Every worry, every need, every desire is connected to the external world. So we are spending all of our energy projecting these negative concerns into three dimensional reality. Added to that are the remarkable conflicting thoughts within about who we are and what we want to do in this lifetime. We can release all of these old ideas and allow the idea of Acceptance to fill the void left by their departure. Just notice how this simplifies the mind. All of the fears and negative self concepts can be replaced with one simple Truth and so eliminate the incredible confusion these thoughts have produced in our minds. Simple and secure like the warmth of the sun on our face and the feeling of Love in our hearts.

Chapter 16
The World We Live In

The Secret of Life

I was working with my grandson the other night to help him deal with the weaning process. I found by observing and feeling that this was a very painful experience for him. There was much discomfort in the areas that had been connected to his mother and which were losing that connection. So I began to encourage him to connect to his Inner Source and he almost got it. He would lie down and relax and begin to let it flow, but then raise up again and be distraught over not having his mother's presence. As we kept working through the layers of his fear and discomfort, he became more and more easy with himself and went deeper within, finally arriving at the Center of Love. He obviously felt he was losing his Source of Love and was having trouble understanding that he had the real Source within him. I was trying to help him connect just as I am helping myself to connect. We had just arrived at the point where he was experiencing the inner flow of Love and I was telling him that, "Love flows from this Center and manifests as Love in many other forms", when his mother arrived. I immediately added, "and here is one now." He didn't seem to have trouble after that and is now weaned and going to sleep by himself. What an amazing experience for a small child to have. And I was thinking how interesting it is that so many of us lose this connection at this tender age but, like Little Bo Peep, don't know where to find it.

This is an amazing misunderstanding of life, the idea that we are now these isolated individuals facing the vagaries of fate all alone. We become lost souls looking for our home with no one to depend on but ourselves. Talk about alienated! Those of us who are strong can do this, for a while at least. By sheer force of will be can become successful and build some kind of secure life. But there are many of us who lack this strength and cower in the shadows of the world, and who desperately seek some kind of connection with anyone because they feel so totally lost and alone. We can help this situation by helping them to connect to the Source of Love within. We can all learn to allow the Light within to manifest its soothing illumination throughout even the darkest parts of our present confusion. The more we focus on this process of becoming Love and Light, the more we will become so, until only Light exists and everything else disappears. These other problems only exist because we have been focusing on them every moment since we were small children. We learned the misguided lessons of the present Age on our parent's knee and now have the chance to learn the magnificent lessons of the dawning New Age.

I was thinking about the time I first began meeting with others to discuss spiritual matters. Those early meetings were more like lectures. I suppose I was trying to impress others with my wisdom as well as wanting to help them grow. I also sense that I felt by being wise I would make them like me. These seems to be a normal phase when we begin to approach the Spiritual Path. Many in our acquaintance expect to achieve ultimate wisdom almost immediately. Indeed, some of them would show up the second session with the Truths of the Ages firmly in their grasp. It is probably a generalization to say all fall prey to this, but many in my experience have. Perhaps it is that so many are so tired of this present life in the Castle of Gloom that they are anxious to be out of it. Plus, our usual desire for instant gratification kicks in as well. While it does make me feel very useful to help encourage this Transformation in others, there is really another level to this process.

Once we begin to experience the Joy of seeing the Light, our own reasons for wanting and needing to see it start to fade. We become assured that we have found the Inner Peace we have been seeking and begin to relax the part of us which has driven us for so long. The very urgent desire to discover something of real value gets replaced by the quiet realization that we have done so. As I began to witness the growth of others in our group, I let go of the need to be considered wise. What was my self centered need for respect compared to the joy of participating in their growth? It was only a manifestation of my need to be loved anyway. By changing my focus from achieving love and respect for myself to simply loving, I not only secured the love I wanted, I also found immense joy and satisfaction in helping them to grow. This movement away from self centeredness produces much more of what we really want and is another key to real change.

World Wide Change

This is the perfect time for world wide transformation to happen. We have marvelous systems of distribution that can move information to all parts of the world in a very short time. It is these very thoughts that need to be communicated and discussed. We have uncannily set up the very systems that are enabling us to spread the word about Inner Evolution. It's like we have established wonderful news and media networks and now we finally have something truly valuable to communicate. I remember Thoreau mentioning that there was a lot of excitement about a telegraph line being established between Maine and Massachusetts, but he wondered whether Maine and Massachusetts had anything to say to each another. The present media focuses most of its attention on negative world events and as such only serves to make them manifest even more. But it has at least produced the necessary hardware networks to transmit the new messages and for that we can be grateful. There may not have been much communication of any real, positive importance in the past, but that should soon change. What excites and amazes me is how the present world system has worked itself into the perfect position for this change. And the first thing we can change is our basis of fear.

Fear and Transformation

I was thinking about my own process of understanding and releasing these fears. Realizing that our desires are only a mechanism to allay fear, we begin to release them and allow Trust to fill the areas they once occupied. Looking back, I wonder how I ever dredged up the energy to go after desires when all of my doubts and fears were constantly dragging me back. It is so much easier this way and so much more successful, that to continue to go after desires is absurd. I realized that this was taking the idea of fear closer to its final resolution.

I began by remembering that when I started this transformation, I was even afraid of it. I was worried about everything so, of course, I was also concerned about my spiritual worth. How long would it take, how painful would it be and, especially, would I actually be able to do it? The answer is yes and no. 'Yes,' because all of us can make this Transformation because it is built into the system. All of us can think, we can all feel Love, we can expand and become aware of the Kingdom of Spirit. The intuition is one of our senses like any of the other five. The only prerequisite is that we allow it to develop. We do not doubt our ability to feel and see, so why would we doubt our intuitive sense? Then there's the 'no' part of it. We can block out intuition by doubting it and by worrying and thinking we might not be able to make the grade. This is our fear that we were raised to exhibit. It is a protective device designed to shield us from what we don't know so we will not be hurt. But in this case, it protects us from the very thing that will set us free.

So fear it is not really any protection at all. It is not selective but more like a force field. To older thinking it is supposedly desirable because it keeps out trouble, but trouble is only a manifestation of fear, and so fear and trouble go round and round in their endless game. Fear is actually harmful because it keeps out love. Many of us have developed huge defenses that successfully do just that, but now that we know there is nothing to fear, we can begin to lower our shields and experience Joy and Love again. So I began to see fear as merely a mechanism that I once used in my pursuit of security. It is really a simple thing. It contains a lot of emotional power, but the mechanism itself is quite childish and extremely dumb. It has very little discernment. It keeps out everything regardless of what it is. When we let someone else close to us, it is usually only after a considerable period of testing to see if they can really be trusted. Not exactly the best way to start a relationship, but perhaps the best that fearful humans can do. What really brought this understanding home was the fact that fear kept showing up regardless of how successful I was or how secure I felt. In other words, fear was not related to anything that was happening in my life, it was only a habitual response to all situations. As such, it must have been fulfilling some conditioned need.

So here was need again. For some reason, fear was among the things I thought I needed. It was obviously something that was conditioned into me, but it was now really getting in the way of everything I tried to do. It was like a third leg I carried around just in case I might need it, totally superfluous and cumbersome. So I decided to figure it out so I could let it go. As this began to happen, I saw many of my desires start to release. All the desires for protection and safety, the desire to stay separate from others in order to safeguard my weak self image, the desire for fame and power and, surprisingly enough, among them was the desire to know.

Knowledge and Intuition

Desire for knowledge makes us think and study, read and learn in order to figure things out. It makes us scrunch our foreheads in the attempt to know things before they happen, usually because we wish to reduce our fear of the future. If we were not so afraid of the future, then we would not be so intent on knowing it in advance. If we could release our fear of survival, then we would not be so consumed with controlling nature. Then we might be able to open up and Trust a little more than we do now. Once we do allow this future fear to subside, our intuition shows us exactly what we need to know about everything, including the future if we wish to look in that direction. Usually though, once our intuition opens we lose interest in the future because the present moment is where all the action is anyway. If the present moment is wonderful, then the future can only be even more so because the present is the foundation of what we call future time. It continually amazed me that humans can experience misery and all manner of negativity today and yet think that, somehow, tomorrow will be better. You would think that we would intuitively perceive the link between the two. Once we begin to develop our intuition, this is precisely what happens. This intuitive sense is the communication link between us and the rest of creation.

With our physical eyes we can see the trees and animals and touch them, but with our intuition we can share their essence. The intuition opens up an entire new world composed of all the various energies of which our physical, emotional and mental experiences are only three. With our physical eyes we can see the beauty of this world, but with our intuitive eyes we can see the absolute perfection of everything, from the smallest corner to the entirety of the Universe itself. Intuition gives us access to the Wisdom of the ages and plugs us into the Source of Love and Light so that we are never, ever lonely or confused again. This may take some getting used to and, in fact, the process of Transformation is the method by which we get used to living with intuitive perceptions. We get used to living without fear and doubt, and without the painful self images we have been carrying around with us like proud tumors. It is a dual process of replacing outworn ideas about Life with more accurate ones and of opening to the wonders of intuitive perception. To begin, we only need to know who we are, where we are, and what we are supposed to be doing while we're here.

The Eternal Questions

Who we are is easy, we are the Children of Light, we are Light expressing itself in human form. Meditating on the simplicity of this self concept helps to open up the remarkable aspects of this Light. Light is positive, it is joyful, it is the Source of warmth and sustenance for all Life forms on the planet. Why should we be any different? Earlier concepts liked to insist that we were somehow different, special and superior to all other forms of Life. Yet this was merely an arrogant misunderstanding that has allowed us to misuse the rest of creation for our own selfish benefits. By seeing ourselves as part of this global expression of Light, we come into our true heritage, a legacy enhanced by cooperation rather than competition with all other Life forms. By knowing ourselves to be dynamically interconnected with all Life, we rid ourselves of the plagues of isolation and loneliness and, by becoming One with all Life, we immerse ourselves in the joyful flow of everlasting Bliss.

Where we are is equally simple, we are manifesting this Light on the Earth, a dimension which nurtures us and allows us the opportunity to express our Light as three dimensional interactive holograms. Only by expressing Light in this form can we truly learn about the aspect of Light we call Love. If a picture is worth a thousand words, then a three dimensional expression is worth a thousand pictures, and our fascination with moving pictures is testament to this Truth. The current debate over whether or not movies have affected world culture is a recognition of the strength of these imitation three dimensional manifestations. Our next step is to view our own lives as extensions of this principle, to see our experiences as projections of our inner scripts which play out the ideas and feelings we have within us, and so help us to understand what is going on inside. Every moment in our lives is the process of our Inner Essence expressing itself so that we can become consciously aware of It. By Understanding who we are, we can align ourselves with these Energies, becoming more positive and expressing more of the Love and Light that brings us Fulfillment and Joy.

That leaves the question of what we are doing, the old cry of 'Why are we here?' That, too, is a simple answer but one with profound ramifications. We are here to learn and to grow, and to help each other learn and grow. Along the way we get to share Love and Joy because that is what we are learning. We also get to experience this beautiful world of three dimensional forms and we get to expand into the new dimensions of Spirit. We are now becoming conscious of what is really happening here and are beginning to allow our old errant beliefs and negative emotions to make way for positive ones. We are becoming in tune with our true essence of Love and Light. This is what we are learning and is the foundation of our new and exciting growth as Humans.

Chapter 17

Beyond Belief

Shame

I was meditating about the idea of shame one morning and my attention was lured to an event that occurred when I was 7 years old. We were playing in the dump at the end of our street when a strange man cornered me and made me take off my clothes. I then had to stand naked in front of all my friends until he climbed up the hill and out of sight. I remember the shame I felt because all my friends were trying so hard not to look as I stood exposed for all the world to see. Because of this simple event, the idea of shame has been very important to me in many situations. This experience added extra clout to the times when my mother and teachers would tell me I should be ashamed for doing whatever they felt was in error. As a result, I remembered always trying to be absolutely perfect so that no one would ever again be ashamed of me. Of course, I had many failures in this attempt and so suffered much guilt and self recrimination. Shame is only a mechanism the old method used to try to enforce good behavior and as such is easy to understand and forgive. They were probably not aware of the life long pain such a seemingly innocent idea can cause to sensitive beings like us.

Guilt or shame is feeling bad about something that we did, or failed to do, in the past, or even in a past life. The idea that being guilty makes sense is absurd. All guilt does is make the whole situation intolerable. We stick ourselves in the position of feeling bad about something we can do nothing about. It doesn't improve the situation, it doesn't make us better people, it doesn't do anything except make us hurt. It is a belief that has no decent purpose and needs to be swept from our minds like an old cobweb. Besides, if we are busy punishing ourselves for things that happened in the past then nothing can happen now because our energies are tied up in useless and unproductive thinking. It is absurd and we need to understand it as such, then release it. We no longer need guilt to enforce appropriate behavior patterns either. Our behavior flows from our deepest Understanding of Life and it is there that changes need to be encouraged. All guilt does is squelch the deed before it manifests physically, but it does nothing about the idea behind it. This results in us having all kinds of unfulfilled ideas and desires in our minds, things that we would have done if we hadn't been so guilty, and creates other delightful things as well.

Those of us who rebel against the inner guilt will do the forbidden things just to prove that we are not subject to the laws and rules we have been force fed. We have a lot of that going on now. Action by rebellion is a logical outcome of using devices like guilt and fear of punishment to control behavior. We know this already and we tell our children that they are going to rebel. Thus we encourage them to do so and then complain when they do. "Well, I didn't want them to rebel that much," we say. They are only doing what they have been programmed to do, what we were programmed to do. We need to change the programming, and the first step is to go to the Center for help and guidance. We need to release our reliance on faulty psychological control devices and realize that everyone has a Center full of Love and Light. From this Center only Perfection can flow, perfect Light, perfect Love and perfect manifestations of Creative Intelligence. Guilt, fear and self recrimination are some of the boulders we need to remove from the stream so that Life Energy can flow unhampered.

If shame keeps us focused in the past so that nothing can happen in the present, planning for the future has a similar effect. Nothing can happen when we are mentally thinking about either the past or the future. We only live in the now moment and it is amazing how few of us actually live here! We spend most of our lives thinking about things that are long gone or yet to be, in other words, things that do not exist. No wonder television is so popular, it doesn't exist either so fits in perfectly with our general illusory experience. If we are so worried about our future or the state of the world, why don't we stop worrying and do something? As long as we focus on these things in the mind, nothing will happen and nothing will change. It is up to each of us to refocus our energies where they will do the most good, in the present moment, actively Centered, here and now.

I would like to repeat one trap here, and that is feeling bad because we didn't figure all of this out before. Self re-crimination for any reason is negative enough, but to feel bad about ourselves because we used to feel bad about ourselves is the height of absurdity, yet is perfectly logical to the ego mind. What is interesting is what happened when I began to release this old guilt and shame.

By using the tools of forgiveness and knowing that my parents and teachers were doing the best that they knew how, I was able to loosen these old emotional memories and allow them to be replaced with Love. But as the shame released, so did my pride. I saw that my pride was really the other side of shame, an overreaction to it, and both of them had only caused me to keep myself away from others and thus isolated and alone. I suppose it seemed better at the time to be alone than be constantly in fear of being humiliated, but what an odd drama to have going on within me for so many years.

As I continued to release and forgive I had the opportunity to relive many old experiences where I shied away from friends or potential lovers because of fear. The idea of humiliation was often stronger than the desire for friendship or love. Then would come the hours of sadness at having run away from interaction with others because they might not like me. I often wondered why I did not ask them if they would be my friend rather than assume the worst. I would get angry at myself and then pride would kick in and I would try to become something that others would admire and thereby gain the love I could not allow myself to accept freely. I began to see the enormity of these insane behavior patterns I had established because of these twin ideas of shame and pride, both of them destructive, both of them painful, and both of them lacking in any true Understanding of the real inner me. I could now see how much of so many of our lives are spent trying to satisfy the incessant demands of these erroneous ideas.

When we realize the insane and destructive nature of these two beliefs, we are ready to release them. As they are such a large part of the self image, this seems like the logical place to start. Instead of trying so hard to make others proud of us, instead of trying to behave perfectly, we go within to find the part of us that is always perfect. There is no reason to be proud or ashamed of the fact that we are Light. It is simply what we are. So we move past these old beliefs to a place where they are no longer issues. We understand that as long as we allow these conflicting ideas to occupy our minds, we will never be satisfied. As long as we focus on pride we will always be trying to do things that will make us proud, yet our sense of shame will shoot us down every time. We will never be able to satisfy these drives, so it is much easier just to let them go, and replace then with a Higher Understanding.

The true test of a Higher Understanding, as with any theory, is whether or not it addresses all the same issues of the earlier theory while being both more accurate and taking it further. This old understanding was based on the desire to control behavior. Because it was believed that humans were basically evil, we all agreed that mechanisms like fear and punishment were necessary in order to insure positive behavior. We didn't particularly like them and even called them necessary evils, but if you know someone is going to hurt you if he gets a chance, then you do everything you can think of to prevent him. So we used direct punishment and its ally, the fear of punishment, to help guard against the inevitable aberrant behavior. But using these ideas to combat negative behaviors has only succeeded in making them worse. And we are presently dealing with the ineffectiveness of this approach, as one look at our prison and judicial systems will reveal.

Later it was discovered that guilt and shame could do even more because they could stop the behaviors from even happening. In fact, some kinds of guilt do so well that we feel guilty about even thinking about misbehaving. But now that we know that we are Light, there is no longer any reason to behave in anti-social ways. It doesn't get us what we truly want anyway. There is nothing to be ashamed of so we have nothing to prove. There is no reason to try so hard to do and become things that will make us proud. So we can joyfully release this entire mechanism and replace it with a simple truth, that we are Light and that this Light manifests in Absolute Perfection. That's a whole lot easier and I, for one, feel relieved to be off that particular stage.

This allows us to be who we are. So far in our history we have been worrying about who we are more than anything else. We have identified ourselves with particular groups that held certain beliefs and it was important for us to stand for something. Often, the things we chose to be were so far from the truth as to be unrecognizable as human. The current rage to be totally different from everyone else comes to mind with all of its bizarre styles and 'life as art.' The desire for notoriety is a poor substitute for self love as well as a very sad and destructive one. We have been trying to please someone, a heavenly father, our parents or our egos instead of just Being who we are. We can end all of this play acting now and watch ourselves expand within the Light.

As I was meditating on this I felt a wonderful sense of well being flow through me. These old beliefs and all of their painful memories of guilt and shame faded away. The sharp pains in my thighs began to release and I recognized that I had been holding my legs tight ever since those early experiences because I had been angry but unable to express it. After all, I had been taught that I should be ashamed and so I had to accept these events as a true reflection of me. I didn't have to like it, but I had to accept it. And so I was angry until I realized what all of this was trying desperately to teach me.

Experience and Learning

It was designed to teach me that my three dimensional experiences were an emanation of me. Everything that I had ever experienced was a perfect reflection of my deepest thinking, how I truly felt about myself and the world. There were times when this was not a very pretty picture I was creating, and there were times when it was inspiring. But coming to the realization that they had all been me has allowed me to assume conscious control. I have begun the process of rearranging my thoughts and feelings into positive, constructive ones. Without all of the pain and confusion, without all of the shame and unnerving pride I might never have looked within and thus would have never seen the Light.

The opposite of Light is darkness. All of my former drives, my motivations and self-images had been full of darkness in its various disguises. Anger, fear, guilt, shame, arrogance, envy and sad loneliness, these dark energies could only produce dark and unhappy results. There are many now on this earth who are trying to manifest these qualities in an attempt to make negativity and despair an acceptable lifestyle. Existentialism teaches that there is no point to existence, anyway, so why not just do whatever we feel like at any given moment? I suppose this would be fine if doing so would make us happy, but it doesn't. Spontaneity without Understanding is not true spontaneity, but rather only an endless repetition of old habits. Our strong cultural heroes have changed from the tough but clever Bogart to the merely ruthless and vicious stars of modern action dramas. 'Might for right' was the cry of King Arthur and was an attempt to replace the earlier and more ruthless 'might makes right.' This legacy now reaches its logical absurdity in violence for its own sake, violence and debauchery as an art form. This is only showing us the true state of these old beliefs. This thinking is manifesting in all kinds of spontaneous act of senseless violence as those without Center try to find themselves in this latest craze. If we recognize the destructiveness of these acts, then it is time to go within and eliminate the central ideas and feelings that have made them possible. If the belief in violence can result in such atrocities, then it is time to release it from our minds and replace it with something we would truly like to experience. Love, for instance, or Joy. And as we replace these outworn and negative ideas, the new ideas will become the collective thoughts which will manifest both in our lives and our art. This is a much more positive set of ideas to live by. Let's allow them to become the next craze by making them the central concepts of our thinking.

This is a major milestone on the Spiritual Path. When we understand that we are Light, then we are on our way along the Path of Enlightenment. It is called enlightenment because it involves Light in all of its forms. Our thoughts become filled with Light, our burden is lightened, our moods become lighter and Light begins to shine from us as from a beacon. All of these common metaphors about Light relate to the process of enlightenment, a process which has been known and undertaken for thousands of years by the spiritually minded. We are all about to become spiritually minded, our minds filled with thoughts of Spirit, with thoughts of Light. This is in sharp contrast to the more common mind today which is filled with fear, doubt and confusion, all of which cover the Light.

We must trust that this new method of Being will produce the life that we really want. There is no way a mind full of doubt can 'know' in advance what it is like to live with Trust. There are a few chronicles like this one and testimonials from various others, but only personal experience will convince anyone that the Light exists within. But when we think about it, the current method doesn't offer any promises either. Sure, everyone 'believes' that contentment is possible and advertisements claim happiness and joy in many vacation spots around the world. Yet the ads generally suggest that you go somewhere and then 'let yourself go,' which is what we have been talking about all along. We only really enjoy ourselves if we let go of our tight control. This is exactly what Trust is, only we do not have to pay thousands of dollars to rent a particular environment in order to feel safe enough to experience it. We can let go here, now and feel the Flow.

Energy and Flow

I was thinking about sexuality. Actually I woke up in the middle of the night with a message, the message that sexuality was one of the most amazing flows of energy that we can experience. This is hardly ground breaking news, but perhaps a deeper understanding of sex would be. If we can imagine the flow of Love and Light from the Center in its strongest form, it will resemble the moment of blissful orgasm, except that it will be constant instead of fleeting. Then I realized how many ways modern humans try to simulate and stimulate this flow. There are, of course, those who specialize in sexual orgies, but there is also danger, violence, drugs and alcohol, competitive sports and movies, fast cars and many, many other substitutes. That is how much we need to feel this flow, a need that is now easily satisfied by going to the Source and plugging in directly. So when we look at the supposed huge problems we have in the world with aberrations of all kinds, we can see that all are merely trying to produce life circumstances where they will be able to feel the flow of Life Energy. There are many paths and yet they all are attempts to arrive at the same place.

We are all doing the very best that we know how. If we truly want to help, then our job is to help educate ourselves to the new methods for discovering the Joy and Love within instead of vainly trying to produce it in outer circumstances. All of these frustrated ones know full well the lack of real happiness they are experiencing and would welcome a way which both promises and delivers. They might be resistant at first, as most of us are when presented with change, but in time all will travel with us on the Spiritual Path, especially when they see the Joyful lives we are experiencing there. In the face of living proof, all resistance fades away and the gap between what is being experienced and what can be will narrow. Everyone will at some time realize that there is now no other real choice but to become Beings of Light. This is the natural process of evolution which is evident in any aspect of living.

Let's take Western medicine as an example and attempt to construct a short history of its development towards the

Light. In the beginning there was nothing we could do about anything. Sickness was a dark mystery and would spur us to look for cures. Early potions and herbs were discovered and dispensed by the shamans and witch doctors. Along with this, there evolved the idea of powers who were responsible for the illnesses and who could be influenced to cure. This created a kind of hybrid system where both Divine and natural sources of healing were utilized, a combination of voodoo, sacrifice and prayer along with herbs and early medicines. This went on for thousands of years until modern medicine emerged with its focus solely on chemical and surgical manipulation. Psychology then added the role of the mind in healing. Through the use of placebos and investigations in psychosomatic illnesses, we began to understand that the body is actually subject to the mind's desires and beliefs. Illnesses can be viewed as the fulfillment of early conditioning, the result of learned responses to life and health. These understandings have spawned many new health techniques as well as the re-emergence of many ancient ones like acupuncture, reiki and massage. Today we have a multitude of ways to approach good health including the use of relaxation and meditation techniques that put us in touch with our own internal Source of Health.

We can see in this brief history a direction that has lead ever closer to the Center. We started by seeking help outside in plants or some supernatural being, then began working on the surface of our bodies, then inside our bodies, then within our minds and finally in the Center itself. We are now at the point of ultimate arrival. We are in the process of learning to cure ourselves of all of our ills, and in so doing will teach ourselves how to utilize the Spiritual Energies that we are discovering along the way.

In a recent health experience, I tried to use these ideas to understand what I was experiencing. I had been very sick with an apparent flu and saw it as a kind of purging of negative energies somewhere within me. It is interesting that the name influenza is from the word influence and was coined because of the belief that illness was caused by the influence of the stars, and the collective consciousness. We are all sick of something and these dis-eases manifest. In my case, I saw this illness as a way to cleanse my mind of some very deep negative beliefs like fear of death and despair. I thought that in allowing them to manifest through this illness, I could rid them from my system. Since part of my problem was an angry inability to love, the illness condensed into coughing and massive congestion behind the heart. I was both gasping for Life and crying for Love. The other area of dis-ease was expression of self, especially as a Divine Being. Since we express from the throat chakra, I experienced a very sore throat and loss of voice. Even in illness, my soul was communicating to me the lessons I needed to learn most.

I have since learned that I do not have to experience severe illness in order to release negative thoughts. Rather, I only need to affirm the positive aspects of myself and let these stronger energies chase the negative ones from my system. In my focused attempts to rid myself of negatives, I was only acknowledging their existence and thus making them stronger. It was this realization that began the cure. I began to affirm the positive, healing aspects of Love within me and my physical form began to respond and heal. Only when I released all doubt about my Divinity and accepted the perfect health within, was I able to feel secure and confident in this world. During this process of healing, I did finally see the deep resentments and frustrations that were the true causes of my discomfort, but by then they were only of passing interest, their former importance usurped by the glorious Essence of Inner Light.

Sexuality

I was thinking about what the lesson might be for sexual guilt. Since sexuality is a very powerful aspect of us, I am sure that it is part of our lesson in self acceptance. The present system stresses that we should discover what is wrong with us and devise the appropriate direction to cure it. So we do not, for instance, talk about sexual acceptance, we talk about ways to overcome sexual guilt, repression and deviance. It's as if the possibility of us totally understanding and accepting this aspect of ourselves is out of the question. We believe that to be human is to be maladjusted. The current rendition of this is that all of us are from dysfunctional families and a lot of that dysfunction is in the sexual realms. So here we are again, focusing all of our attentions on the negative, on the problems. And this propensity is easily explained.

In trying to understand sexuality, we are so used to focusing on the negative that this is what we usually do. Since being positive and adjusted never seems to be the case, we assume that there is something wrong with us and desperately try to find a cure. We look everywhere we can think of, but since we are so used to thinking negatively, we usually assume the worst. If we are not sexually satisfied, then we change partners or try for more frequency. We use drugs to increase the intensity or perversions to add an additional element of forbidden thrill. And all of this looking is in the negative direction. If we would look towards the inner us who is experiencing our sexuality we might find a different way to approach our rather rampant dissatisfaction.

When we go within, we get closer to the Center of things. It's like getting close to the boss to find out what is really going on in the workplace. The feeling that we really want, the satisfaction that we crave is found by opening to the deeper levels of us. We might settle for having sex more often and in different ways, but what we really want is to feel Love more deeply. The moments of orgasm are so wonderful that we want more, as indeed, we should.

There has been a lot of doubt about the benefits of sex in Western culture, but that is only because we have focused on the surface attributes of it. We see the illegitimate children the broken homes, the disease and apparent moral degeneration and want to blame something for it. Since sex is involved, we simplistically name it as the cause of the trouble. But the sexual act only puts us in touch with feelings that we are capable of having. In fact, the orgasm has historically been the closest feeling we have had to the feeling of Oneness with all Life. We call this feeling intimacy, and it is this spiritual connection, when we allow it to happen, that is the rush. We are able, even if only for those few moments, to feel connected to something strong enough to override our normal confusion and pain. It thus provides both incredible pleasure and welcome relief from our everyday stresses. But as we go deeper within, we begin to see that we can connect to the Source in many other ways as well. The musician connects with the Muse, the artist with creativity and the dancer or athlete through the exhilaration of physical performance. In meditation, we connect directly and thus more surely, and when we do all aspects of our life deepen. We begin to feel more connected to every aspect of us, including our sexuality. Thus we experience a perceivable gain in our life quality. So sexuality and its omnipresent guilt has really been a blessing in disguise because it has driven us to open up to deeper feelings and made us quest to find their true Source within. Or we might say that the intense pleasure of sexual ecstasy has kept hope alive for deeper feelings, and deeper meanings to Life during the dark ages of learning through competition and selfishness. Either way, like all other aspects of modern living, it has played its part in the evolution of our Conscious Understanding of Life.

Tension and Release

I was playing some music tonight and paying attention to the range of emotions which traveled all the way from peaceful and serene to hard driving. There seems to be a part of us that likes both the calm and the intense, the cool summer walks and the heated contests, the soft touch of a evening breeze and the intense sexual embrace. From my theatre training I recognize the existence of this tension and release, a reenactment of sexuality or day following night. We structure our lives along these lines because we perceive that this is how the larger world is structured. So we have activities because we're antsy, relationships because we're lonely and thoughts because we need to figure things out. Everything seems driven by need. As discussed before, we see ourselves as empty vessels that need to be filled, but I think the whole idea is misplaced.

Just because we are hungry for food doesn't mean we have to be hungry for companionship, knowledge or wealth.

We could just as easily manifest companionship because we are naturally loving beings, knowledge because we are curious and wealth because we plug into our natural Abundance. All of these apparent hungers can only be based on the belief that we might not get what we need if we don't go after them.

I think that we view life this way because we still believe life is hard and we are thankful for the releases, the Sundays, vacations, birthdays and other moments of relaxation from the grind. It may very well be that our sexual experience appears as tension and release only because our minds habitually respond that way to all facets of living. Like any other part of life, sexuality responds to our mental programming. As we expand into the soft and peaceful realms of spirit, our experience in all aspects of living will automatically soften and become peaceful. So the present releases we crave only appear to be necessary because we are so conditioned to experiencing tension. Without tension there would be no need for release and our lives might enjoy yet another expansion, an expansion into continual peacefulness. However much we might enjoy the ride as the pendulum swings from low to high, the high to low part is always uncomfortable. And anyway, it is always so much more enjoyable in the Center. After forty years of such extremes in my life, the peacefulness reminds me of the calm that settles in when a group of teenage boys finally go outside to play. And, indeed, the beliefs of the present system are quite adolescent, full of exuberance and passion, but completely lacking in depth.

Each area of life has its own habitual way of operating and while the hunger/satisfaction explains eating fairly well, it does not apply to relationships. Relationships have their own set of interactions that cannot be explained without other qualities like companionship, sharing and Love. Our desire for knowledge also needs additional qualities like curiosity and discernment, while spiritual learning requires other more expansive qualities like openness and Trust. It is Trust which can satisfy all of our desires while yet being unconcerned with their outcome. We are, in effect, satisfying all of our desires by looking past them to the Source of Abundance.

As I looked within myself and asked to release the hunger and know that all is well, I found myself thinking that I am satisfied with who I am. For the first time in forty-five years, I like the activities in my life and the people with whom I associate. I appreciate my Understanding and enjoy sharing love with others. But most of all, I like myself. I have become a person that I would like to know, and I would like to know more about this person that is me. There is no longer any reason for me to strive to become someone different from who I am. It is vitally important for us to learn to Love ourselves. We must appreciate who we are and who we are becoming instead of wishing and trying to be someone else. We can help ourselves immensely by allowing our inner qualities of Love and sharing to manifest in our lives. These will then start to replace some of the other concepts we have built our lives upon. Qualities like bravery and will power, cleverness and tenacity can be released and replaced with a calm acceptance of all that we are. We are all wonderful expressions of Light with endless and remarkable possibilities. This is a given, a verified fact. By realizing this Truth about ourselves, we open the door to becoming so.

What a blessing this is at this moment to understand the ancient Truth that we are made in the image of God. When we correctly interpret this to mean that we are full of the same qualities as Divinity, however we might conceive it, then we see that we are made of the same Light and express the same Love. This Truth is reappearing when the world needs it most. When all seems lost and hopeless, the new way appears, as has been foretold for countless centuries, and it is simple and easy with immediate and positive results.

It is a new Understanding of what it means to be a Human Being. Everything else that is happening on the earth at the moment is of minor consequence when compared to this. Only when we become Centered and Serene Beings will the world become what we all wish it to become. Everything that we like about the earth will continue. All that is good and beautiful will remain and even become more so. All the kindness and Love will only increase along with our knowledge and wisdom. And everything that we do not like about the earth now will change. It will soon become apparent to all that the anger, frustration and hatred are not reliable ways to get what we want and they will be abandoned along with all the rest of the tried and tired methods we have fruitlessly employed. We are only just beginning to understand the first things about Love. Perhaps we should give it a real chance before we dismiss it as some pipe dream of the New Age. We only resist Love as a method of change because of our unfamiliarity with it. It's like offering a caveman a powerful computer or a new stone ax. He would take the ax every time because within his belief system it has more value. To most humans at this time, power appears to have more value than Love, but that is only because we have not really experienced Love, not yet. We crave it, but we have no idea what it is. It is time we admitted our lack of Understanding and allowed ourselves to expand into this new and exciting dimension.

In my life, I was amazed at the Joy I experienced when I was finally able to open up and feel Love flow. Those first few moments were more meaningful than all of my anger and drive engendered successes of the past. In just a few moments I had felt more wonderful healing emotion than I thought possible in a lifetime. All of this was brought on by the simple decision to become joyous. And it was only the beginning.

Love

I began to think about other things like how we understand Love. We see it as what saves us, a protective device that we acquire to help us along our way. We even say, "With you beside me, I can do anything." You can almost see Kirk Douglas and Lana Turner gazing at the city below them and making their pledge to take on life full front. "Let's go get it," is the cry and love is the helper in the struggle for survival and happiness. But real Love is so much more than this, and nothing at all like what we think it is. It is not just what saves us from our many fears and helps us through the rough spots, or even the salvation from our world of woe. It is our Essence. Love has only been seen as salvation because we felt we were being attacked and needed help with the struggle. Without dangers there is no need for protection. So we can release this rather severe limitation on Love and allow it to be more of what it truly is.

The social ramifications of this idea are immense, but the operating mechanism is simple. If we think that Love is protection, then as soon as Love grows to where it protects, it has fulfilled its purpose and we stop encouraging its growth. When Love grows until it satisfies our needs, it stops growing because we don't think to allow it to become anything more. Only when we open up to the possibilities of Love will we be able to experience and understand more of its true nature and capabilities. We say that 'Love heals all' but we rarely give it a chance. Our preconceived notions of what it is keep it manifesting in its present limited expression. It's what we expect, so it's what we get. In essence, we are settling for a mere fragment of Love while imagining that we have tasted it all and yet feeling dissatisfied, or regretting that we haven't and feeling that we've missed something.

When modern people say Love, they usually mean romantic love. This is a wonderful and marvelous form of Love that we love to experience, even with its aspects of illusion and unrequited disappointments. But there are many other forms of Love all equally wonderful in their own way. Why should we settle for a part when we can experience the whole quite easily? We are now able to expand into experiences of Love that only the Masters have known before. If this one form of Love we know is so wonderful even with its faults, imagine how these others must be that are by their very nature faultless. By expanding, we do not lose the foundation we have built, we use it instead as the basis of an incredible new growth.

Murphy's Fear

One of the oldest adages in the world is that everything we need will be there when we need it. It is said various ways, 'the good Lord provides,' 'the universe provides,' 'good things happen to those who are in the right place at the right time,' and many other variations. They are all talking about Trust, the kind of Trust that knows that all will be provided and made clear to us when the time is right. How different this is from the fear of so many that they will be lucky to survive. This is the Murphy's Law approach to living and represents one of the most destructive games we have been playing. If we believe, however jokingly, that this is true, then it becomes true in our life. Such a belief is a self-perpetuating syndrome designed to produce constant mishap and disaster. While it may be a distillation of common life experiences up until now, it represents a total misunderstanding of the underlying Laws of Energy. Yet this is the experience of many I have known.

Murphy's 'understanding' is based on the fear of death. 'I'll be lucky to survive because death is right around the corner,' is how it runs, 'and if I die, the hearse will probably run out of gas.' We fight this 'down on my luck' concept for a while but eventually we give up. It becomes not worth the fight and we die. So we experience exactly what we think we will, hardship, suffering and death. We get tired of the fight, tired of the misery or boredom and tired of the apparent senselessness of existence. What kind of thinking is this? By thinking these things we have produced these results. One would think that since we know about this situation we would stop thinking these things immediately. But these thoughts run deep within us and the emotions connected with them are even deeper. They run all the way to the Center of our Being, where they surround the Light with their dark clouds of confusion and misery.

These deep emotions of fear and anger seem powerful. They are powerful enough to move people to be cruel to each other for personal gain. They are powerful enough to move men to go into battle against their own brothers. This dark energy is doing exactly what it should do. Dark energy manifests in darkness, but its apparent power is only the shadow of the Light it covers. If we think these emotions are powerful, wait until we experience the Love that lies beneath them. We have been living in a world of cloudy, overcast days and thinking they were sunny because we didn't know any different. Wait until we get a glimpse of the full sun shining on our path. Wait until we feel the healing warmth of the Light within radiating from our Center. We have not yet experienced Light, we have only seen its shadow and mistaken that filtered warmth for the actual encounter.

We have created the world we now see before us. If we think it is a monster, then it reflects the monstrous thoughts we have been thinking. It isn't a monster because it's negative, but because it is not under our conscious control. That's the definition of a monster, something destructive and out of control. It is the primordial dragon, the ruthless invaders, the epidemic without a cure. Life is only a hologram for our learning so whatever death or destruction our thinking has caused is immaterial. All that truly matters is that we learn from these experiences in the ever brightening Evolution of Consciousness. That's evolution, not evil-ution. So far, most of us have been ignoring what we are learning because we have been so focused on the day to day, surface reality. We have been concentrating so hard on what we do not have or do not feel or are not experiencing, that we are not even aware of what is really happening within our own minds, let alone on the deeper levels of Soul. We have been an integral part of this gigantic play without knowing it and although two of its major themes have been Love and Happiness, they have remained as elusive as ever.

The Search for Love and Joy

We have been looking for just the right person to share love with when we can just as easily share Love with everyone. We have that much Love within us, and the more Love we allow to flow the more we have to share because the Source is an endless fountain. We have looked on Love as the rarest and most precious commodity on this earth and have thus made it so. If we deepen our awareness and see that it is as Abundant as Life itself, then we will no longer expend all of our efforts in the frantic search for our meager share of it. We will realize that we are Love and that this is the Truth we have been trying to teach ourselves throughout the ages of recorded history. We will find the Source of Love within us and this Love will heal the deepest wounds of everyone on the planet. This is the Love that the Master Jesus tried to show us so many centuries ago. And as he was filled with this Love, so can we be, and even more so can we be like fountains overflowing. There is only room to feel one emotion at a time, so why not let it be Love?

The only impediment to feeling Love each moment is the belief that we can only feel Love if we have someone close who makes us feel it. There it is again, trying to make something happen, but this time we want someone else to make it happen for us. How lazy can we get, and where did we ever get the idea that Love comes from someone else? We need to release these fallacies from our minds before we go completely crazy from Love starvation. The last few decades have seen a remarkable upswing in disenchanted and unsuccessful relationships. This presents us with a wonderful opportunity, the opportunity to find the true Source of Love within ourselves. All this failure should be teaching us that it does not exist in someone else, so what choice do we have? And that's the point. The old ideas about Love have forced us into a corner where Love is all but non-existent. We have become a world that is both Love starved and Love crazed. There are all kinds of poor substitutes on every street corner and available by mail or phone, but real Love continues to elude all but a few. This has forced many of us to turn within. Willing to try anything to ease the pain, we have tried meditation and there have seen the Light shining like a beacon in the darkness of our journey. We have found home at last. And so will every one of us.

When confronted with the choice
between two roads,
always take the middle path.

WILLINAK

Chapter 18

The Journey Home

The Source

This vision of the Source within is life changing. When we realize that we can feel Love at all moments, we begin to spoil ourselves by feeling it. When we see that our minds can think thoughts of Joy and thereby create Joy, hopefully we allow it to happen. Why not? We can easily allow our Inner Selves to flower and become the fountain of beauty that we truly are. And so we become.

When this began to occur in my life, I felt that I had been given another chance. Since I was able to think and so manifest anything I wanted, I had the opportunity to decide what I wanted to let happen. So I gave myself the gift of volunteering to help others. This might seem like an odd choice at first. After all, I could have asked for a new career, bunches of money or a complete change of lifestyle. I could even become a star! But if anything was now possible, I was stuck with the job of deciding, and knowing that I would get whatever I asked for made me cautious. I had had enough experience in the past of really projecting for things and then backpedaling like crazy when they started showing up. It's like the old adage that there is more unhappiness at answered prayer than at unanswered. Sometimes the things we believe we want the most turn into the biggest pains. So I wanted to be careful. I wanted to ask for and receive something that would not only be wonderful, but also help me grow even more. That seemed like a very safe bet.

I was happier than ever before because I had let go of some of my desires, and because I was growing and learning quickly, it only seemed obvious that to continue on this path would be most desirable. So I quietly asked to be allowed to help others, knowing full well that by doing so I was helping myself. In a couple of days a young man showed up with questions about Spirituality, about relationships, about Life, about everything. At first I was going to suggest some books he might read, but then I had the intuition that Ellyn and I should meet with him and discuss whatever he needed to talk about. So we suggested a Sunday afternoon in the park rendezvous. He showed up promptly and brought some friends with him. We discussed everything under the sun. Being sixteen year old boys this ran the gamut from what are girls all about to why are we here. We talked about why we feel the things we do, where scary thoughts come from, and what we can do to make them stop. Over the past 6 or 7 years, this has developed into a way of living. This is not done with a self-sacrificing attitude, but rather with the very present realization that we learn as much as or more than they do. Now I have been given the opportunity to share these experiences through this writing. I have watched these young people grow from confused and insecure teenagers into emerging adults. In a world where many kids get lost in the latest craze or get swallowed by convention, they are treading the new path of enlightenment and finding there a sustaining sense of joy and satisfaction. It is rewarding in that we not only get to see their Love and Light begin to manifest, we also learn so much about ourselves. And this process continues to expand.

At first it was only once a week, then twice, and then there were the birthday celebrations and dropping in with new friends. These kids have become part of our family, sometimes closer than our own children. After all, we are all each other's children. What a simple beginning to a wonderful experience.

It has challenged us to continually give more and open up to ever deeper layers of our inner selves. We are constantly meeting with new friends and observing how our old friends are now beginning to have groups of their own. The message of Love and Light once planted in hearts and souls grows quickly and spreads like Morning Glories on spring fences. And this is a natural thing. We only have to allow ourselves to expand our Love and it happens. We only have to be willing to help and we will be given the opportunity to do so. Without these experiences, I might never have had the impetus to grow, because it is in trying to help these young people find the answers to their questions and their problems that I have found the answers to mine.

The Spiritual Path

One of the more useful answers I have received through these experiences has to do with the Spiritual Path itself, with the concept of the Spiritual Path. As soon as we begin talking about a path and about taking the first step on that path, we immediately begin to envision the goal, the place where the path leads. This is where the metaphor breaks down, because the older mind is so used to seeing goals that it doesn't know how to see anything else. Yet the first step on the Spiritual Path is more like letting go of the idea of a path altogether, and substituting the concepts of adventure and growth. We release the linear concept of beginning, middle and end in favor of the concept of expansion, an expansion from the Center of Light. So I must continually remind my mind that I am not becoming more successful, I am moving past the idea of success altogether. On the Spiritual Path there are only successes, only growth and amazing progress, so much so that the idea of success becomes another non-issue. There is no possibility of failure on this path any more than one can go swimming and not get wet. We are immersing ourselves in the Spiritual Sea of Energy that surrounds us and in which we have our Being, and we can only expand and grow within their nurturing glow. Success and failure are only terms we use within the limited minds we now possess. With Spiritual Growth we expand past these concepts to an Understanding of our complete and automatic perfection.

This expansion is one of the processes we go through as we grow in awareness. All of the concepts we have been discussing appear as dualities, doorways with opposing ideas on either side. Whenever we try to expand our consciousness we are met with our current limits. We then have to grow beyond these ideas, pass through these doorways into the realms of inner space. One of the first ideas we run into is the idea of making things happen. Many of us ask ourselves, "Why are you wasting your time doing this stuff when you could be out there making your dreams come true?" Or we doubt our ability to grow, or we doubt that there is anything more than what we are now experiencing. Fear, lack of trust, uncertainty, confusion, there are many ideas, but they are easily expanded beyond when one is connected to the Center. Success and failure are a common example. We need to understand that they are only ideas and not realities. They only have bearing on our lives if we think they do. Considering all of the pain and worry these twin ideas produce, it is a blessing to leave them behind and emerge in the true Light of our Spiritual Essence. And this process teaches us about the nature of the mind itself.

The Concept of Opposites

Of the many things that mind can do, thinking in opposites is one of the most original. Opposites like hard and soft, light and dark, hateful and loving. Because we have thought all of these opposites, we have created them in three dimensional forms. We are seeing exactly what we are thinking. Obviously, thinking in opposites only causes conflict, and conflict is both destructive and unnecessary. We do not enjoy these conflicts and we are ready to release them and replace them with experiences we do enjoy, like sharing. These old ideas have taught us how this system works. So now that we know that we have produced all of this with our thinking, we can go into our minds and find the center between all of these opposing thoughts. Between success and failure lies the concept of Perfection. Between the ideas of good and evil there is only Being, existing as expressions of Love and Light. We are learning that the concept of opposites has been merely another learning experience for us, another step in the evolution of human consciousness. In leaving it behind, we surround ourselves with the idea of Oneness. When we dive into this unified sea of Spiritual Perfection there is no question of whether or not we will be immersed. We can only be what we already are, Spiritual Beings of perfect Love and Light.

If we look closer at the idea of failure, we can see that it is really only another form of fear, fear of being able to produce or be something. It is feeling unable to make the grade, unworthy of sitting at the right hand of the Father. It is all of the ideas of fear as they apply to our performance as humans, humans who must please someone in order to survive or in order to receive the supposed blessing of eternal life. The fear of failure attaches itself to the self image, and thus we fear that somehow for some reason we are not endowed with the necessary intelligence, talent, courage, etc., to be up to the task at hand. Even being a human is too much for some of us. There is too much to do, too many responsibilities, too many stresses for one person to deal with. For many of us, Life is terrible and yet, paradoxically, there's not enough of it. I don't see how more of something awful would be better, but this seems to be one type of common thinking. These peculiar ideas then manifest as a life with these major characteristics. Perhaps we can replace these particular ideas with some that are a little more positive, like that we are Centers of Love and Light, and that the adventure is only beginning and we will experience lives of so much wondrous Joy and incredible events as we have never dreamed possible. We only have to allow ourselves to manifest this kind of life for us to experience it fully. We must decide that we are these Centers of Light and so worthy of these Joys and capable of feeling and sharing this Love. If we do not choose to change, then we must be getting some other kind of payoff by thinking in these old negative ways.

The Payoff of Negativity

I realized in my own life that I had been very proud of my anger for a long time. I thought it made me tough and I liked the image of myself as strong and potentially violent. It was a useful image to have growing up in a tough neighborhood where the obviously wimpy were picked on by the gang members. I was also so used to my sadness that it seemed odd to even think of letting it go. There was such romance in being star-crossed lovers and dreaming of some future romance that would someday sweep me off my feet. I had built a life around these ideas along with others like fear of the future and unworthiness. I had a vested interest in these and it was difficult to release them even after I began to notice how destructive they were to my own happiness. Again and again they would surface and threaten to destroy what little joy I had managed to allow in my life. After all, it is much more romantic to lose a love affair at the height of its passion than to enjoy one for a long time. It is also much more romantic to pine for a long lost love than to accept and grow with someone day to day. With this scenario, I also got the added benefit of anger at myself for losing and the inevitable feeling of unworthiness. I had it all! It took much inner searching before I finally saw through the veil of my own illusions.

When I did, I saw the fear that resided in the middle of all of this madness. It was my fear of being intimate that had resulted in my developing the romantic aspect in the first place. The romance of the ages was unlikely to happen in my life, especially considering how much I did not deserve anything, so it was much safer and kept me alone. For many years my fear of letting anyone see the real me was stronger than my desire to share love. But how foolish that was. The me that I was protecting was only this imagined personality self, this romantic, lonely, undeserving illusion who had no relation to the true self I really was inside. By meditating on the Source of my Being, I was finally able to pierce through this illusion and see the Light that I truly am. That is why I know it works. I have come from the depths of despair and self imposed loneliness with the worst self image in the world to a direct knowledge and experience of who I really am, and thus who all of us really are.

Only because of my dark despair did I have the desire and will to seek for something better. Only because of the huge hole I sensed within would none of the present world's panaceas help. It could not be filled with pleasures or possessions, with extravagance or exciting experiences. I needed to find the source of the pain that exuded from this hole. In discovering the hole, I saw that it was not a hole at all, but a doorway leading to self discovery. It only appears to be a hole because the filter is so dark that most of the Light on the other side is blocked. Each of us has this Source of Light within us, and in many of us this Light is highly filtered. We must allow these filters to fall away and let the Light shine forth in its true and amazing brilliance.

Humiliation

I was thinking today about humiliation. Humiliation is a crime against our humanity. It makes us feel violated as Human Beings and very angry, an anger which usually covers up the sadness we were made to feel. Many groups on this earth have intense racial humiliations to overcome. The Blacks and Native Americans in the United States, the Israelis and Arabs in the Middle East, the Croats, Muslims and Serbs in Eastern Europe have ages old animosities going all the way back to Cain and Abel. This only keeps the conflict going because at some time or another, someone treated one of their ancestors badly, made them and us feel bad about ourselves, and so we are angry at them forever. Let's look at what we might be learning from all of this.

Most areas of the world are embroiled in some form of this conflict and eight out of ten people don't like who they are. Eight out of ten! Self image, or racial image, is so very important and when humiliated, it gets angry and needs to feel something in return. Usually we settle for a mixture of pride and anger. Pride covers the wound and anger keeps us from feeling the hurt by focusing on the person or group who humiliated us in the first place. In personal events, we usually resent our parents, the most likely perpetrators, while at the same time feeling guilty for our resentments. Racial events are a little easier to keep going because we can continue to view this other group as the enemy and so justify the continued anger and aggression without any guilt. It is interesting that today, so many of these deep racial hatreds are breaking out again. The veneer of culture and governmental controls are breaking down under the weight of stronger and deeper emotional commitments. We are again seeing what has really been happening beneath the surface of our supposedly ordered world. We are learning that we can no longer just suppress these older forms of self or racial expression. We cannot ignore them and then pretend that they are gone from our lives forever. What is buried deep eventually surfaces again until it is finally understood and released.

Rather than simply another indication of the failure of modern thinking to improve life, this situation has the potential to improve our lives by showing us how collective thinking works. What we are learning is that the old idea of 'out of sight, out of mind' does not work. Thoughts, even subconscious thoughts, manifest and need to be dealt with on a conscious level. The days of suppression as a means of insuring the status quo are ending because they are being proven ineffectual. The lack of personal respect and the uncontrolled violence throughout the world is evidence enough of this condition. These thoughts are only doing what they are designed to do. Negative, hateful thinking by design produces the very world events we are now witnessing, and it doesn't matter whether these thoughts are right on the surface, deeply buried in the psyche or justified by some massive cultural heritage. Thoughts always manifest and these thoughts are manifesting to the detriment of all who think them. This is the nature of reality. We had better learn this now while we have a chance to reverse the current self defeating trends. Fortunately, we are.

A New Image of Self

The model that we use for this new adventurous Life is that of a fountain. We are fountains of Love and Light that we allow to flow out and manifest. This is far different from the current concept of life as a commodity that we must use to our best advantage. This older model is more like a hose that we direct anywhere we wish and with successes and failures depending on where we direct the nozzle. The new model of our Center as a fountain releases us from the stress of having to constantly monitor and direct it. We can simply observe the wonderful patterns the fountain produces, knowing that we are seeing the true inner nature of ourselves. This is a tremendous amount of struggle that we no longer have to worry about. If we look at the world situation, we can see that all of the current conflicts can be understood as aspects of this struggle.

Every group is fighting for its autonomy or to redress previous wrongs. These are all matters of self image, a self image that is focused on external circumstances rather than internal essences. All of these conflicts will ultimately be unsuccessful in producing the 'grand dream' of the particular group because they are all based on unimportant aspects of the self. This is all fighting between egos who are trying everything they can think of to be different from anyone else. But the fact is that we are all One, we are all beings of Light, and no amount of bombast or victorious marches will ever prove differently. I would hope that at some point leaders with some vision would emerge out of the ashes these conflicts are producing, and lead these people to the true path of Happiness, Joy and international Brotherhood. Until then we are not Human Beings, but only human egos behaving like a bunch of children who will do anything to get their way. The way to cure these ills is to move past the ideas that are causing them.

When we realize that the ego and its petty, personal desires is really destructive, then we do not hesitate to let it go. We no longer wish to produce the effects that thinking on these ideas produces. We move through these doorways flanked by these erroneous ideas of the self, ideas like success/failure, deserving/undeserving, pride/unworthiness, to the point where we merely are. Beingness. We can skim past the idea of feeling good or bad about ourselves to where we feel wonderful just to be who we are. No one needs to be the top dog, the richest scoundrel, the wisest priest or the strongest warrior. We can all be these incredible manifestations of Light Eternal. Instead of spending all of our energies on ideas that don't really matter and that do not produce anything of real value for us, we can release them and concentrate on ideas that create the kind of life experiences we would like to have. We can focus our attention on allowing Love and Happiness to flow and so experience them in our lives.

I, for one, would like to experience these things at all times. I don't see why I should have to wait until I achieve some kind of success, or acquire a certain amount of goods, or even become wise. I should be able to experience all of it right now, right here. So I have developed a kind of mantra that says 'I am Love, I am Light, I am One with all Life.' These thoughts move through my mind in various forms and are producing these realities in my life. They will do the same for anyone else who cares to join in the fun.

We can use the power of our own thinking to create the Life of Happiness and Joy that we really want to have. We are joining together and raising our Love-filled voices in a celebration of Life which we have only dreamed about before. We are creating a tremendously joyful noise and observing how it rings throughout eternity. And we are just now really getting started. In my life, I feel like I have been released from centuries of oppression and suffering and have emerged into a world of brilliant possibilities. And this oppression has not been at the hands of some particular person or group, but rather has been the result of my own limited thinking. So I am releasing my choking association with the ideas of the past. Let the old ideas of justice for my people or anger at my early years be hanged. I will not expend any more effort in the pursuit of those goals because I know they will never produce any Happiness or Joy.

True Success

I was thinking about the way we think about success. When we talk about becoming successful, we usually mean finding the perfect job, developing a new product or better skills, or just being at the right place at the right time, on top of the world. But success is not an acquisition or the result of luck or good timing, it's an attitude. It's a set of ideas which establishes an environment where the right skill is developed or we stumble upon the perfect idea or situation. Having our focus on finding something that will make us successful keeps us from developing the very attitude of success that we need in order to succeed. We are never successful, we are only going to be when our ship comes in. This is backwards thinking and helps produce all the failures we witness in our modern world.

When you really think about it, true success is expanding our Love. It is wanting to help because we are the most joyous and Love-filled when we are helping to make things better, helping others and helping ourselves. The feeling of being of Service is the most magical emotion on Earth and is why most of us love to teach our children and help them grow. It lends an aura of beauty and grace to every situation and produces positive results for all concerned. It is the secret of success, the Secret of Life. To be loving and helpful instead of fearful and selfish creates an environment where only success is possible. The only problem we have is getting our egos our of the way.

Only our egos want to continue being selfish because that is all that they know, they weren't programmed to be anything else. Egos are only habitual ways of approaching existence, and we must leave them behind before we will be able to experience Life in any better way. Besides, they do not help produce success because they do not encourage us to Love or share. They actually insure ultimate failure by interfering with our natural intimacy with all Life. We don't understand egos nor do we enjoy the world the ego mind has produced, yet we continue to hold onto them even when there are better, more successful alternatives. Perhaps it's just that we haven't yet learned how to let go. That may be what we're trying to teach ourselves now.

Knowing that we can do anything we want opens up tremendous possibilities. We could use this knowledge to go after our cherished ego goals with new vigor, but that would only produce the same reality we have now. We can instead open up to a totally new experience based on our new Understanding of who we are. We can become involved in building a better world for ourselves and for everyone that we meet, a world built on the twin ideas of Love and Light. There will be plenty of things to do. When we begin to move past the old ideas of what needs to be done in order to survive, or to keep the status quo in place, or to fulfill our lifelong dreams, then we can allow ourselves to become manifestations of something larger than all of us. But we must move past these old ideas first. We must release our commitment to old ways of thinking and living before new ways can emerge from our deeper Center. Our Center is like a chrysalis just waiting to open and release the Magic it contains. We must allow this to happen before we will be able to experience it.

So we are in the process of changing the rules by which the game of life is played. Those who wish to continue in the old game may do so, but they will have to put up with the limited benefits it provides. Since so many on the earth at this point are clamoring for more than they presently have, it seems clear that most are dissatisfied with the present game. We need to help them see that the key to their success lies within their own thinking and not in some scam, government program or in the ultimate defeat of their perceived enemies. These old approaches to improving things for specialized groups are as much a part of the present game as the abuses that have spawned them, and equally off center. They both are focused on the external circumstances instead of on the erroneous thinking that has caused those circumstances in the first place.

The Light at the End of the Tunnel

I'm beginning to see that this process of becoming aware

of concepts and releasing them is not endless, but one which finally stops when we get to the core beliefs. When we reach these central icons of the mind and replace them with more positive thoughts, then we have allowed the mind to change. This is the point in our inner evolution when we are thinking about Love and Light much more than we are thinking about fear and selfishness. Our new thinking creates the environment for change and the feedback from the change encourages us to expand further and further into perfect manifestation. All of our present tensions melt away. We are no longer engaged in proving anything, or doing anything to make things happen. Our lives relax and become the beautiful expressions of Light that they truly are.

I have begun to stretch again lately, but rather than just stretch my muscles, I also stretch my emotions and mind. It is a sort of total stretch meditation, an expansion of all aspects of the self beyond the narrow confines of my comfort zone. As I do so, I begin to loosen and realize that I am no longer held in by the old patterns. We do not need to adhere to the old patterns nor do we need to rebel against them. We can find the doorway between these two concepts and emerge free and clear of both of them.

Rebellion Revisited

I remember my youth in the late 60's when rebellion first became so fashionable. The idea of being forced to live in a culture whose values were so ego centered and lacking in Spiritual Understanding led many to flee to communes and other countries. It was the idea of having to surrender to forces of culture with which we did not agree and which are now creating their final destructive tour de force, hastening their own demise. Yet the rebellion we employed has turned out to be equally destructive in the long run because it has kept the focus riveted on the old system. It really doesn't matter whether one is actively producing old ways or fighting against them, no new thinking is taking place so no substantial progress is being made. Both points of view are limited to aspects of the current system. Only when we release the current system, gratefully acknowledging what it has taught us, can we move into something new and more wonderful.

Thinking about my life in retrospect, I see that I have always been the philosopher type. I have always tried to explain life in terms of larger concepts. I remember my parents telling me that I was too proud and needed to just have faith until the day (after death, no doubt) when all would be explained. This is the old, 'we'll understand it all by and by' routine. I refused to do that because I felt that the mind was capable of understanding more of what was going on. Somewhere I knew there were concepts that would satisfy the mind's quest for knowledge and understanding. I knew that it was possible and that this knowledge would help to make the world a better place. On becoming an adult, I remember being appalled by the paltry life being offered. The middle class life is not fun, and it should be. As the Children of Light, Life should be a gas! We should be these Beings full of all the Love and Joy that Divinity contains, and yet everyone I knew was not. We were all told to make the best of it and told to wait for Joy in some future place or time. Surely, I felt, there had to be something more than this endless struggle of acquisition and somewhat satisfying achievement.

I was eighteen in 1965. The anti-war movement was coming into full swing and here at last was something that made sense to me. 'War is not healthy for children and other living things' became a motto of a generation confused by contradictory beliefs within the cultural structure, both of which were offered as 'the truth.' The idea of going to the other side of the world and coercing other people into becoming free and democratic seemed absurd, a contradiction in terms. Free people should be allowed to be whoever they want to be. Pursuit of Happiness seemed to apply only to Americans and only if it was good for business.

It was a couple of years later that the Hippie movement introduced the ideas of free expression of self, including Love, and of Spiritual Expansion into other dimensions of experience. The introduction of meditation as a means of expanding the mind's awareness of other levels of reality has had a profound effect on the way we view ourselves as humans. Before this time, our mental understanding was limited to input from the five senses and the major belief systems of our particular culture. Other realms were discussed in traditional Western religion, but these realms were inaccessible to the general public until after death. When we wanted to know about God, we would ask the priest or pastor because it was their job to know about such things. This idea of only clergy being able to access spiritual energy can lead to a monopoly of the worst kind. This is not the mere monopoly of goods or services for common consumption, but a monopoly of vital information about Life itself and direct connection to its very Source. This is selfishness of the worst kind because it is an attempt to deny everyone else what they truly deserve while trying to keep it all for the a limited group of clergy. It was and continues to be the ultimate power trip in some religious structures.

So we, as travelers on the road of Life, had come upon a central contradiction in the general belief patterns of all human cultures. If Life was so abundant, why was everyone, including the clergy, trying to hoard it, and mistreating their neighbors and brothers in the attempt to secure as much as possible to themselves? Obviously, the answer is, selfishness! When all of us were selfish, only a very few saints were pure and selfless. They came along in all cultures at one time or another and lived a life dedicated to teaching us about how life worked. We would listen to them and duly record what they said, yet without understanding much of it. It is only now that we are finally listening to and following the steps that will lead to our purification and ultimate success.

Before now, most of us were too busy being fearful humans to be able to cope with open Trust. We were too focused on the future to notice the present moment. We were too busy living according to the rules we had learned to even question them. 'I am the way I am,' the old adage says. and indicates a person for whom change is impossible. Without change there is not growth and without growth there is not real Joy. We cannot live without growth and expansion yet we fight it with every fear filled trick we can think of, almost with every breathe that we take. We need to learn to breathe differently. When we breathe out the energy that we think will make us happy, let's fill the void with Joy and Love instead of selfish gain and fear. For just once, let's try something that we are not all that familiar with. It takes a little Trust to open up to our true inner selves but we soon see that our fears are ungrounded. We are afraid of something that we know nothing about. Why are we like that?

Observe what kind of thinking this is. We could just as easily be excited about something we don't know anything about as to be afraid. These are both possible thoughts and should have a 50/50 chance, yet we consistently choose to think fearfully. These fearful thoughts over the ages have produced many fear filled events for all of us in many lifetimes. So we have developed the habit of thinking in this way. It is habit based on experience, but not on fact. This is a case where experience is not the best teacher.

Experience as Teacher

Experience is only the contents of our memory banks. It is only our perceptions of the small part of this lifetime that we have experienced. Meditation opens up a whole new part of us that we can explore and draw upon. It lends us a strength based on a secure knowledge, knowledge of what Life is and what in the world we are supposed to be doing here. With this foundation, we can begin to operate as Human Beings filled with Light, expressing Love and living with Joy.

The way we think has been unalterably changed by the introduction of meditation and the new concepts of Life outlined in this short chronicle. We are now to the point of more fully implementing these ideas through daily meditation and focusing on the Center at all moments. When I began this process of studying and meditating on spiritual things, I had no idea that it would be an almost total reprogramming of the conscious mind. Little did I suspect that it would bring about a complete transformation of myself and the world. But about a year ago, in early 1992, I was given the idea of recording my thoughts on tape. After about ten months I began to transcribe these into the computer. I liked what was being written in these transcriptions, but I had no idea that I would be going through the transformation I was writing about. I intentionally started just recording what I thought about Life and Spiritual Growth, a kind of compilation of the first 45 years of my observations about Life. In these few months I have changed my perspective on the process of Spiritual Growth. A year ago I probably would have argued that since it was the mind thinking all of these negative thoughts that were causing all the problems, the cure was to reprogram the mind with new and positive thoughts. All change would take place within the mind and this would be very safe and comfortable for one such as I who was unused to being very emotional. Yet I have come to see that the mind is really only involved in part of this inner Transformation

We only need to release and replace the old ideas with enough new ones so that we can shift our focus to the Center and allow the Love and Light to flow. It is actually this flow of energy from the Center that produces the change in consciousness. The mind really only clears in its attempt to catch up. The Soul is the Source and our focus is the key. By shifting our focus to the Center we open up those realms of experience that we call the Spiritual World for our exploration and ultimate benefit.

Authority Figures

I was thinking about the question of authority figures in our cultures. Ellyn and I have been reading about the people who write books and travel the lecture/workshop route and so spread the good word about Spiritual Growth and transformation. Some have said that they are dissatisfied with the responses they get and feel they can be of more benefit by writing. The idea being that if one curls up with a book, there is time to read and meditate, then read again and so assimilate the information presented. They can also reach more people whereas with a lecture the information speeds by and each listener maybe picks up a few thoughts out of the hundreds offered. Besides, they all agree that the lecture tour is a grueling schedule. But I began to see something different as the real limiting factor.

While lectures, books and workshops by known specialists may be all well and good, it is still a manifestation of the old way of doing things. These 'experts' are merely taking the place once occupied by the clergy and we still all flock to hear the latest truths from those who supposedly 'know.' It is actually more important that we learn that we are all capable of knowing, all capable of teaching and sharing this knowledge and experience with others. So rather than bringing in a constant procession of experts, we need to develop our own local groups where we meet to learn and grow in Understanding. This approach has many benefits.

First of all it is very personal. Anyone attending has the opportunity to ask questions that are of particular importance to them. I suppose workshops are a little more one on one than lectures, but experts can only use the shotgun approach and hope that everyone will get something from the general spattering of ideas that are presented. But in the individual attention and sharing within the group, there is much more opportunity for growth and progress. All that it takes is for someone in each locality to quietly, within themselves, volunteer to be a Center for Love and Light. Of course, we are all Centers of Love and Light so we do not have to do anything we are not entirely capable of doing. Yet in the act of acknowledging this truth, in the simple act of saying 'yes,' we open up the gate that allows this reality to flow from us.

None of the current crop of spiritual authors would argue that they are the one and only source of spiritual truth, yet the way that we habitually think makes us think that they are. We did the same thing to Jesus of Nazareth. Rather than seeing him as an ordinary man with Divine Understanding, we turned him into the one and only Son of the Father, and so cut ourselves off from ever achieving the same level of consciousness that he had attained. Let's not make this same mistake again. We are all the Children of Light and we all have equal access to all forms of Divine Energy. Jesus told us that everything he could do we can do also and even greater things, and we are just beginning to understand what he meant. We are all healers and channelers of Divine Energy. If we wait for someone famous to tell us what to do, we will never get anywhere. The main idea here is that someone coming to tell us about it is someone coming from outside of us. It is too much like entertainment, an event we go to because it is the latest fashion. Lecturers cannot do it for us. They may be able to help point us in the right direction, but the work of transformation must be done within each of us and we must do it. We can go to hear the words of inspiration and the read about the personal experiences of others, but in the end we must, like Dorothy of Oz, do it for ourselves.

So if the lectures and seminars reach too few and the books are too impersonal, then we need this local, grass roots approach. I imagine that everyone's experience will be similar to anyone who has ever tried to teach. In helping someone else to learn and grow we learn and grow as much ourselves. As we help others understand spiritual lessons they become clearer to us. This fits in with spiritual truth, because it is in the absorbing and making the thoughts one's own that the mind begins to change. We must help each other replace this old thinking with the new and so help this Transformation proceed. It is the sounds and meanings of these new ideas which will change the vibration of our Inner Environment. Like music, the sounds of words are very powerful and move us in many ways which we are only beginning to discover. The controversy over certain modern music and its lyrics is the most obvious indication of the emerging awareness of the power of words to shape our lives. So, the idea is to change the words we think to our self all day long every day and so change our Life experiences. And the idea is also to share this experience of growth with others. It is time to take Spiritual Transformation out of the realms of entertainment and bring it into every day life in our own neighborhoods.

As Centers of Love and Light we become interested in growth and sharing instead of the outcome of our own personal desires and goals. Our awareness of Life expands with this change of focus and we become involved in helping the planet to evolve into its next phase. In establishing these local centers we create places where those who have questions, where those who wish to grow spiritually can come for help, guidance and sharing. There are probably such places now in addition to the larger centers where workshops and retreats take place. If we want this transformation to happen on a global scale then we need to make it available in all areas. We cannot wait for someone else to do it, for the government or the international council of churches to do it. We get to do it. We are building a new world culture based on the idea of sharing and the first thing we get to share with each other is this process of Spiritual Transformation. When we do this, our consciousness expands to include the new ideas of sharing and growth we are employing. The rest of this scenario of world change grows from these simple roots. We do not have to set up vast institutions for spiritual learning, we only have to gather together in our living rooms and backyards to discuss these things. All we have to do is allow our Love and Light to expand and the Universe will take care of the details. We will soon find ourselves surrounded by others who wish to share these things and so the growth and expansion proceeds. Like any flower, the flowering of our Souls emerges from the inside out. This is the purpose for which we incarned as Humans in the first place.

Perfection

In my own life I have watched myself and others change overnight. I became an almost instant Hippie in the 60's and have witnessed young people become Punks, Skin Heads or Generation X denizens with a simple haircut. Within hours these new personalities are spouting all of the major thought forms of the group as if they had belonged for years. This is the same process we have been talking about. By saying 'yes' to the new form they wish to emulate, these young people become them overnight, in the twinkling of an eye. But the change is usually only on the surface. I have witnessed new age people become enlightened overnight as well. Instead of torn clothing and spiked hair they don colorful robes, bead necklaces and change their name to 'Effervescent Morning Star', but it is still put on the outside which is no guarantee of inner change. It may be a beginning of inner change, but why expend energy with outer trappings when we can go right to the heart of the matter. Change from the Center happens by allowing, not by putting on. It is a subtle yet significant difference.

For one thing, none of these personality trips goes anywhere near Joy. There may be moments of ecstasy especially with the help of drugs or alcohol, but a sustaining and abiding Joy is not possible. Thus the level of frustration is the same as in more conservative subcultures. They both operate from the same personality level and so are guaranteed to produce the same unsatisfactory results. And of course, the personality operates mainly from fear, the fear that we are not going to get what we need. All of this effort to try to become someone that will satisfy desires. All of this effort is beside the point. Everything we need is provided when we are connected to the Center. We do not have to worry about who we are and if we are cool enough to attract a lover, talented enough to get a good job, or clever enough to fool everyone into believing our charade. It is all acting. No wonder we worship the movie stars. They are doing a better job of being who they aren't than we are and so we reward them immensely for their efforts. Yet this all stems from need. We act out because we think that we need to. We can change that and eliminate a lot of effort, pressure and stress from our lives and be more successful in every way.

I suppose the saddest cases are those who act out for more than just survival, or normal love and respect. There are many whose needs are so great that they need the world to bow at their feet before they can feel good about themselves.

Many of our entertainers are in this category and far from being less stressed, which you think they would be being so rich and famous, they actually drive themselves harder because their needs are greater. The feeling of being powerful or influential is another substitute and many fall for it. There are others ranging from the psychotic to the dissatisfied lobby groups. They are all ways to get what we need and none of them work worth a darn. They do not work because they are based on limited ideas of what Life is and how one goes about living. They are merely the only games we have known until now.

So we replace these ideas. Instead of worrying about who we are, we become who we are. Instead of being concerned with our appearance, we concentrate on our Essence. And instead of being these carefully crafted works of art we call personalities, we allow ourselves to become the Centers of Love and Light that we truly are. This is what is going on in my life and what I hope will be going on in many other's lives soon. And we get a lot by becoming these Centered Beings.

For one thing, this is knowledge about the world, the key to Happiness and Joy for which we have been searching since the beginning of time. This is how to create for ourselves everything that we want by a process of allowing the Soul to manifest. The Soul knows the plan for this Life and can easily create everything that we need if we just get our egos out of the way. We can have everything that we have now if we like and we get rid of everything that we now fear. We can also add everything wonderful that we can imagine. Anything that we can imagine can happen. This is the nature of our energy and how it manifests. Our energy takes the shape of whatever we think. To become conscious of this is to become conscious creators. We are all creators of our Life experiences and our medium is Light. We are what we say we are. This is just the beginning of our growth into the Light, and if the first taste is this wonderful, if the first moments are this joyful, imagine what it will be like when we are in full swing.

When we open up the Source of Light and Love within us, our backyard garden becomes paradise. Everyone we meet becomes angelic and all of our relationships become Holy. We share our Love and Light and we help others to find theirs. There are many ready to learn this now. It is important that we all becomes Centers and observe how we gather together like moths, attracted not to the flame, but to the Light. It is a simple process of knowing who we are and allowing that to manifest. It's like walking through a door and emerging out in this new experience full of exciting possibilities.

For me, I see a return of the surge of creative energy I felt when I was working so hard to be an artist, but without the struggles and doubts of that personality game. The wonderful creative flow that the artist feels is the flow of energy from the Center that we can all feel all of the time. What we create with this flow is a world filled with beauty and Light, with Love and with Joy, a world that even the best art we have only begins to express. The other nice thing about this kind of creation is that, unlike the artist, this creation is not separate from ourselves. We won't fall into the trap of thinking that we can only feel the flow if we are producing something artistically beautiful. Our medium of creation is ourselves and the exhibition is our everyday lives. We can enjoy our creations every hour of every day. We already do, although 'enjoy' may not be the right word for some of us, at least not yet. Our lives are the creations of our thinking and emotions, so let's make them works of such Love and Joy that the rest of the world will be astounded.

This is what I intend and suggest. I know it is partially self centered, but since I can experience whatever I can imagine, I wish to imagine my Life full of Love and Joy. I would also like to help others do the same so that we can share it. Why not? This is what I think about most of the time, and this is what is happening. These are the kind of groups I envision springing up all over the globe, the coming together of many to share in this positive expansion of Light. We thus become fellow travelers on the Spiritual Path.

We are these Centers of Love and Light, brilliant rose pink stars dotting the surface of the earth. And when others look at us they will see our Light and be encouraged in their struggles, or better yet, encouraged to expand beyond struggle altogether. Many will choose to join in the Transformation because they will see their own Light reflected in our eyes as our is in theirs. And they will know this Light is in them and will begin to allow it to flow. Thus each of us becomes a brilliant testament to the beauty of the Light within and helps it spread like wildfire in all directions. And with the Light comes Love, the healing, uniting force that will transform us and the entire planet. I can see it happening, I can feel it flowing. And that's the point. When we see it and feel it, then it shall come into Being, for each of us and for the entire world. This is what I think is happening on this planet at this moment. It is my Understanding of What in the World is Going on Here?

May all our moments be filled with Love and with Light.

Epilogue

We finally did find our house. One day, we could feel it coming so Ellyn started calling about houses in the paper. After several calls with little apparent result, she asked the Universe for help, and the next day met Kathleen, a wonderful beginning agent who was very eager to help. She and Ellyn went on the road for a while looking at the various houses for sale, but none of them answered our needs. While most of them had all the normal rooms with a narrow hall, they lacked the versatility and character that we knew was so essential to our purpose. We needed guest rooms and places to meet with friends After looking at a dozen or so of these prospects, we thought maybe the time wasn't right after all. We should not have to work so hard to find this place, it should just be there. So we decided to let go if it, at least until the latest Branson projects were completed. But Ellyn felt differently the next day and continued to look and magically, a few mornings later, there it was. She didn't have to even look inside because she knew the moment she and Kathleen pulled up in the driveway. What was interesting is that after seeing the perfect porch and upstairs, they came into the tiniest kitchen the world has ever seen, hardly enough space to handle everyday things, let alone the gatherings we enjoy. After half an hour of vainly trying to think of some way to make it work, they decided to look at the rest of the house and rounded the corner into the biggest, most gorgeous kitchen imaginable. There was obviously still a little doubt that the perfect house existed, but only enough to stall it for a few minutes

The next morning I was hauled there myself complete

with entourage of daughters, boyfriends, grandson and even one of our old neighbors. What an entrance we made and if ever there was a sign that this was our new house, this was it. It was obvious to me on the first glance as well. The next week Ellyn began to seek financing, and after being shown the door at one place, requested help in finding the perfect bank. The next morning she met the perfect loan lady, also eager to help, who offered us exceptional terms and the deal was made with a minimum of effort and complete lack of worry. In July we moved in while this book was being edited and began the next phase of our adventure in three dimensional experience.

We are really incredibly powerful Beings once we learn how to utilize our energies efficiently. And it's really the simplest thing. We only have to Love and it will all happen. Our connection to the Center shows us who we truly are and this produces Joy and Excitement. We can easily be happy and creative, and be thrilled about the growth we are experiencing right now. Learning to express Love is the easiest thing I have ever done yet has produced the most amazing changes I have ever experienced. It's like gong home but a hundred times more satisfying, or like getting our Heart's desire but without all the waiting, work and unbearable stress. It's like falling in Love with everything, with all forms of Life. Love heals and expands everything, so it is the best medicine to both correct perceived dilemmas and encourage positive growth. Using any other type of focus is self sabotage from the start. Only Love can hold things together. I hope you agree and will share my enthusiasm for the Spiritual Path. We have a lot to learn, but the learning is exciting and full of Joyful Adventure. Our positive, Love-filled energies will create a world where nobody loses and we all gain everything we have ever wanted. It may sound crazy, but I'm glad to be here and grateful that I get to experience this era of Spiritual Expansion. It's the greatest discovery the world has ever witnessed. It is Us. We are emerging into the Light. Let's shine together!

Index

A

A New Image of Self 277
A New Understanding 47
A Positive Attitude 176
Abundance 239
  desire and 186
  Ease of access to 239
  essence of new way 148
  Jesus' miracles and 148
  Mental blocks to 240
  Need and 237
  new understanding of 118
  ours for the asking 37
  Simplicity of 240
  striving and 146
  violent acquisition as opposite 179
Acceptance 57, 220
  our need for 97
Accomplishment
  joy and 174
Achievement 75
  idea of 78
Acquisition
  path of 4
  violence and 180
Addiction
  cultural limitations and 181
Adventure 192
  as challenge to fear 193
  Western culture and 193
Aggression and violence
  irony of 207

Alcohol
  search for Joy and 180
Alienation
  Isolation and 242
All that I have done ye can do also 37
Allegiance
  difference from unity 83
  roots in tribal consciousness 81
  two directions of evolution 81
Allowing
  benefits of 127
Ambition 77
  ideas behind 78
  Spiritual Path and 77
  vehicle to spiritual path 79
American Dream
  based on unworkable ideas 224
American way
  verses Spirituality 43
Ancient truths
  Current resurfacing of 262
Anger 24
  as tangled layers 25
  lack of justification for 115
  reason behind 162
Anger and Love 232
Appearance
  surface vs. inner 73
  Vs. Essence as focus 290
Aquarius
  New Age of Spiritual Man 178
Arafat, Yassir 12
as it is within, so it is without 9
as we think, so we become 192
Ask and it shall be given 109
ask and ye shall receive 37
ask and ye shall receive' 59
Assuming the worst
  Aspect of guilt 251
Attachment
  lack mentality and 186
Attainment
  joy and 174
Attitudes
  results of change 46
Auras
  imbuing with energy 100

Authority
  source of power 169
Authority Figures 285
Authority figures
  How we view them 286
  Vs. inner knowing 287
Awareness
  of how Life energy works 201

B

Beauty of Life
  Suffering and 222
Becoming
  current concept of 202
Becoming a Center 168
Being
  achievement and 202
Being and Becoming 202
Beingness
  Central image of new image 278
Beings of Light
  deciding to be 159
Belief systems
  acceptance of 203
Beliefs
  problems with changing 203
Better safe than sorry 35
Big Bang Theory
  as expansion of Light 202
Bishop Sheen 113
Blame
  forgiveness and 196
  no one is at fault 231
Blindness
  symbolic 125
Book
  As chronicle of growth 284
Branson
  displays old thinking 59
Buddha
  teachings of 67

C

Centered
  two definitions 109

Centers of Light
  becoming 169
Centers of Love and Light
  Neighborhood 288
Challenge 116
  to see world struggles clearly 117
Change
  and pride 11
  as part of our nature 230
  as replacement of key ideas 30
  as result of new thinking 5
  challenges of 63
  emotional aspect 17
  fear of 11
  resistence to 17
Change of Consciousness
  two aspects of 58
Change of consciousness
  paradox of 58
Channeling
  misunderstandings of 168
Children
  enthusiasm for Life 221
Children of Light
  humans defined as 50
  we as the 79
Choice
  What to ask for 269
Christian cosmology 16
Clergy
  Monopoly of 283
Close mindedness
  insecurity and 203
Committment
  fear of 35
Competition 189
  and failure 45
  as central manifesting principle
    189
  benefits of releasing 189
  present world system and 190
  self image and 189
Competition and fear
  major lesson of 192
Concept of Opposites 272
  limiting aspects of 28
Connecting point

to spiritual energy 236
Conscious creators
  Becoming 290
conscious creators
  we as 12
Conscious mind
  as quarreling factions 35
  birth of 14
  limitations of 27
Conscious thinking
  benefits of 37
Consciousness
  control and 162
Consumerism
  as obsolete Life model 35
Control 12
  as means of acquisition 3
  idea of 88
  of our minds 110
  perceived lack of 7
Control issue
  consciousness and 162
Cooperation
  flawed by selfishness 81
  with Higher Self, aspects of 58
Course in Miracles 113
Creative power
  of mind 36
Creative process
  ego and 39
  Magic of 38
Creativity 144
  current problems with 145
  doubt and 215
  In every day Life 291
  newly defined 38
  our essence as 144
  saying Yes to 140
  what shows true genius? 144
Cult of the personality
  defined 23
Cultural conditioning
  positive aspects of 110
Cultural frameworks
  limitations of 225
Cultures
  different approaches of 218

Current thought system
  based entirely on fear 17

D

Darkness
  Old understanding of 231
Deep desires
  longing to satisfy 125
Demanding
  vs. allowing 220
Deserving
  and need for approval 44
  identity and 132
  opposite to Divine Law 45
Desire
  as impetus for Spiritual growth
    185
  fantasizing and 187
  true fulfillment of 186
Desire, Accomplishment and Failure
    185
Desire and Fear
  paradox of 22
Desire fulfillment
  three paths of 186
Desirelessness
  attachment and 185
Desires
  as flaw in old method 95
  melodrama aspects 132
  produce continual failure 187
Destiny 13
  as Humans 93
Devil
  concept of Evil and 195
Disappointment
  new understanding of 133
Discontent
  Need and 237
Discussion group
  Our early ones 270
Dissatisfaction
  as peculiar habit 61
Divine Perfection 12
DNA
  internal source of structure 57

Doing nothing
  Zen paradox of 95
Doubt
  many layers of 182
  of ability to change 15
  paralyzing paradox of 86
  scientific method and 87
Doubt and Control 86
Dreams 173
  coming true 174
Drug use
  aspects of cure 180
Drugs
  search for Joy and 180
Dualities
  Process of growing past 272

E

Eastern meditation
  beginnings in modern culture 177
Econony
  shifting away from defense 208
Education 73
  breeds confusion and alienation
    153
  limited by focus on facts 153
Ego
  As block to success 279
  as center of old way of thinking 21
  as Growth motivator 139
  as master of fear 235
  benefits of releasing 151
  control issue and 157
  desire for control by 4
  Destructive habits of 279
  discussed 150
  eternal conflict of 40
  sharing and 83
  Spiritual Path and 103
  structure of 150
  Transformation and 188
  true function of 152
Ego mind
  limitations of 129
Ego recognition
  destructive aspects of 45

Emergence
  as new Beings of Light 94
Emotional evolution
  trinity of values 156
Emptiness 238
  Concept of discussed 238
  Fear of 238
  Illusion of 275
Encouragement 95
End justifies the means 5
Energy and Flow 256
Enjoyment
  marred by pressure of goals 184
  purpose of life and 130
Entertainment
  concept of 34
Essence
  as creative 144
  Love as our true 159
  Our deepest 238
  Vs. appearance as focus 290
Eternal punishment
  source in Christian theology 120
Eternity
  Time and 199
Ethic hatreds
  Why they do not disappear 232
Eve's apple 121
Evil
  as realm of Devil 195
  as self manifesting idea 66
  belief in as basis of fear 194
  Central idea of present system 233
  Glorification of 233
  Old understanding of 231
  True lesson of 233
  true source of 66
Evolution
  current mental growth 149
  four phases of 155
  next logical step 107
Evolution Revisited 155
Existentialism
  as breakdown of old order 82
  Paradigm of negativity 254
Experience and Learning 254
Experience as Teacher 284

Experts
    fallacy of 168
Exploration 161
    intuitive nature of 49
    new spirit of 22
    purpose of Life 65
Exploring a New Method 155
Expression
    as expansion of Light 175
    as natural expansion of Life 172

F

Failure
    A closer look 273
    syndrome discussed 187
Fame
    problems with 23
Farmers
    disdain for 205
Fear 190, 227
    as cause of difficulty 7
    as protective sheath 135
    As protective shield 244
    as simple habit 194
    as source of fearful world 190
    as unfounded prejudice 195
    at tip of pyramid 60
    based on concept of evil 194
    basic belief behind 61
    current fascination with 193
    ego's part in 235
    Emptiness and 238
    Fulfills a need 245
    guilt and sexuality and 123
    ignorance and 194
    Inner essence of 228
    Memories and 229
    Modern dilemma of 228
    narrow focus of 61
    of being alone 52
    of intimacy 134
    of what lies within 193, 229
    Simplicity of mechanism 245
    two parts of misunderstanding 61
Fear and Doubt
    as the old gods 87

Fear and Transformation 244
Fear of Failure
    striving and 196
Fear of God
    absurdity of 17
Fear of intimacy
    Romance and 274
Fear of the unknown
    Insanity of 284
Feeling connected
    importance of 13
Fighting
    and personal success 2
    and self-centeredness 3
Focus 200
    as key to change 109
    as key to transformation 285
    key to manifesting 200
    on good, not bad 54
Force
    as fear 197
    use of for peace 82
Forgiveness
    key to change 25
Fountain
    As model for new Humans 277
Freedom
    answer to our needs? 106
    selfishness and 107
    spirituality and 160
Friend
    becoming our own best 107
Future
    as home of fear 62
    as our major concern 104
    hope and 155
    projection of present thinking 191
    tarot readings and 104
    the past revisited 84
    worry and 5
Future faith
    Described 234

G

Games the old way plays 133
Garden of Eden 138

Generation gap
   old way and 153
Getting Hurt 114
Giving up
   as key to joy 51
Goals 127, 163
   confusions surrounding 127
   vs. the journey 183
God
   as supreme repair man 69
   present concept lacks Unity 90
God and Devil
   as basis for culture 16
God Will Provide
   Need and 237
Good Ol Days
   Fallacy of 224
Growth
   as purpose of Life 34
   as source of Happiness 219
   concept of Perfection and 175
   opportunities for 220
   Signs of 227
Growth and Light 91
Guidance
   inner vs. outer 96
Guilt
   Absurdity of use for control 249
   And assuming the worst 251
   Effectiveness of 253
   Negative aspects of 250
   punishment and 121
   sexuality, fear and 123
Guilt and Pride
   Beyond these ideas 252

H

Happiness 147, 219
   as goal of all endeavor 13
   in everyday events 147
   key ingredients of 65
   key to 9
   Pursuit of 219
   search for 97
   searching for 64
   true state of 93

Hard Work
   idea of as block to achievement 35
Hard work
   latent meanings of 205
   present fallacy of 206
Hardships
   modern versions of 53
Hatred
   lack of justification for 115
   What it is showing us 232
He who finds his life shall lose it 24
Heaven on Earth
   Christ Consciousness and 171
heaven on earth 28
Higher Self 1
   and Personality 24
   cooperation with 58
Hippies
   spiritual aspects of 282
Historical events
   true causes of 116
Hitler 123
Holograms
   Paradigm for us 247
   paradigm for us 217
   paradigm of Humans as 165
Holy Grail
   happiness as 64
   Secret of Life and 193
Homeland
   struggle of groups for 13
Hope
   as aspect of fear 18
Hope and Fear
   major ideas of mind 29
Human
   pressure of being one 163
Human Being
   defined 217
Human Beings
   as 3-D transmitters 98
   created in God's image 70
Human Race
   vs. Human Beings 164
Human-centeredness 21
Humanity
   task of 100

Humans
  as transmitters of energy 8
  Beings, not Doers 47
Humiliation 275
Humiliaton
  Responses to 275
Hunger/satisfaction metaphor
  limitations of 261
Hurt
  dealing with 114
Hurts
  as test cases 116

I

I die daily 133
Ideas
  as tools for growth 223
  Major
    as obstacles 4
  power of 124
Identity 128
  and purpose of Spiritual Path 33
  deserving and 132
  limited understanding of 128
  Soul's agenda and 131
  the real world and 131
If it isn't broken, why fix it 181
Ignorance
  fear and 194
Illness
  As purging of old thinking 258
  Curing with positive thinking 258
  Manifestation of negative beliefs
    258
Imperfection
  problem of focusing on 175
In my father's house there are many
    mansions 37, 118
Industrial revolution
  promise of 204
Infatuation 158
  lesson of 158
Injustice
  Abundance and 118
Injustices
  as test cases of understanding 116

Inner change
  as only way out 66
Inner exploration
  resistance to 41
Inner Joy 181
Inner peace
  problems with finding 52
Inner void
  Concept discussed 238
Innocence
  protection of 223
Intention 213
International conflicts
  Self image aspects 277
Intimacy 134
  fear of 111, 134
Intuition
  Aspects of 246
  dawning of 14
  how to develop 204
  source of knowledge 203
  spiritual vehicle for wisdom 100
Intuitive sense
  Discussed 246
Isolation
  Feelings of 242

J

Jesus
  As fountain of Love 267
  as Master teacher 152
  From teacher to authority figure
    286
  misunderstanding of his teachings
    98
  Simplicity of teachings 98
  teaches Abundance 148
  teaching of 67
  transformation and 141
Jobs
  how to improve them 206
Joy
  accomplishments and 174
  secret of finding 163
  starvation for 186
  Why we want it 231

Justice
   as block to evolution 116

K

Kingdom of Earth
   New Age as 173
Kingdom of Heaven within 9
Knowledge and Intuition 245

L

Lack
   manufactured by thinking 146
Lawlessness
   Result of guilt and punishment
     252
Lecture/Workshops
   Disadvantages of 286
let go and let it happen 133
Let thine eye be single 32
Let yourself go
   Part of Transformation 255
Letting go
   decision making process and 130
Life
   as conflict of good and evil 9
   as seen when I was 18 282
   as series of projections 48
   as theatre 125
   conflict between good and evil
     195
   hologram model 30
   misconceptions of 7
   new paradigm 8
   old rules of 46
   purpose of 12
   repetitiveness of 222
   Secret of 165
   two major lessons of 27
   underlying forces of 105
   Understanding of 231
   versus things 53
Life direction
   Cultural choices 236
Life Energy
   conscious awareness of 201

Life Experience
   making every minute count 184
Life experiences
   as feedback 8
Light
   as our Essence 95
   central idea in mind 30
   equality of expressions of 163
   finding vs. growing in 136
   our uniqueness as expressions of
     164
   Strength of unfiltered 234
Living in the Present
   oddness of 18
Local groups
   Advantages of 286
Love 263
   2 % more is all it takes 206
   as impetus for everything 137
   as key to Abundance 206
   as prime motivating force 166
   As rare commodity 266
   Beauties of its expanded forms
     264
   Beginning of a true understanding
     263
   Cosmic Joke and 162
   deeper aspects of 136
   desperation for 159
   expanding concept of 159
   history of search for 160
   Limiting ideas about 264
   Meaning discussed 263
   Necessity of 3-D form for expres-
     sion of 247
   of self, importance of 262
   old fantasies of 158
   old habits of 157
   Old ideas about 267
   our true Essence 159
   power to change 108
   secret of finding 163
   sex and 158
   sharing the best within us 166
   sharing vs. trading 137
   Source in someone else 267
   stronger than fear 17
   True strength of 233

vs. infatuation 158
Love and Happiness. 30
Love and Joy
   power of 79
Love and Light 11, 48, 113
Love, Joy and Celebration 33
Low self esteem
   how it starts 176

M

Making decisions
   as probabilities 36
Making every minute count
   experience and 184
Making it happen
   source of idea 57
Manifestation
   complete freedom of 7
   three dimensions of 6
Manipulation
   aspect of fear 25
Media systems
   Positive use of 227
Medicine
   As example of spiritual evolution
     257
Meditation
   addiction and 181
   as change of focus 18
   as retraining the mind 114
   on heart center 101
   our true being and 185
   problems with 184
   spiritual value of 101
Memories
   fear and 229
Mental evolution
   trinity of values 156
Might makes right
   Vs. Might for right 254
Mind
   as tool for creation 8
   bypassing to facilitate change 113
   conscious control of 1
   creative power of 36
   full of love 9
   layers of 63
   need for quieting 2
   pyramid model of 29
   storage house for memories 62
Mind control
   positive lesson of 110
Missionary zeal
   modern twist of 223
   respect for others and 167
Modern culture
   coldness of 52
Modern life
   paradox of 130
Mohammed
   teachings of 67
Money 209
   as manifestation of lack 209
   as manifestation of lack mentality
     146
   as only block to sharing 209
   limiting aspects of 210
Mother Teresa 182
Motivation
   importance of 215
Motivation and Growth 215
Movie stars
   Paid to be who they aren't 289
Movies
   Debate about affects of 247
   display false ideas of Life 72
   safe haven for adventure 63
Murphy's Fear 264
Murphy's Law
   Distillation of negative concepts
     265

N

Napoleon 123
necessity is the mother of invention
   181
Need 236
   Abundance and 237
   Concept of defined 236
   Discontent and 237
   Hunger as metaphor 261

Negative beliefs
   apparent strength of 216
   ease of changing 216
   unworthiness and 217
Negative ideas
   inherent weaknesses of 216
Negative thinking
   Hurts those who think them 276
   self created Hell 62
Negativity
   absurdity of 216
   Personal inventory 274
New age
   traditional religions and 171
New Understanding
   criterion for 48
New way
   as expression of thought 36
   built in safeguards 123
   contrast with old way 211
   ease of Being 152
   freedom of 36
   simplicity of 26
No
   as negation of Life 35
No man cometh unto the Father 83
Nostalgia
   analyzed 50

O

Observer
   neutral guide within 144
Old system
   basic contradiction of 43
   futility of significant change within
      225
   reason for failure 42
Old thinking
   letting go of 112
Old Truths
   failure of 153
Old way
   contrast with new way 211
   dangerous aspects of 36
   destructive nature of 207
   emotional attachment to 170

limitations of 50
   playing along with 133
   Releasing our commitment to 280
   rewards of 85
Olympic Figure Skating scandal 46
Oneness 12
   Concept of opposites and 273
   journey towards 15
   need to learn now 116
Openness
   to Inner Self 201
Opinions
   that others have of us 229
Opportunities 165
Opposites
   Concept of Oneness and 273
   idea of 16
   idea that creates conflict 189
Opposites, concept of
   as source of male/female conflict
      32
Original sin
   sexuality and 121
out of sight, out of mind 276

P

Paradise
   finding within 161
Past
   conditioning and 74
   learning from 28, 165
   misconceptions of 11
Path of Service
   reluctance to begin 170
Payoff of Negativity 274
Perfection 288
   concept of and growth 175
Personal growth
   change of focus and 92
Personal responsibility
   importance of 205
Personality
   and Higher Self 24
   as weak reflection of Light 23
   Built to satisfy desire 289
   Illusion aspects of 274

limited perspective of 136
looking beneath 135
need for control 23
problems as focus 218
Soul and 63
Personality voices
analyzed 63
Plato
allegory of the Cave 93
Positive
apparent struggle to become 176
Positive change
as reprogramming 11
governmental attempts at 99
Positive feedback
Transformation and 177
Positive thinking
as way out 109
importance of 1
Power of 278
power of 113
process of utilizing 222
Posture
result of attitude 219
Power
and Abundance 4
as means of attainment 3
as result of focus 7
desire for 4
of our thinking 5
path of, flaws 85
spirituality and 76
Power of Darkness
Illusion of 265
Present
Foundation of future 246
Present system
limitations of 30
Present world
As created monster 266
Pride
As balance for shame 251
stops change 11
value of 64
Pride and Allegiance 81
Pride and shame
Beyond these ideas 252

Problems
focus on 43
how we approach them 181
result of our thinking 181
Progress
idea of and Spiritual Growth 164
Prometheus 25
Proof
need for 20
Prophecy
ancient, as Transformation 145
Psychological models
many voices of 32
Psychology
trauma and transformation 177
Punishment 119
as expression of love 119
deserving and 121
essential part of life 119
guilt and 121
power of idea of 120
roots in sexuality 121
true lesson of 120
Purification 170
as process of saying "yes" 36
defined 170
process of 37
Purpose 12
of Life 14
sense of 155
Purpose of Life
in present system 33
on Spiritual Path 33
Pursuit of Happiness
positive aspects of 106
Pursuit of Wealth
Abundance and 146

Q

Quest
for Love and Joy 226

R

Racial hatreds
as major lessons in love 117

Discussed 275
Rainbow Bridge 113
Real world
 limitations of belief in 204
 limitations of that belief 143
Rebellion 54
 As cooperation with current
  thinking 281
 incapable of helping anything 55
 intuitive aspects of 80
 Logical outcome of using fear and
  guilt 250
 new way and 85
 potential growth in 54
 self destructive aspects of 54
 weapon of the weak 55
Rebellion Revisited 281
Rebirth
 As Spiritual Beings 239
 spiritual 42
Recognition 110
 desire for, benefits 111
 reasons for drive to attain 112
Redress of grievances
 foolishness of 231
Regret
 limiting aspects of 51
Relationships
 as vehicles for learning 28
Releasing the Old Method 95
Religion
 as conditioned thinking 66
 compared to Spirituality 65
 concept of Evil and 66
 defined 47
 failure to produce happiness 75
 Western concept of world 66
Religious teachings
 error of focus 67
Renunciation
 as misunderstanding of Spiritual
  laws 31
Resentment
 anger and 25
Responsibility
 various aspects of 205
Retribution

the modern dilemma 114
Risk 195
 as form of fear 195
Romance
 Fear of intimacy and 274

S

Safety
 use of force and 82
Salvation
 of others, discussed 167
Scarcity
 manufactured by thinking 146
Science
 analysis of 88
Scientific method
 control aspects 88
Search for Happiness
 problems with 130
Search for Love and Joy 266
Searching
 history of 106
Seek and ye shall find 163
seek and ye shall find 109
Seek ye first the Kingdom of Heaven
 21
Self Centeredness 137
 irony of 137
Self centeredness
 Moving away from 243
 vs. world centeredness 213
Self doubt
 absurdity of 216
Self Esteem
 love and 159
Self Expression 172
Self expression
 as allowing Light to flow 95
 low self esteem and 172
 vs. expression of Divinity within
  172
Self image
 competition and 189
 Importance of, discussed 253
 New vs. old understanding of 230
 Source of all conflict 277

star worship and 72
survival and 53
the real world and 131
Self images
negative, how they start 176
Self love
importance of 262
Self recrimination
Ultimate foolishness of 251
Self reliance
misconceptions of 142
Self-centeredness
opposite of Abundance 21
reasons for 21
Selfishness
freedom and 107
Key to cultural contradictions 283
obstacle to love 21
Seminars and Workshops
value of 168
Senses
over reliance on 124
Separateness 140
allegiances and 83
Separation of Church and State 191
Serendipity
as flow of Light 88
Sex
Feeling the Flow and 256
Love and 158
Sexual guilt
As spur to inner exploration 260
Sexual orgasm
As potential feeling of Oneness 259
Sexuality 258
Focus is on negative issues 259
major lesson of 122
Programmed misunderstanding of 261
Why acceptance is so rare 258
Shame 249
Mechanism to control behavior 249
Negative aspects of 250
Pride as opposite 251
Shame and Pride

Beyond these ideas 252
Sharing
ego and 83
lack of and fear 140
Simplicity
Abundance and 240
Simplicity.i.Jesus
Simplicity of teachings 98
Sixties
Cultural ideas discussed 282
Soul
as Essence 80
Center of personal Universe 202
old concept 9
perspective of 64
superior perspective 156
true function of 157
Soul centered
vs. personality centered 218
Soul manifestation
positive effects of 211
Souls
natural purity of 149
Western attitude towards 66
Source of Love
search for 160
Spiritual Beings
building a community of 155
Spiritual Energy
understanding of 58
Spiritual evolution
trinity of values 156
Spiritual Growth
international interest in 178
progress and 164
Spiritual growth
four steps of 123
Spiritual Life
way of perceiving 77
Spiritual Path
ambition and 77
identity and purpose as benefits 33
paradox of 169
Spiritual path
Aspects of 271
Next evolutionary step 256

Spiritual perspective
    changes in 77
Spiritual Revolution
    the 60's and 177
Spiritual transformation
    produces Heaven on Earth 67
Spiritual Understanding
    as centered sight 151
    personality and 146
Spirituality
    as renunciation 31
    basic concepts of 59
    differences from religion 65
    essence of 65
    Grass roots approach to 286
    power and 76
    simplicity of 59
Spontaneity
    paradox of 89
Star crossed lovers
    Romance and 274
Star Worship
    beliefs behind 72
Stress
    attitude and 59
Stress and release
    Two sides of same false belief 261
Striving 196
    Abundance and 146
    as fear of failure 196
    New method and 197
Struggle
    idea of 69
    releasing inner 69
Sub cultures
    Personality manifestation galore
        288
Success 143
    Blocked by ego 279
    Concept of discussed 279
    damper to creativity 143
    human spirit and 192
    performance and 163
    self centered aspect 144
    Spiritual vs. worldly 221
Success and failure
    Common duality 272

Suffering
    as cycles of memory 162
    as the great teacher 115
    caused by misunderstanding 40
Superiority
    fear and 142
Superstition and Evil 233
Suppression
    Technique for control 276
Survival
    of world 171
Sympathetic Magic
    and modern star worship 72

T

Tarot
    the future and 104
Teachings
    ego centric vs. soul centered 66
Television
    Paradigm for our illusion 251
Tension and Release 260
The Challenge of Change 148
The Control Issue 110
The Cult of the Personality 22
The dead in Christ shall rise 42
The Devil Created 194
The Ego 139
"The end justifies the means" 13
The Energy Matrix 217
The Eternal Questions 247
The Fifties
    America's golden era 224
The Four Steps of Growth 123
The Future is Now 104
The Inner City Puzzle 179
The Kingdom of Heaven in Within
        you. 16
The Light at the End of the Tunnel
        280
The Missionary Tradition 167
The new way, defined 19
The Observer 151
The old way
    as habitual thinking 20
    defined briefly 19

The Process of Transformation 68
The Pyramid.i.Mind
  pyramid model of 29
The Real World 131
The Religious/Spiritual Life 65
The Search for the Center 84
The Secret of Life 241
The Source 269
The Spiritual Path 271
The Truth Shall Set Us Free 225
The Two Paths
  complimentary nature of 32
  fallacy of 31
Theories
  True test of 252
Thinking
  as collection of habits 7
  normal reservations of 149
  opposite of living 188
  our belief in 62
  process explained 62
thinking
  as the true enemy 107
Thought expansion
  described 217
Thoughts
  as script for life movie 6
  benefits of changing 99
  creative nature of 37
  creative power of 208
Three dimensional form
  Necessary to experience Love 247
Time
  concern with 199
  Eternity and 199
Traditional religions
  Heaven on Earth and 171
Transformation 1
  and old ideas 68
  as change of consciousness 100
  as emergence 67
  as prophecy 145
  aspects of 176
  beginning process 164
  Expansion of 292
  experience of 214
  Fear of 244

getting out of the way of 184
Jesus' teachings and 141
Next evolutionary step 256
simplicity of 26, 79
swiftness of 141
thought aspects of 223
two aspects of 18
Two major aspects of 285
vision of 214
Trinity
  during four phases of Evolution
    156
  new interpretation 124
True Source
  paradox of finding 94
True Success 279
Trust 60
  and fear 5
  as key to Spiritual Growth 60
  as scientific fact 200
  based on fact 36
  basis of new way 19
  contrast with hope 19
  courage to 200

U

Unhappiness
  source of 140
Uniqueness
  as humans 140
  our true 90
  true expression of 104
United Nations
  step towards unity 81
Unity
  idea of, discussed 89
Universe
  as reflection of Light 61
Unworthiness
  ambition and 78
  source of negative beliefs 217

V

Victim mentality
  as block to growth 109

as self destructive 43
leading to truth 44
popularity of 182
Violence
competition as source 189
Inner causes of 254
irony of 207
problem with controlling 179
problems with 12

W

We are what we think
Love and 162
Weaning process
Sense of loss and 241
Western culture
conflicting ideas of 184
true lesson of 120
What are we doing here?
Question discussed 248
when the student is ready, the teacher
will appear 167
Where are we?
Question discussed 247
Who are we?
Question discussed 247
Who We Are 49
who we are 12
Why are we here?
Question discussed 248
Will
bending to higher will 68
presumed importance of 228
Will power
vs. Soul power 229
Work
finding joy in 206
hard as description of 205
improving enjoyment of 206
Work and Freedom 204
Work ethic
basis of 204
World
reality of 8
World centeredness
vs. self centeredness 213

World changes
what initiates them 262
World healing
simplicity of 99
World problems
as ideal lesson 44
media image 2
way to change 2
World situation
as perfect success 105
caused by misunderstanding 7
forcing us to look within 10
World Transformation
personal involvement in 173
World violence
True lesson of 233
Worry
perplexing aspects of 61

Y

Yes
as affirmation of Life 35
Key to change 289
key to starting the Flow 215
Youth of Today
plight of 74

Z

Zoroaster 194

Suggested Readings

Creative Visualization   Shakti Gawain

Excellent introduction to meditation and visualization

A Course in Miracles

The Definitive Long Term Study Guide

Real Magic   Wayne Dyer

His best work so far.

Ageless Body, Timeless Mind Deepok Chopra

Takes concept of 'We are what we think' to its logical limit. Especially first and last two chapters.

You Can Heal Your Life   Louise Hay

Discusses how thoughts manifest as illnesses with excellent affirmations for starting the healing process.

Illusions   Richard Bach

One of the first and best.

The Only Dance There Is   Ram Dass

One of my favorites.

The Seat of the Soul   Gary Zukov

These are only a few that we have personally read and would like to recommend. There are many other excellent resources that we know nothing about, but which you can easily discover by following your intuition. The best resource is, as always, Within.

About the Author

Coburn Tuller likes to describe himself as a '3-D interactive hologram but to me the best adjective is comfortable. He seems equally at ease whether writing books, building stage sets, composing and performing music on instruments of his own design, leading discussion groups on higher consciousness or petting a cat. Since first meeting Coburn, I have watched him dismantle, block by block, the false foundations that keep us all from allowing joy to overtake ourselves, our communities and our planet. Observing this process has inspired my own spiritual catharsis which has led to the realization of many personal goals, all achieved by changing the ideas that inhabit my mind. This book represents a continuous dialog that has gone on within Coburn for many years,and over that time many around him have been directly, and indirectly, comforted by his generosity, his wit and his humanity. We have all gained much by Coburn's courage to confront his own mind.

Ken Boschert

Order form

IF YOU NEED AN ADDITIONAL COPY OF

What in the World is Going On Here?

FOR A GIFT OR FRIEND, CHECK WITH YOUR LOCAL
BOOKSTORE, OR USE THE ORDER FORM BELOW:

SIMPLY FILL OUT THE INFORMATION BELOW AND
MAIL TO:
BUTTERFLY PO BOX 2001
SPRINGFIELD, MO 65801

OR CALL 1-800-727-1636

I wish to order:

_____ copies of What in the World is Going On Here? $20

Price includes shipping and handling.

Name ____

Address ____

City_________________________ State ______ Zip __________

Total________ Check Enclosed ☐   Mastercard ☐   Visa ☐

My card number is:_________________________________

Expiration Date________ Signature______________________

Daytime Telephone_________________________________